Quo Anima

Akron Series in Contemporary Poetics

Akron Series in Contemporary Poetics
Mary Biddinger and John Gallaher, Editors
Nick Sturm, Associate Editor

Mary Biddinger, John Gallaher, eds., *The Monkey & the Wrench: Essays into Contemporary Poetics*
Robert Archambeau, *The Poet Resigns: Poetry in a Difficult World*
Rebecca Hazelton & Alan Michael Parker, eds., *The Manifesto Project*
Jennifer Phelps and Elizabeth Robinson, eds, *Quo Anima: innovation and spirituality in contemporary women's poetry*

Quo Anima

innovation and spirituality in contemporary women's poetry

Jennifer Phelps and
Elizabeth Robinson, editors

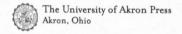

The University of Akron Press
Akron, Ohio

ISBN: 978-1-629221-57-1 (paper)
ISBN: 978-1-629220-74-1 (ePDF)
ISBN: 978-1-629220-75-8 (ePub)

A catalog record for this title is available from the Library of Congress.

The paper used in this publication meets the minimum requirements of ANSI NISO z39.48–1992 (Permanence of Paper). ∞

The views contained herein are those of the individual authors and do not necessarily reflect the views of the editors, the Akron Series in Contemporary Poetics, or The University of Akron Press.

Cover: Painting, *Untitled*, Lourdes Sanchez. Courtesy Sears Peyton Gallery. Cover design by Amy Freels.

Quo Anima was designed and typeset by Amy Freels. The typeface, Mrs. Eaves, was designed by Zuzana Licko in 1996. The display type, Mr. Eaves, was designed by Zuzana Licko in 2009. *Quo Anima* was printed on sixty-pound natural and bound by Bookmasters of Ashland, Ohio.

Produced in conjunction with the University of Akron Affordable Learning Initiative. More information is available at www.uakron.edu/affordablelearning/

Dedicated to the memory of kari edwards, Barbara Guest, Joanne Kyger, Colleen Lookingbill, and Leslie Scalapino

Contents

Introduction

"There is always something in poetry," Barbara Guest observes, "that desires the invisible."[1] Guest suggests that the poem and its various modes of agency make space for what she alternately calls metaphysics or spirituality. She writes:

> Do you ever notice as you write that no matter what there is on the written page something appears *back of everything that is said, a little ghost?* I judge that this ghost is there to remind us there is always more, an elsewhere, a hiddenness, a secondary form of speech, an eye blink [. . .] it is the *obscure essence that lies within the poem that is not necessary to put into language, but that the poem must hint at, must say 'this is not all I can tell you. There is something more I do not say.' Leave this little echo to haunt the poem, do not give it form, but let it assume its own ghost-like shape.*[2]

Guest's sensitivity to the unarticulated "essence" of the poem arrives as a useful counterpoint to the poetics that emerged with L=A=N=G=U=A=G=E poetry in the 1970s and 1980s. As a reaction against, and critique of, conventional lyric poetry, and even the lyricism of the New American poetries, the poetics of the L=A=N=G=U=A=G=E writers raised a number of influential critiques. The potential spirituality within a poem was often seen as a problem to be avoided at all costs. The easy epiphanies of lyric-inflected poetry, the valorization of the speaker as possessing some kind of elevated priestly insight, the elitist transcendence of the religious or metaphysical, the lack of engagement with a world whose practical problems should no longer be separated from the making of art—all of these are fair criticisms of (some) poetries that have essayed (some forms) of the spiritual.

And yet. In *Quo Anima*, we have revisited the terrain of the spiritual as it has been explored, enacted, and exploited by a varied range of resourceful and intrepid women poets. There we've found poetries characterized not by dogmatic certainties, but irresolution and wonder, and by insights that make no triumphalist claims. In the work of women writers, we are impressed by the fluidity with which feminist commitments enter terrain in which subjectivity is ambiguous, malleable, and willing to upset gender conventions. Many of the poets we consider also use language as a vehicle to engage and reenact embodiment. This may occur via maternity or the erotic, but it may just as easily transpire through an attunement to the materiality and history of language. We've come to better appreciate the profound intersubjectivity and relationality that mediates—even as it gestures toward—transcendence in so much contemporary poetry by women.

Importantly, these women poets, adept scholars of contemporary poetry and poetics, defy not only conventions of feminine experience and spirituality but go on to defy the patriarchal authorities of experimentalism. In so doing, they remake poetry that speaks not just to women, but provides for poetic possibilities previously unexplored. Indeed, many of the poets whose work is addressed in this anthology were significantly influenced by the formal freedoms of the L=A=N=G=U=A=G=E movement, but departed in a variety of ways from the theoretical discourse of that cohort. Susan Howe not only opened the page as a visual field, she excavated marginalized, often feminine, histories. Leslie Scalapino introduced Buddhist thought and practice into her poetry. These are only two instances from a rich body of writings by women. A generation on, women writers are boldly making (for example) affect, maternity, and the nature of gender itself intrinsic to the poetry they write—all while continuing to apply pressure on the nature of sign and subject that began with their L=A=N=G=U=A=G=E poet antecedents. Following the legacy of innovation that embraces the ethos of the reader as co-creator of the poem, the poetries discussed in *Quo Anima* venture further into poetry as a site of inquiry for which there is no final conclusion. Fanny

Howe's foundational essay, "Bewilderment," distills this approach, lifting up a poetics that "doesn't want to answer questions so much as lengthen the resonance of those questions."[3]

Indeed, the extra-paradigmatic "swerves" that Joan Retallack describes in *A Poethical Wager* demonstrate the ways that making art can renew the meaning of "transformation" and, in so doing, transform the project of poetry itself. The risk entailed in such questioning and mutability results in writing that forges an embodied, politically engaged poetry that nonetheless approaches the question of the mystical and spiritual boldly. What therefore emerges are creative works (and, correspondingly, poetics) that unsay obstructions that have beset poetry—insofar as conventional definitions of poetics tend to constrain the speculative nature of the inquiry that arises in *any* poetry. In this way, innovation is a necessary element of this poetry, for poetry becomes inquiry rather than assertion, hypothesis rather than assumption. By their very fluidity and responsiveness (as evidenced also in their formal suppleness), the poetries considered in *Quo Anima* retain spirituality as an active endeavor and not a static category. The material in this anthology indicates that a wide variety of commitments shape what is most crucial to the act of making poems: intersubjectivity, justice, a relationship to ineffable and the incomprehensible, and even the possibility of saying or unsaying language itself.

This range of concern clearly makes any study of spirituality difficult to essay. We can no more give a comprehensive definition of spirituality than we can of feminism. "Spirituality" is itself a vexed word. Yet a general orientation to what we mean by the term is a complex and evolving network of metaphors, symbols, and practices that compose a constellation of affect, belief, and cognition. These operate in ways that both stabilize and disrupt meaning and structure. Such a definition, we feel, supplies a useful sense of poetics as a process and practice: it thereby opens the imagination to both a poetics *and* a spirituality that are elastic and dynamic. Innovation, then, as it is conceived of here is not limited to formal decisions and crafting. Nor is innovation synonymous with transgression. Many of the poets studied here are quite formally accessible, while others are formally wild. What is important is the poet's willingness to revisit material from many domains, whether formal, historical, ethical, or spiritual and her ability to experience and convey it in a renewing manner.

Imagination becomes central to any poetry of spirituality insofar as it opens to perceptions (or modes and practices of perceiving) that are not typically acknowledged, widely shared, or granted legitimacy. (Or which, alternatively, are overdetermined and limited by tradition and practice.) We value the affinity of this approach with Retallack's aforementioned *A Poethical Wager* in enlarging the compass of art-making systems with other value and meaning-making systems. Importantly, we understand such processes and systems—whether artistic, religious, or ethical—as entailing risk, ambiguity, and change.

Ultimately, our commitment to studying the intersection of spirituality and writing by women speaks to a changing understanding of feminism. Certainly, we wish to affirm women's full humanity and range of expression. The conclusion of Kathleen Fraser's essay, "The Tradition of Marginality," is still cogent:

> It is precisely in proposing a poetics of sufficient depth and complexity to satisfy our own hungers—as well as participating in the "dig" for a female tradition of linguistic invention—that we began to starve the larger-than-life figures who dominated and denied us [. . . .] Thus, from the edge or brink or borderline we call the margin, we are able to create another center . . . a laboratory in which to look for the unknown elements we suspect are there.[4]

Within that shifting, reforming center, the question of women's subjectivity cannot be static. Indeed, some of the poets in this anthology (kari edwards, Olga Broumas, and T Begley, for example) question what it is to be a woman and if such a category can be clearly delineated. Spirituality, too, is a site in which the boundaries of the subject can blur, efface, and become elastic. In that way, feminism and spirituality are ideally suited to overlap and interact—swerve—in a genuinely revelatory manner.

*

Within the past two decades, poetry anthologies and essay collections have signaled increased energy and interest in the relationship between experimental poetry and spirituality. Andrew Schelling's *Wisdom Anthology of North American Buddhist Poetry* came out in 2005, while Autumn House Press published *Joyful Noise: An Anthology of American Spiritual Poetry* (edited by Robert Strong) in 2006. Devin Johnston's *Precipitations: Contemporary American Poetry as Occult Practice* (Wesleyan, 2002) and Hank Lazer's *Lyric & Spirit* (Omnidawn, 2008) have opened a necessary critical discussion on ways that poetry can demonstrate resonance with, as well as resistance to, the spiritual. Fanny Howe's *The Wedding Dress* (2003) and *The Winter Sun* (2009) are foundational texts for contemporary writers interested in poetics and spirituality. Simultaneously, powerful individual reflections and essays that interact with theology and mysticism have further invigorated the conversation ensuing within contemporary innovative poetry.

This anthology intends to address what we perceive as a gap in critical conversation in order to study more intensively how *women* have participated in raising a variety of questions pertinent to mystical, spiritual, theological, or otherwise speculative strains of writing. Despite the heartening emergent body of work, we note the relative scarcity of critical response to women who are writing in this vein. Indeed, poets such as (for example) Fanny Howe, Jean Valentine, Brenda Hillman, Lissa Wolsak, Mei-Mei Berssenbrugge, Cecilia Vicuña, Barbara Guest, kari edwards, Laynie Browne, Brenda Coultas, Olga Broumas, and Joanne Kyger manifest gratifyingly varied responses to the interrelations of the spiritual and the poetic. Others, both those whose work is considered in this anthology and a growing community of vital women writers whose work awaits further critical consideration, have contributed richly to contemporary poetry and its potential for a heuristic metaphysics or spirituality. The gap in critical study remains significant between women and their male counterparts. In another context, the theologian Grace Jantzen noted that "while oppression runs deep, it is also true that from within the mystical tradition . . . from some of the women mystics came creative and courageous efforts at pushing back the boundaries of thought and action so that liberation could be achieved."[5] Similarly, within the evolving legacies of contemporary poetry, we attempt to ameliorate the relative critical silence with which women's subjectivity and the spiritual has been met.

In *Quo Anima*, our intention is to track the ongoing processes through which women poets struggle with, and remodel, central questions of spirituality, legacy, and meaning through their poetry. As we compiled responses, we made some decisions that are relevant to the shifting and multifaceted nature of our inquiry. Firstly, we asked poets to write about other poets. That is, though many of the authors of these pieces do indeed have scholarly bona fides, we sought respondents who are actively engaged in the making of poems themselves and who would address other poets with a practitioner's insight and sympathy. It may be that there are few fields more subject to skepticism than poetry, spirituality, and feminine experience; our approach was to create a field of empathy in which to explore these topics. As we proceeded with the culling of materials, we found that traditional essay responses were not always the most satisfactory way to get at the richness of experience and formal originality that characterizes the poetry under consideration here. Slowly, we began adding interviews, personal statements, and, finally, even some poems into the mix. The results, though they differ from those of a conventional scholarly collection, excite us: our hope is that they will invite ongoing discourse (both creative and critical) in a manner that builds on and augments the work of all the writers who participated in this project. Where there are lacunae (and we are keenly aware of these), we hope with some optimism that this collection will open to an extended and more comprehensive study of what Elizabeth Savage helpfully cites as a "theopoetics."

As the essays, statements, and interviews that comprise this collection began to arrive, themes and preoccupations became manifest. Fascinatingly, these themes often overlap from poet to poet but are deployed in contrasting ways. In Section One, *the silent thing that has to be expressed*, we track the recurring thread of apophasis: the unsaying of language where language is insufficient to reference. The poem, suffused with doubt about its ability to achieve stable reference, opens to a site of mystery and instability: referential openness. As Michael Sells writes, "Apophasis moves toward the transreferential. It cannot dispense with reference, but through the constant turning back upon its own referential delimitations, it seeks a momentary liberation from such limitations."[6] Certainly this struggle is apparent in the poem that opens the section. Here, giovanni singleton undoes, through the character of a single letter [I/i], the stability of the speaking agent. Other wranglings with the apophatic may not be as graphic, but are equally as urgent. Studying Fanny Howe's long-term relationship with the work of Simone Weil, Brian Teare considers Howe's "bewilderment" and the necessity of the apophatic pilgrim to wander in a way that (to quote Howe) leads to "progressing at one level and becoming more lost at another."[7] Similarly, Hank Lazer studies the formal complexity of Lissa Wolsak's poetry, through which he tentatively defines spirituality as a "rising into consciousness (of an understanding, however incomplete or fleeting, of being)." That is, this consciousness requires "slippage in which spirit, by a kind of self-opposition, becomes a way of knowing." Sara Nolan understands the gaps of the unsaid in Jean Valentine's poetry as receptivity: an acceptance of unresolved strangeness that both offers, and requires of the reader, profound empathy. Laura Moriarty, describing her turn to Zen practice as her husband died, also encounters an inexplicable, unsayable world:

> One feels the cut. Existence leaves off from time to time. History is what we are left with. Reality is conflict. It is compromised. It is and is not the case.

The world becomes no less perplexing, but an empathetic attendance upon its disorder makes, Moriarty claims, a sort of a refuge. Neither her writing nor her meditation practice negates her grief; they create a site in which suffering finds its way to a different kind of meaning.

Indeed, the risk of emotional connection, of an affective ethics, becomes an important means by which traditional poetries can be unsaid and reconfigured. Other poets study the overlap of the affective and the spiritual as these inflect the experiences by which we understand the world and make meaning. This is the subject of Section Two, *the memory of the journey unraveling*. Faith Barrett's essay on Leslie Scalapino's *The Tango*, one of the most politically engaged poetries discussed in the anthology, confronts the devastation wreaked on Tibetan Buddhist monasteries and the universal nature of suffering. Scalapino's repetitive poetic patterning begins to efface the subject, yet, as Barrett shows, this poetry, like the tango, underlines "the extent to which both cultural rituals rely on gesture and movement rather than language to communicate." Emotionally charged patterns and rhythms leap outside traditional poetic conventions but connect the reader powerfully with the text. Perhaps moving past what we assume to be language is one way of mining our linguistic resources. Similarly, Tracie Morris recollects her childhood context—the ways she did and did not absorb the religious and spiritual resources of her environment, including the ways her African American family both absorbed and stayed outside the church. This is continuous with her creative work. There, Morris sometimes goes so far as to eschew words in favor of nonsemantic sound, the "sounds that lead me to being moved to utter some *thing* beyond my sense of what I *think* I know, going back to that family place *before* I was from anyplace." Morris cannily moves within resource and restriction. In an excerpt from *Penury*, Myung Mi Kim, too, uninscribes the language of both personal and historical grief by overwriting it and replacing it on the page with a pattern of slashes that are visually rhythmic. Kythe Heller illuminates the ways that Cecilia Vicuña's poetries also break open poetry, finding the core of human history, myth, and meaning that both create and unravel the words we use to address each other. The patterns of language are revelatory of the patterns of the world. This process is deeply ethical and participative. The poets working in this mode build practical and spiritual community through their deep attentiveness.

Section three, *continually dispersed along the web of the inter-relation*, is focused on relationality, whether within the intimacies of familial or erotic relationships or as transacted the complex dynamics of interaction between the human and natural worlds. In other words, these essays focus less explicitly on the character of language itself and more on the relationships that can be created within language. Sasha Steensen, reading Mei-Mei Berssenbrugge's *Four Year Old Girl*, looks into the particular form of transcendence that arises in the intimacy between mother and child, "this possibility that something *of* us *exceeds* us." Thus, whatever divine presence we may experience will occur via intersubjectivity. That intimacy can transform becomes clear in Kazim Ali's ecstatic investigation of the collaboration of Olga Broumas and T Begley.

Ali opens to the eros of collaboration, to the larger utterance that comes of the twining of two voices. Indeed, the tensions of embodiment continually inform spiritual understanding, whether erotic, maternal, or through the sensuous rhythms of speaking. Turning to the natural world, Rusty Morrison shows how Melissa Kwasny uses the sensory, particularly by way of the image, to open to the extrasensory. In each of these instances, embodied experience commingles with both pleasure and limitation. Joanne Kyger clarifies this, linking elemental processes such as breathing with spirit and place:

> If one thinks about the origins of the word "spirit" coming from "spiritus"—breath or "spirare"—to breathe—then one understands that in a "bioregion" we all share the same air. So yes, there is a "coexistence" with the spirit realm. We share the same arena of breathing existence.

The final section of the book, *all things leave themselves behind*, responds to questions of epistemology and the transformations that ensue when we look deeply into the nature of what we know and believe. Poetry's work with innovative form, we see here and elsewhere, enacts and opens the possibility for multiple forms of transformation. Indeed, form makes inquiry possible even as inquiry alters form itself, opening ever more provocatively into the irresolvable mysteries that inhere within and around us. Jennifer Phelps traces Brenda Hillman's poetry through a series of shifts that originate in personal experience and emerge as radical formal experiments. Phelps understands Hillman's poetry as resulting from an ongoing alchemical transformation. Claudia Keelan eloquently undoes epistemological questions; she envisions, instead, a mode of working that allows for "seeing in the one the human, seeing a *process* by which something whole is seen." Kimberly Lyons's poem echoes this:

> It's the fragments held by a few threads
> to the larger body
> of the Gnostic cloth

The erratic weave of presence amid absence reminds the reader, once again, of the apophatic, that whose existence abides outside the sayable. Yet some poets approach the challenge of presence from a slightly different angle. What if the presence is only dubiously present? What traces are we tracking? Exploring the ghost story in *Gravesend*, Cole Swensen develops a poetry that, Elizabeth Robinson claims, locates itself between the poles of belief and unbelief: "In affirming that she does not believe, she is not exactly saying that she *disbelieves*." The disrupted knowing, the suspension, this creates is its own form of beguilement. As Dan Beachy-Quick says of Susan Howe's writing, the pull of this poetry comes of "words putting themselves in this difficult and impossible grace called *delay*."

In conclusion, poem and essay, interview and statement come together here to gesture toward practices that venture forth into spirit and mystery as women poets understand these at the juncture of twentieth and twenty-first centuries. This is an endeavor that, we would argue, requires all the imaginative and formal resourcefulness that one would find in any poetry of our time. As Alice Notley says, "I find out everything I believe through writing." *Quo Anima*, then, reads and writes into being a new avenue of belief.

Notes

1. Guest, *Forces of Imagination*, 19.
2. Guest, *Forces of Imagination*, 100–101.
3. Howe, *The Wedding Dress*, 20.
4. Fraser, "The Tradition of Marginality," 38.
5. Jantzen, *Power, Gender and Christian Mysticism*, 23.
6. Sells, *Mystical Languages of Unsaying*, 8–9.
7. Howe, *The Wedding Dress*, 16.

Bibliography

Berssenbrugge, Mei-Mei. *Four Year Old Girl*. Berkeley: Kelsey Street Press, 1998.

Guest, Barbara. *Forces of Imagination: Writing on Writing*. Berkeley: Kelsey Street Press, 2003.

Fraser, Kathleen. "The Tradition of Marginality." In *Translating the Unspeakable: Poetry and the Innovative Necessity*, 25–38. Tuscaloosa: University of Alabama Press, 1999.

Howe, Fanny. *The Wedding Dress: Meditations on Word and Life*. Berkeley: University of California Press, 2003.

Howe, Fanny. *The Winter Sun: Notes on a Vocation*. St. Paul: Graywolf Press, 2009.

Jantzen, Grace M. *Power, Gender and Christian Mysticism*. Cambridge: Cambridge University Press, 1995.

Johnston, Devin. *Precipitations: Contemporary American Poetry as Occult Practice*. Middletown: Wesleyan Press, 2002.

Kim, Myung Mi. *Penury*. Oakland: Omnidawn Publishing, 2009.

Lazer, Hank. *Lyric & Spirit: Selected Essays, 1996–2008*. Oakland: Omnidawn Publishing, 2008.

Retallack, Joan. *The Poethical Wager*. Berkeley: University of California Press, 2004.

Scalapino, Leslie and Marina Adams. *The Tango*. New York: Granary Books, 2001.

Schelling, Andrew, ed. *The Wisdom Anthology of North American Buddhist Poetry*. Somerville, MA: Wisdom Publications, 2005.

Sells, Michael A. *Mystical Languages of Unsaying*. Chicago: University of Chicago Press, 1994.

Strong, Robert, ed. *Joyful Noise: An Anthology of American Spiritual Poetry*. Pittsburgh: Autumn House Press, 2006.

Swensen, Cole. *Gravesend*. Berkeley: University of California Press, 2012.

part i.

the silent thing that has to be expressed

eye of the be/holder
giovanni singleton

giovanni singleton

The Apophatic Pilgrim

Simone Weil and Fanny Howe

Brian Teare

i.

The apophatic pilgrim is, at first, a hard character to describe. She was born in the West in the twentieth century, and though many of its conflicts shape her, its wars in particular forge her conscience, vocabulary, and destiny. Her desires are largely spiritual; her aspirations are political; her problems are material; her situation is existential. She is an atheist who thinks disbelief might be a way of purifying the notion of God almost fatally tainted by her century, and in this way never stops praying. Bourgeois by birth, she courts social change by letting material scarcity's limitations teach her compassion and selflessness and hopes to share this method with those in need. Justice is her cause and love her central motivation. Her ethics are drawn from ancient traditions whose values strike others as anachronistic, masochistic, or unrealistic; thus, though her politics are thoroughly contemporary, her political aims remain largely misunderstood and undervalued. As often characterized as a misguided naïf as she is a radical visionary, she lives on the margin of whatever society she finds herself in. Yet she persists, convinced that suffering might lead her further inward, out to knowledge of God. Hope makes her strange. Paradox makes her possible.

The portrait of the apophatic pilgrim I'm drawing is a composite; a composite by nature blurs important distinctions and fails to make features precise, and this portrait begins as no exception; I've derived the pilgrim's features equally from the lives and writings of both Simone Weil and Fanny Howe. And though this essay will first describe some of Weil's thinking and its influence on Howe before going on to focus on a reading of Howe's book *The Quietist*, it's worth emphasizing that Howe's writings on Weil encourage us to read backwards from Howe to Weil and forwards from Weil to Howe and back again, a cycle that creates the palimpsestic blur that emerges from one writer's deep identification and engagement with another. "I have read SW for so long, and so intensely," Howe writes in her essay "Work and Love," "I often don't remember what she believed, stated, or knew. In a sense my stupidity is a sign that I have incorporated her work into myself."[1] But to apprentice one's own body and mind to the work of another is only one of the ways the pilgrim tries to convert doubt and suffering into what Weil in her *Notebooks* calls "a *negative* sovereign good."[2] The pilgrim believes her physical labor, intellectual pursuits, creative and spiritual practices, and everyday domestic life also prepare her for possible apophasis; she supposes that the suffering inherent in unskilled manual labor or a life lived in continual service to others might serve as the lever that lifts up the worker or mother into a union with divinity beyond human conceptions of the divine and an attendant dissolution of self.

"We must seek," writes Simone Weil in her *Notebooks*, "that form of transference which transports us outside space."[3] For Weil, who experienced a wordless visitation from Christ in 1938, the *Notebooks* might be the most profound record of such transport, though they characteristically omit a straightforward account of her visionary state. Rather, the *Notebooks* could be said to constitute a theory of the apophatic.[4] Structured as an almost endless series of logical proofs, the *Notebooks'* semantic surface resembles philosophical grammar, but its unspoken "meaning event" introduces apophatic paradox and syntax into her propositions. Weil's dependence on analogy, simile, metaphor, and correspondence to structure her thinking means that she makes progress by replacing the central term of her argument with another, analogous term in her attempt to get ever closer, through language, to an inexpressible source of knowledge—a form of argument that paradoxically conceals through continual revelation. "Writing—like translating—negative operation," Weil writes, "setting aside those words which conceal the model, the silent thing that has to be expressed."[5] This model at first appears to refer to a Platonic ideal, but over time its silence begins to function more like Christian mystery, what Michael Sells in *Mystical Languages of Unsaying* calls "a referential openness onto the depths of a particular tradition, and into conversation with other traditions" of mysticism.[6]

Weil's *Notebooks* return often to the question of the nature of that unexpressed "model, the silent thing," and they do so by examining the nature of reading, taking for a given that "the world is a text containing several meanings, and we pass from one meaning to another by an effort."[7] Because her interdisciplinary and cross-cultural epistemology depends upon correspondences between ancient and contemporary philosophy and science as well as classics of Eastern and Western theology and mysticism, Weil perceives meaning's multiplicity as problematic because potentially unlimited interpretations of the world obscure the only road to God, the destination upon which the pilgrim has set her sights. If it is "real difficulty, choosing from among the readings,"[8] she might "read *doubt* in all outward aspects,"[9] or she might "read in all outward aspects—God,"[10] but she nonetheless "must study a reading very closely"[11] because of the potential for narcissistic wish fulfillment:

> To read in outside things what we carry within ourselves—inevitable. How manage to escape it? Or even turn it into a means of reading truly? Possible resource: analogy.[12]

Because analogy depends on logical similitude, but is also like metaphor in its ability to stretch plausible likeness in service of intuitive knowledge, analogy allows Weil in her *Notebooks* to "break away . . . from hypotheses" in favor of reading the "inexpressible analogy between inexpressible things,"[13] rendering "Each thing reflected, transposed in every other thing."[14] On the one hand, Weil's reliance on analogy for such transpositions is consonant with an apophatic language that "cannot dispense with reference, but through the constant turning back upon its own referential delimitations . . . seeks a momentary liberation from such delimitations" in order to gesture toward a spiritual truth beyond signification.[15] On the other hand, Howe's essay "Doubt" characterizes

Weil's *Notebooks* as "a superhuman effort at conversion to a belief in afflic-
tion as a sign of God's presence" and questions the actual results of Weil's
apophatic operations: "Is this possible? Can you turn 'void' into 'God'
by switching the words over and over again?"[16] As with most pedagogi-
cal relationships, Howe's doubt concerning her master's methods could
be said to mark the end of her apprenticeship and the beginning of her
own journey—one that takes its core concerns from Weil's life and writ-
ings even as it departs from Weil's assumptions about the power of lan-
guage to perform a negative sovereign good.

ii.

To switch one word for another suggests a process of substitution,
one whose ultimate goal, for Weil, would be a kind of linguistic tran-
substantiation: as wine into blood, so void into God. Indeed, Weil in
her *Notebooks* attempts to make them one, to forge a union between the
ineffable and the demonstrative, carefully hammering out each link
in the chain of analogies that leads from one to the other in the hope
of making them one. As Howe points out, Weil's insistence on and
faith in the operations of logic forces a paradoxical marriage between
transcendence and immanence that changes "void" to "God" over and
over without necessarily succeeding. Howe's writings, however, most
often address the relation between mystery and revelation by insisting
on the gap between them, demonstrating that one of the central terms
of apophatic experience is that it can't really be "translated" into lan-
guage, and can at best only be approximated. In a passage from *Winter
Sun: Notes on a Vocation*, Howe details her contemporary sense that

> The quest for a condition that exists in two separate states is what
> confuses people like me. The person looking for a fixed identity is
> often the same person looking for God (escape into emptiness). This
> split search can only be folded into one in the process of working on
> something ... with a wholeheartedness that qualifies as complete atten-
> tion. In such a state you find yourself depending on an unknown
> model to supply you with the focus to complete what you are doing.
> Your work is practical, but your relationship is always potential in the
> range of its errors and failures.[17]

Howe's narratives and lyric sequences are poignant and powerful as theology because they never cohere into legible allegories and their image patterns never totally convert into symbolic systems—her pilgrim is not quite Christian in the same way that her journey is never quite progress. "Bewilderment circumnavigates," Howe writes of her own apophatic theory, "believing at the center of every errant or circular movement is the empty but ultimate referent."[18] In fact, the very "errors and failures" of Howe's bewildered narrative structures enable her writing to communicate both the presence of "the unknown model" or "ultimate referent" *and* the lived experience of how "relationship is always potential." And though a late novel like *Indivisible* uses plot to render visible the "practical work" of narrative that testifies to "secret" theological significance, Howe eschews neat equations between events and theological meanings. In general, she prefers to work through inference and indirection, to render dramatic a pattern that suggests cause and effect but ultimately refuses legible or logical denouement. In the absence of the values of allegory, the existential logic of action retains only a trace of *deus ex machina*, an off-stage grace that, it's inferred, gives the shape to Howe's prose logic.

And though her lyric sequences share many of the same postmodern narrative values as her late fiction, Howe's poems attempt the "escape into emptiness" in ways that her narratives can't. "For poets," Howe writes in her essay "Bewilderment," "the obliquity of a bewildered poetry is its own theme."[19] Howe uses lineation to emphasize not just the individual words and syllables within a line, but also the montage-like effects inherent in line and stanza breaks. In the same way that her narratives refuse to embody allegorical values, the juxtapositions wrought by her line breaks suggest metaphorical relationships that never quite develop into conceit and grammatical logic that never quite develops into sentences. Her lines' apparent parataxis and non sequiturs either undermine or hyperbolize conventional prosodic musicality and linguistic beauty, perhaps in the hopes that truth might reveal itself, tricked out by obliquity. Rather than rely on traditional poetic forms or conventional figuration, Howe uses the heightened aural, prosodic and morphemic materiality of the poetic line as the perfect medium with which to perform her own rituals of substitution:

Much of my writing has been the effort to rearrange, rewrite the word "God" by filling up the pages with other names . . . when I write, I rewrite that name, and then what I write, if it is written well, becomes not a new "God," but a new person, a human face. If a face does not gaze back at me from the page, there is only paper and wood, the static object empty of the divine spark. The human face in repose and in silence is what I see, when what I have written approximates the unspeakable.[20]

Here Howe shows how truly a student of Weil she has been: starting with the word "God," she rewrites it "by filling up the page with other names" that, if written well, nonetheless contain the name of God as a kind of "divine spark." In other words, over and over again Howe turns "God" into words that reveal, "in repose and in silence," their origin in "the unspeakable." Given Howe's doubt concerning the efficacy of Weil's substitution of "God" for "void," it seems fair to wonder whether or not Howe's process is equally beset with futility. It's important, however, to note that, though at first her writing seems to be performing a series of substitutions, Howe calls the relation between "God" and its rewriting a form of "approximation." The task she sets herself is not a kind of transubstantiation; writing and rewriting fold the split search into one process whose terms nevertheless never fuse. "God" and the "other names" never cancel each other out, and never become equal, but remain in a dynamic relation characterized equally by mystery and demonstration, writing and rewriting a perpetual circumnavigation around the ultimate referent. "I can keep *unsaying* what I have said, and amending it," Howe writes in "Bewilderment," "but I can't escape the law of the words in a sentence."[21] Poised between unsaying and the law, Howe's poetic language serves not as a translation of the unspeakable, but as a site for the articulation of the knowledge that arises from the tension between unmaking and making. Rather than sites where we might encounter certain immanence or transcendence, her poems remain "places to learn about perplexity and loss of bearing."[22]

iii.

A lyric sequence that spirals around a central visionary experience narrated in three prose poems, *The Quietist* is perhaps Howe's most explicitly apophatic text. Its structure carries out the "sublimations, inversions, echolalia, digressions, glossolalia and rhymes" of bewilderment by pacing the prose poems out across the sequence of eighteen lyrics, thereby juxtaposing "a maximum amount of randomness . . . against a minimum amount of order."[23] The prose sections create the illusions of scene, temporal progress, and narrative continuity, but the juxtapositions and non sequiturs of the lyrics undermine referential stability and traditional narrativity through dramatic shifts in diction, imagery, and prosodic structures. Moved by the same "heave, thrill, and murmur of the nomadic heart"[24] that guides the lyric sequence, the pilgrim's journey formally begins with the first prose poem, which narrates her entry into a visionary state:

> I will tell you how it happened. The hour was the break of dawn and I was lying with a lonely man. We lay on my narrow bed looking out the window onto the sloping slate roofs of a monastery. The damp cheek of the stranger rested by my breast and I felt the sorrow that nursing would very often bring me. I didn't doze but let my sad feelings drift away until the whole of my innerverse had been sucked from my body out the window. While my limbs then lay like wood or paper which has fallen from a great height, my sight looked back. Or of the two souls which occupy the person in a sort of figure eight, the upper one looked back at the lower one. It observed that I was being transported by a quality—magnetic mercy?—which would not be deterred by the white building, or its occupants, or our habits, ethics, acts.[25]

Though the scene at first seems self-explanatory—an assignation between our pilgrim and a stranger that triggers a vision—the details the narration gives and those it withholds quickly give us pause: is this an erotic relationship, or a platonic one? Why does this particular moment of melancholy lead to a vision of the upper soul leaving the pilgrim's body? Does the sorrow of nursing elicited by the stranger's cheek by her breast provide a link between the erotic and the maternal? And does this chance link grant the pilgrim's upper soul access to an exit? The pilgrim's upper soul observes that it is being drawn forth by a force outside itself, and suspects that this is the result of mercy—but why has such mercy been granted? The mystical narrative continues through two further prose poems that mark the middle and end of the series, but the experience leaves the pilgrim without language to interpret cause and effect: "It was just an out-of-body experience . . . but since it left an imprint, as firm as the taste of a lover's tongue, it was also an experience outside of common language. I had died before my own eyes!"[26] If this begins to sound something like apophasis, later on she'll recall the experience as a "mystical path" leading to a moment when bliss and abyss were the same, and "PLENTITUDE was the name of the condition."[27]

But the mystical experience narrated by the three prose poems is ultimately remarkable not for its few congruencies with apophatic literature, but for its notable departures from traditional narratives of apophasis: 1) it is depicted as the result not of piety but of a random act of mercy; 2) it happens in the presence of another person; 3) it happens in the context of physical intimacy; 4) the felt presence of divinity is absent from the report of the experience. These departures from traditional narratives of apophasis could be directly linked to *The Quietist*'s portrayal of the pilgrim's embodiment, a state in which the spiritual, erotic, and maternal are represented neither as metaphor nor as allegorical figure, as they are in a classic Medieval apophatic text like Marguerite Porete's *Mirror of Simple Souls*, but as literal and felt experience. This particular departure from Christian orthodoxy could also be said to articulate a struggle central to the life of the apophatic pilgrim: between being "a physical body // With subjective needs" and attaining through faith "Pure equilibrium amounting to enough."[28] Throughout the sequence, Howe indeed places her pilgrim between need and equilibrium where she must make a choice whose outcome might seem to resolve conflict; however, bewilderment ensures that she is always "progressing at one level and becoming more lost at another."[29]

Howe's pilgrim usually progresses spiritually while becoming erotically or romantically lost—though many of her texts suggest that romantic loss may lead to spiritual gain—and thus the shape of her journey gains its contours and trajectory from a traditional conflict between earthly desires and the Christian soul. But in *The Quietist*, as in much of her work, Howe allows a Christian vocabulary to be muddied by an existential one, which, she seems to say, disguises temptation and sin within a discourse of free will. Because "You can't make a choice without a temptation," and "temptation has the same momentum as fire,"[30] any choice her pilgrim makes reveals itself to have been a desire in disguise, a situation that leads to an outcome familiar to all of us:

Then sex shuts the door
With the words:
"Advance to the fire and play with it."[31]

It makes sense that Howe characterizes the erotic as a hot and poten-
tially wounding distraction from a pilgrim's spiritual attention, especially
given that the sequence is titled *The Quietist*. A late seventeenth century
French Catholic heresy, Quietism as it was then practiced involved a
form of meditation called "orison," which the scholar Marie-Florine
Bruneau describes, in *Women Mystics Confront the Modern World*, as "the aban-
donment of cognition, representation, conceptualization, the memory
of God and oneself," [32] qualities shared by traditional apophatic mysti-
cism, Weil's religiosity, and Howe's conceptualization of bewilderment.
Quietist heretics such as Madame Guyon are linked to Medieval apophatic
mystics like Porete by a shared emphasis on the value of private medita-
tion and "a quieting of reason and of discursive thought" [33] that was seen
by the Catholic Church and its officials to undermine its authority as a
social, political, and theological institution. Despite the radical nature
of their spiritual practices and religious beliefs, these women nonethe-
less remained inheritors of a doctrinal tradition in which, as Amy Hol-
lywood writes in "Suffering Transformed: Marguerite Porete, Meister
Eckhart, and the Problem of Women's Spirituality,"

> women are associated with the bodily aspect of human nature. Under-
> stood as intrinsic to human personhood, the body is subject to both
> sin and redemption. The association of women with bodiliness is
> therefore not only, or even primarily, a means by which women are
> denigrated and a debilitating hierarchy of male over female inscribed
> within the social order, but also the means by which women achieve
> sanctification.[34]

Given that Christian theology depends, like Weil's, upon its own
chain of analogous terms—woman is to body is to sin—whose misogy-
nist logic inheres in even the most radical mystical practice, the ques-
tions remain: what links remain strongest in the chain that binds
historical apophasis to contemporaneity? What does it mean for con-
temporary feminist theology that a mystic like Porete subverted "the
association of women with the body," as Hollywood argues, "through
the transfigurative operations of apophasis,"[35] operations in which the

body is altogether rejected as a site of possible sanctification? Does a subversion in which the body entirely disappears count as a useful feminist solution or is it an even more radical problematizing of the role of women's bodies in Christian mysticism? In what ways does *The Quietist* use the conflict between bodily need and spiritual equilibrium to dramatize this problematic historical inheritance?

iv.

That the apophatic tradition depends upon a certain amount of antagonism toward embodied eroticism should come as no surprise: not only did the Beguine Porete take the traditional voluntary vows of chastity that befit her calling, but her *Mirror of Simple Souls* employs tropes of romantic and sexual love to serve her allegorical text as errors in the soul's search for union with God. This reading of the erotic is perfectly consonant with apophatic theory. As Hollywood notes, Porete "refuses the path to the divine which lies through humanity, and demands instead the renunciation of all createdness in order to become divine herself."[36] And though she could not have known herself to be a reader of Porete's *Mirror*, as the author's true identity had not yet been rediscovered, it's clear that Weil's thinking recuperates negative theology's implicit rejection of the flesh in even more explicit terms: "Our true dignity is not to be parts of a body, even though it be a mystical one, even though it be that of Christ."[37] But scholar Ann Pirruccello is right to suggest in her essay, "Making the World my Body: Simone Weil and Somatic Practice," that Weil's apophatic orthodoxy not only constitutes "a blatantly negative strand in her regard for the body, which often echoes traditional Western philosophical and religious views of the body," but that it belies a negativity "both philosophical and personal."[38] It is indeed hard to ignore the zealous inventiveness behind some of Weil's writing, apophatic aphorisms that sting with inverted wit:

Nothing belongs to me except my wretchedness.
Nothings belongs to me, even my wretchedness; it belongs to my flesh.[39]

Given that in many texts over many years Howe claims Weil as her teacher, it seems safe to assume that she's familiar with Weil's attitudes toward embodiment, but she has had little to say about this aspect of Weil's theological legacy. It's hard to imagine what such asceticism could mean to Howe as a lived aspect of daily spiritual practice, given that her politics were formed by the Civil Rights Movement as well as Women's Liberation, and her faith was articulated in the crucible of motherhood, from which, she writes in the introduction to *The Wedding Dress*, "I learned everything I ever hoped to learn about consequence."[40] If it is hard at first to gauge both Howe's proximity to and distance from Weil, perhaps reviewing some contemporary context might help us measure from mid-century to millennium.

Given the enormous force orthodoxy possesses even within heretical traditions of Christian mysticism, "the body" has for two decades at least been at the center of scholarly debate concerning the lives and writing of women mystics, and, likely because of this groundbreaking work by feminist religious scholars, it has recently become a key concept in reappraisals of apophatic theology as well. From Caroline Walker Bynum's seminal 1987 volume *Holy Feast, Holy Fast: The Religious Significance of Food to Medieval Women* to Chris Boesel's and Catherine Keller's 2010 anthology *Apophatic Bodies: Negative Theology, Incarnation, and Relationality*, embodiment's embattled place in women's religious history and contemporary theology has been revisited so often it's almost become a site of pilgrimage. For many feminists, negative theology's general antagonism toward bodies—and women's bodies in particular—remains a troubling legacy because it's difficult to distinguish between theologically prescribed misogyny and attitudes adopted in the wake of true apophatic experience. As Boesel and Keller point out in their introduction to *Apophatic Bodies*, the problem inheres in apophasis itself, which "seems to *say away* the language of the bodily, the creaturely," but "does not negate bodies as such,"[41] only rather "our false knowledge, the idols formed in the confusion of the finite with the infinite."[42] This distinction, however, is cold comfort if embodiment, as figured by apophatic literature, always plays an important role in forming this confusion and keeping the individual soul from *true* bewilderment. Thus when reading Howe in light of Weil, it still makes sense for us to wonder if it's at all possible for the pilgrim's body—let alone her eros—to contribute positively to apophasis.

V.

At first, *The Quietist* would seem to provide the easy answer: no. An inheritor of theological sanctions against the body, Howe's quietist pilgrim at times seems as vehement as Weil in her assessment of embodiment: "Bones & cartilage / Under clothing show what hunger / Has in store for all garbage."[43] This characterization of the body as a form of garbage is in keeping with other passages in which sex is figured in terms of physical discomfort and implied martyrdom: "Sex is made on a bed which is too loose / Or too hard. / Arrows & burning thoughts included."[44] At other times, however, Howe's pilgrim distinguishes herself from these apophatic orthodoxies by associating sex not with temptation or suffering but with outright evil, as she does in several passages linking the male body and sexuality with the devil:

> A man's erect
> nipples
>
> It was enemy class
> travel
>
> with the devil
> who's red for a reason.
>
> Pleasure bloodies his underskin.[45]

The mixed diction of these stanzas is built to shock, and its hard enjambments insist on the conflation of anatomy, arousal, advertising language, and cartoonish images of evil that nonetheless suggest great violence. But taken as parts of the whole lyric sequence, these three brief quotations participate in the partial articulation of latent beliefs about erotic embodiment that structure much of Howe's writing: sex is a site of egocentric power plays and domination associated with male "masters of the military & amorous arts."[46] But such sentiments and representations form only one aspect of *The Quietist*, which otherwise attempts to revise traditional theological readings of body and soul by breaking the links of the chain of analogies that equates only women with body and sin, thus recuperating the pilgrim's body as a potential site of wisdom, compassion, and spiritual insight and subverting apophatic theology's dependence on the total negation of embodiment.

First the sequence works hard to split the concept of "body" into two by differentiating between male and female embodiment; it aligns the former with violence, power, and sexuality, while it associates the latter with maternal love, selflessness, and spirituality. This connection between male sexuality and violence is in keeping with Howe's startling linkage of "A man's erect / nipples" with "enemy class / travel" and "pleasure's bloodied underskin." And the direct connection between female embodiment, maternity, and spirituality is in keeping with what Howe in her novel *Indivisible* calls "the three virtues of maternalism": "the love of one's neighbor, detachment and humility."[47] But the sequence also works to split soul or spirit in two as well, assigning each a corresponding set of associations consonant with those of their bodies: "Boat for her spirit: canoe & baby. / Boat for his spirit: ship of state."[48] This couplet underscores the fact that *The Quietist* forges very different chains of analogies than either traditional apophatic theology or orthodox Catholicism. For Howe, woman is to mother is to humility is to selflessness is to transcendence, while man is to sex is to law is to power is to violence is to devil. And even though Howe borrows much of the logic behind her representations of maternal spirituality from Mariology, these parallel chains nonetheless lock the text into a very different set of attitudes toward gender than those that characterize a Beguine like Porete or a Quietist like Madame Guyon. And yet, like them, her pilgrim looks elsewhere than the Church for the true life of the spirit; like them, her pilgrim experiences men as more likely to be allied with institutional power structures that inhibit rather than empower women's spiritual experience.

But what makes Howe's text so extraordinarily rich with insight and trouble is that it presents neither the pilgrim's body nor her spirit as stable entities. "When she was alone in her cell," Howe writes, "she didn't exist. Only bliss," and yet "she was dying / to join in . . . with the post-Christians."[49] Ultimately Howe's pilgrim exists in a spiritual state of embodiment that is radically contingent, both open to and dependent on relationality for its definition. Such embodiment further complicates a traditional reading of the apophatic experience at the center of *The Quietist* by offering us a glimpse of what scholar Krista Hughes calls "incarnational apophasis."[50] One lyric in particular returns to the central spiritual drama of the sequence—being both a body ruled by necessity and a spirit desiring peace—but refigures that conflict in embodied terms that paradoxically suggest apophasis:

> Zero built a nest
> In my navel. Incurable
> Longing. Blood too—
>
> From violent actions.
> It's a nest belonging to one.
> But zero uses it.
> And its pleasure is mine.[51]

If "zero" equals the ideal sum at which apophatic knowledge aims, this poem surprisingly finds the body's center at the center of apophasis, its "incurable / Longing" an affect more reminiscent of sensible mysticism than quietist detachment. The poem also asserts that apophasis derives a kind of sensual pleasure from the borrowing and "use" of the pilgrim's navel, which conjures an almost natal relationship—the navel's characterization as a "nest" further heightens its connotations as an anatomical site of fusion with the mother, and subtly connects this lyric with the maternal spirituality upon which the rest of the sequence depends. It's for this reason that this lyric in particular shows evidence of sympathy with a feminist vision of incarnational apophasis that extends back, argues Krista E. Hughes in her essay "Intimate Mysteries: The Apophatics of Sensible Love," to the fourteenth century mystic Julian of Norwich, for whom "the body was never to be left behind in this process [of union with God] but in point of fact was at the very center of the process."[52] Howe would likely agree with Hughes that visionary experience can "facilitate... relation *with* the world rather than severing the mystic from her material context;"[53] she might also agree with Hughes' assertion that "fragmentation of the sensual and the substantial" might constitute "a fall away from God"[54] for the incarnational apophatic. The final three lines of this lyric assert that, though the nest belongs "to no one," it's used by zero, "and its pleasure is mine," a series whose vocabulary suggests both an alliance with traditional apophatic theology ("no one" and "zero") and a significant departure from it ("nest" and "pleasure").

Howe's pilgrim reminds us that vocabulary problems remain with us in the wake of apophasis, incarnational or not; language ever after interposes itself between the body and spiritual experience, thereby inserting a swerve between each theological or narrative interpretation and the apophatic encounter it serves. If this makes things tricky for the scholar and theologian, it's business as usual for both pilgrim and poet, given that the lyric, Howe argues in her essay "Bewilderment," "is a method of searching for something that can't be found."[55] Lyric language becomes a co-participant in the pilgrim's journey, serving both to elucidate and further complicate what would never have been a simple narrative anyway. "Words made voices," Howe writes early in the sequence,

> In their terminal search for content—
> for what's contingent on the reason
>
> For being in the world.[56]

Insistently polyvalent, words' "terminal search for content" suggests that their search ends with the attainment of *content* or *content* or that the search for *content*/*content* kills them. Given that this search is "contingent on the reason // for being in the world," Howe gives us reason to believe that language embarks on the same journey as the pilgrim, and likely experiences the same kinds of confusion: between content and contentment and God. But the parallel between pilgrim and word, journey and writing, suggests the possibility of a language charged with a kind of incarnational apophasis. The line, "You know by writing that what you know, writes,"[57] offers the paradoxical possibility that apophatic knowledge makes its way into language only through writing, and only by writing is it possible for the pilgrim to know something of the apophatic experience that remains always outside of knowing.

Notes

1. Howe, "Work and Love," 126.
2. Weil, *Notebooks of Simone Weil*, 21.
3. Weil, *The Notebooks*, 637.
4. In her "Spiritual Autobiography," 69, Weil reports that, when in the middle of a violent headache, she recited George Herbert's poem "Love," and "Christ himself came down and took possession of me." Of the actual experience, she says only, "neither my

senses nor my imagination had any part; I only felt in the midst of my suffering the presence of a love."

5. Weil, *The Notebooks*, 29.
6. Sells, *Mystical Languages of Unsaying*, 8.
7. Weil, *The Notebooks*, 23.
8. Weil, 47.
9. Weil, 39.
10. Weil, 40.
11. Weil, 41.
12. Weil, 45.
13. Weil, 69.
14. Weil, 71.
15. Sells, *Mystical Languages*, 8.
16. Howe, "Doubt," 27.
17. Howe, *The Winter Sun*, 51.
18. Howe, "Bewilderment," 20.
19. Howe, "Bewilderment," 20.
20. Howe, "Well Over Void," 78.
21. Howe, "Bewilderment," 14.
22. Howe, "Bewilderment," 15.
23. Howe, "Bewilderment," 17.
24. Howe, "Bewilderment," 21.
25. Howe, *The Quietist*. Because *The Quietist* is unpaginated, no page numbers shall be referenced when quoting from it.
26. Howe, *The Quietist*.
27. Howe, *The Quietist*.
28. Howe, *The Quietist*.
29. Howe, "Bewilderment," 16.
30. Howe, *The Quietist*.
31. Howe, *The Quietist*.
32. Bruneau, *Women Mystics*, 143.
33. Bruneau, *Women Mystics*, 143.
34. Hollywood, "Suffering Transformed," 87.
35. Hollywood, 88.
36. Hollywood, 96.
37. Weil, *Waiting for God*, 80.
38. Pirruccello, "Making the World my Body," 485.
39. Weil, *Notebooks*, 128.
40. Howe, *The Wedding Dress*, xxvi.
41. Boesel and Keller, Eds., *Apophatic Bodies*, 4.
42. Boesel and Keller, Eds., *Apophatic Bodies*, 5.
43. Howe, *The Quietist*.
44. Howe, *The Quietist*.
45. Howe, *The Quietist*.
46. Howe, *The Quietist*.
47. Howe, "Indivisible," 563.
48. Howe, *The Quietist*.
49. Howe, *The Quietist*.

50. Hughes, "Intimate Mysteries," 349-366.
51. Howe, *The Quietist.*
52. Hughes, "Intimate Mysteries," 354.
53. Hughes, 355.
54. Hughes, 354.
55. Howe, "Bewilderment," 21.
56. Howe, *The Quietist.*
57. Howe, *The Quietist.*

Bibliography

Boesel, Chris, and Catherine Keller, eds. *Apophatic Bodies: Negative Theology, Incarnation, and Relationality.* New York: Fordham University Press, 2010.

Bruneau, Marie-Florine. *Women Mystics Confront the Modern World.* Albany: State University of New York Press, 1998.

Hollywood, Amy. "Suffering Transformed: Marguerite Porete, Meister Eckhart, and the Problem of Women's Spirituality." In *Meister Eckhart and the Beguine Mystics: Hadewijch of Brabant, Mechtild of Magdeburg, and Marguerite Porete*, edited by Bernard McGinn, 87–113. New York: Continuum, 1994.

Howe, Fanny. *Gone.* Berkeley: University of California Press, 2003.

Howe, Fanny. *The Quietist.* Oakland: O Books, 1991.

Howe, Fanny. *Radical Love: Five Novels.* Callicoon, NY: Nightboat Books, 2006.

Howe, Fanny. *The Wedding Dress: Meditations on Word and Life.* Berkeley: University of California Press, 2003.

Howe, Fanny. "Well Over Void." *Five Fingers Review* 10 (1991): 77–80.

Howe, Fanny. *The Winter Sun: Notes on a Vocation.* St. Paul: Graywolf Press, 2009.

Hughes, Krista E. "Intimate Mysteries: The Apophatics of Sensible Love." In *Apophatic Bodies: Negative Theology, Incarnation, and Relationality*, edited by Chris Boesel and Catherine Keller, 349–366. New York: Fordham University Press, 2010.

Pirruccello, Ann. "Making the World My Body: Simone Weil and Somatic Practice," *Philosophy East and West* 52.4 (October 2002): 479–497.

Sells, Michael A. *Mystical Languages of Unsaying.* Chicago: University of Chicago Press, 1994.

Weil, Simone. *The Notebooks of Simone Weil.* Translated by Arthur Wills. New York: G.P. Putnam's Sons, 1956.

Weil, Simone. *Waiting for God.* Translated by Emma Craufurd. New York: Harper and Row, 1973.

Thinking of Spirit and Spiritual
Lissa Wolsak's Squeezed Light
Hank Lazer

> Consciousness breaks with its own imaginative skeleton to exist
> inside and outside the manner of things and can inquire through
> matter, energy, space . . . time, in anti-totalitarian postulates to the
> impinging nakedness and origins. Each dream follows the mouth.
> To let . . . to culture . . .
> —Lissa Wolsak, *An Heuristic Prolusion*[1]

> There is a sloppiness around the public use of the words "soul" and
> "spirit" which is evidence of their disappearance. These words are
> odd now and it is perhaps only their oddness that charges them. . . . We
> need not return to them, and cannot in any sense that we now under-
> stand, but they haunt us. And they are, so to speak, tossed up by our
> task in language. They propose a binding and an entangling with
> the essential unknown that is part of the life of the known.
> —Robin Blaser, "The Practice of Outside"[2]

In *Otherwise than Being or Beyond Essence*, Emmanuel Levinas writes that
"the birthplace of ontology is in the said," and he prods us to think about
what might lie before "language contracts into thought."[3] In Lissa Wol-
sak's poetry, we live and breathe and achieve awareness in that state. Call
it liminal or *chora*, call it the cloud of unknowing, it is a domain that is
ethical, mystical, pedagogical, spiritual, and profoundly etymological.

Lissa Wolsak is an importantly unoriginal original poet, and *Squeezed
Light*, her collected poems, is a major event. It begins:

Girl   with vase of odors

Cradle   one's own head . .

squinches, pendentives,   oculi,   groin

cri imaginaire   pity

the river myth

was there ever

a father field[4]

As Wolsak writes a few pages later, it is writing built on the "swerve word   with / silence at its core."[5] It is rare to find a poetry where the open space is so essentially and carefully deployed; on that note, in their thoughtful introduction, George Quasha and Charles Stein suggest

> The text converses with itself to make space for reading. In fact, reading is what it's already doing, by way of textual self-dialogue and inquiry into its own conception. In the very density of the text is an always unknown kind of spaciousness. Perhaps something like this is carried by the Japanese word *ma* which can be rendered as space, time, gap, emptiness, negative space, or the space (time) between structural parts.[6]

The interval of the unwritten, the space between words, the space that we cross over to arrive at the moment when language contracts into thought, are crucial to the making of Wolsak's poetry. In the poems, we arrive at a kind of temple of reading, a place where we reflect upon how and what we are reading.

Wolsak came to poetry by means of many other activities. As she says in an October 2000 interview with Pete Smith (included in *Squeezed Light*), she had already been a "mother, adventuress, beekeeper, volunteer friend to imprisoned people, volunteer friend and bridge for severely challenged persons, surgical nurse, hotelier, impresario, and recently free-lance artisan of ikebana, and a goldsmith."[7] I note Wolsak's background—born in 1947, she grew up in southern California, never went to college, and moved to Canada in 1969—because I think that an under-recognized quality of current American innovative poetry is its self-taught quality. (Think, for example, of Susan Howe, Charles Bernstein, Jack Foley, and Ron Silliman, to name just a few. There are considerable affinities with "outsider art," art forms not dependent upon learning a particular credentialed craft, though the artists tend to be quite knowledgeable and well-schooled, autodidactically.)

Wolsak's work, though it feels like it came suddenly out of nowhere—her first book did not arrive until she was in her late forties (and we should remember that there are other important instances of great poets late arriving into the book-publishing world, including Wallace Stevens and Robert Frost—a model very much at odds with today's quest for rapid, repeated book publications by young writers)—has many important kinships. Her originality does not come from the void, however; in fact, Wolsak's first purchased book of poetry was Zukofsky's "A," and she acknowledges Stein, Olson, Susan Howe, Beckett, and Celan as important to her, as well as the work of Douglas Oliver, Alice Notley, and Allen Fisher, among others. Reading Wolsak today, in retrospect, her connections to the work of Susan Howe, Jake Berry, Zukofsky, Arakawa and Gins, and many others are evident.

In writing about Lissa Wolsak's poetry[8]—as with that of several other contemporary writers such as Peter O'Leary and John Taggart—I am claiming that this writing is essential to a new mode of spiritual writing. Wolsak's poetry in particular places a demand on me to explore more fully the terms "spirit" and "spirituality." In my writing, I know at the outset that I will not settle our understanding of these terms, for they are terms with long and complex and contradictory histories in the writing of poetry, poetics, philosophy, and religion. These key terms rub against equally complex and contested concepts such as the holy and the sacred. Even so, I offer here some preliminary writing—influenced by my recent readings in Emmanuel Levinas and Robin Blaser[9]—with the hope that these thoughts and juxtapositionings might sharpen the focus upon "spirit" and "spiritual" when I assert that an innovative poetry such as Wolsak's makes a fundamental contribution to a contemporary writing of spiritual experience.

For Levinas, "our question is how and to what degree one can be affected [*affection*] by what is not equal to the world, how one can be affected by what can be neither apprehended nor comprehended."[10] The poem, then, becomes the record of that affection—the wording and manifestation on the page of an engagement with "what can be neither apprehended nor comprehended." The innovative appearance of Wolsak's poems offers a "new realism," a credible, faithful, even somewhat mimetic way to embody those moments of affection. But as with virtually every suggestion or approximation that I will offer for "spirit," the suggestion remains haunted by skepticism: how/why is that approximation—in this case that which "can be neither apprehended or comprehended"—related to "spirit"? Is that really what constitutes "spirit," and why should I call the incomprehensible by the name "spirit"?

In Levinas's lectures (in the collection *God, Death, and Time*), Hegel's writing occupies a central position, and the elements of Hegel's thinking that Levinas addresses often turn out to be pertinent to explorations of Wolsak's poetry: "In Hegel, the manifestation of being to consciousness is a moment of the unfolding of that being."[11] The poem might then be thought of as an occasion or instance—a giving form or shape—for that moment of manifestation, that profound and fleeting and inevitably incomplete (and often emotionally moving) experiencing of the tangibility of being. The poem, then, offers a specific language instance as a temporary insight into (and experiencing of) the nature of being. This may not exactly result in a rigorous or traditional philosophical investigation of the question of being, but a lateral consideration of being. The poem becomes a manifestation of a matter at hand that is of fundamental interest to philosophical thinking. Thus perhaps another key approximation for "spirit" is being itself, a conceptual invisibility, an evasive fundamental that defies specification.

In turning to Blaser's essays to help refine my sense of "spirit" and the "spiritual" in the poetry of Wolsak and other contemporary innovative poets, one key starting point that all share (though to differing degrees) is with a decisive avoidance: "It seems necessary to say that I am not writing about religion in the ordinary sense. That institutionalization of imaginary forms has become an immobility of foregone conclusions."[12] In fact, it seems to me that one of the most exciting developments in contemporary innovative poetry is this multifaceted exploration of new modes of writing spiritual experience in an a-institutional or non-institutional context,[13] from the work of John Taggart to Peter O'Leary, from Fanny Howe to Lissa Wolsak, and including the work of many other poets. As Blaser argues, while many other domains of thought and art-making have abandoned entire terminologies of the "spiritual," such is not the case for poetry. Blaser asserts, "Poetry, however, has never let go of a 'discourse of cosmos' that keeps the attention of the old vocabulary of God, gods, and goddesses intelligent at least."[14] Blaser, by way of the writing of Mark Taylor, summarizes the essential discourses:

> "God, self, history, and book are ... bound in an intricate relationship in which each mirrors the other. No single concept can be changed without altering all the others" (Taylor 7). Each of these four terms represents a category of discourse and each involves a poetics, even if in one instance it may be the history of poetics. This in turn draws us into what I have called a "discourse of the cosmos," the complex poetics of the other, large and small.[15]

It is this poetics of the other that may be the essential term/concept for my exploration of a new poetry of "spirit" and "spiritual" experience. As Blaser points out, "Poetry always had to do with consciousness."[16] My reading of or *feeling* for Wolsak's poetry suggests that it occurs at a kind of tipping point, at that moment that Levinas (via Hegel) describes as a rising into consciousness (of an understanding, however incomplete or fleeting, of being).

Indeed, the poem can be seen as a kind of commerce, a trade, a tracking, a means of moving back and forth, a shuttling to and fro. There is a metric to such motion, a metric of shifting location, a metric as well of engagement and disengagement. As Robin Blaser observes, "the divine is resituated in a composition where belief and disbelief are composing elements of its meaning."[17] If one is to write a credible phenomenology of "spiritual" experience, it must, in my opinion, be composed of both belief and disbelief. A contemporary writing of "spirit" may indeed be characterized by an endlessly unpredictable movement in and out of belief, with a relationship to the divine being (perhaps being itself) as an unsteady but palpable (and invisible) adjacency:

Awing us in

the open place

which inflects

being   as in union or rapture[18]

This passage from Lissa Wolsak's "A Defence of Being, *Second Ana*" suggests that being doesn't really need defending, but by defending *being* we enter into a different, more intense awareness of it. By being *being*'s partisan, one might actually develop a facility for *feeling* being. Participating in the writing as a reader, one is simply allured by Wolsak's poetry—that is, her poetry invites the reader to partake of an experiential or phenomenological pedagogy toward a certain spirituality of being. Would it be too odd to suggest that writing or reading in this manner—in a way that has no fixed activity or outcome in mind—is itself a mode for developing a feeling for being?

One such wormhole toward a feeling for being—which would be the sum of any defense needed for being: a *savoring* sense of being, and thus a defense of the *value* of being—is etymological reading. So in the passage quoted above, as we are checking into "inflection" (as in "the open place / which inflects / being") we might begin our residence in the word by considering a shift in voice, a modulation of pitch, and then think that inflection is the means by which grammatical difference is enacted—tone, tense, person, aspect, mood, gender, number. Yet we still have not arrived at a middle English sense of the word, as in + *flectere* to bend, and thus "to turn from a direct line or course." Is the poem not an instance of inflection? In and by means of language, one turns away from one kind of certainty of saying to a more exploratory bending toward. Such experience is a kind of tropism, as a reader leans into the poem, leaning toward that feeling for being, which may, as Wolsak's poem suggests, be "the open place," wherein we feel inflection itself occurring. This, apparently, in awe, in "awing us in," must be akin ("as in union or rapture") to what *being* is.

Though this union or rapture would seem to bespeak the transcendent, Wolsak's poetry shies away from lapsing into a conventional ontology or transcendent. Elsewhere she writes, "in cold mischief / I insculpt / the gasp of individual perception."[19] In her interview with Pete Smith, Wolsak declares,

> I choose, rather, to activate consciousness, and to keep a loose hold on the smoky, beguiling and sometimes fatuous muse of controlled meaning, but not to exclude the genuinely intended or navigable. I am more a receiver of shape and form than an architect of same.[20]

Correspondingly, Levinas, in summarizing Hegel, describes stages in Spirit's development:

> ... Spirit is thus like a sort of nature [comme une nature] before being opposed to itself. Hegel calls this stage of Spirit's immediacy substance. Spirit is substance, and it has before itself a progression whereby it must become a subject.
>
> It is substance insofar as it makes its own history, develops itself "insofar as its spiritual content is engendered by itself." It will become a subject, become the Knowledge that Spirit has of itself, that is, absolute thought or the living truth that knows itself. From the Spirit that simply is, it will become the Self-Knowledge of that Spirit.[21]

Wolsak's poetry positions itself at this tipping point, where spirit as substance is becoming a realm of experience (and of awareness verging on knowledge) of the reading/writing subject. As and within this poetic experience, one sees the advent of history, event, time.

Certainly, Heidegger picked a great pair: *being* and *time*. His writing made us intensely aware of a kind of gap in western philosophical thinking: our presumption that we knew what we meant by these two vexing terms. Post-Heidegger, it is nearly impossible to think about *being* without also thinking about *time*. Thus in Wolsak's poem:

then ... ought each of

the said things intrude upon us now?

being scient is of

minute moment

loom-shuttles still[22]

I'll repeat about time what I claimed about the pedagogical dimension of Wolsak's poetry with regard to being: the poem and its slowly considered etymologies enact and encourage that feel for time. As a reader we become scient or scientist of that being-opened looming of time and its minute durations. Scient as "knowing," from Latin *sciens*. As also "prescient," a kind of foreknowing. We see Wolsak's lines, in their varied indentations, a kind of loom-shuttle on the page. The reader looms over the page, and thus our experience or feel for time, by means of the peculiar duration of reading (and its minute moments of transport), is illuminated. The poem, by the welcome intrusion of said things (and written things), is turned into a knowing.

Wolsak's spacing of words on the page, her loom-shuttle, becomes an array that invites the kind of slow reading (analogous to slow cooking, and slow eating) that invites a dwelling with the word, a locale that we too often read (and speed) through. That residence in and on and with the word, I am arguing, is analogous to the kind of thinking or feeling of being and time that is the "defensive" or provocative action central to this distinctive poetry.

Wolsak's poetry, for example, has less emphasis on the individual image (or the conventional visual image/analogy) than it does on the overall mode of composition—the poem-series, or the book—as constituting a more comprehensive, indirect "image." The poem itself—its eccentricities of shape/form—becomes a perhaps more comprehensive image or twin of our relationship to the world. In Wolsak's writing, there is a scrupulous tentativeness, an ethically exact desire not to overstep or overstate what is known. Or, as Robin Blaser puts it, "our poetic context involves relation to an unknown, not a knowledge or method of it."[23] I find that it makes sense to think of this ethics of relation as a kind of faith or over-arching image of a relationship to "spirit." Blaser, again by way of Olson, concludes "that all method is belief."[24] I concur and point to Wolsak's poetry as a crucial example.

Continuing my sampling of the "A Defence of Being, *Second Ana*," I find Wolsak asking

> whose bis-
>
> muthous chain of
>
> globes are we ten-
>
> anting?[25]

The page/passage which includes the four lines I have quoted begins, "If we say . . . *deep sea*." This is an apt image, as I believe that the reading I provide is simply one of a nearly infinite number of similar experiences if one dives down and into the word/moments provided throughout Wolsak's poetry. The words become a chain of globes (as in the molecular models one sees in any chemistry textbook), and indeed they

are places we are "tenanting," or, more precisely, "ten- / anting," as
the carefully placed syllables crawl from one line, hyphenated, to the
next. This experience of the word opening up onto a complexity of
association and definition and use is analogous to our learning to
invoke a similar ethical opening up of the elements of *being* and *time*.
That is perhaps how one defends these (and other elements): by teach-
ing and learning an ethics of slow, heuristic residency.

A few pages later—"later" being both a location in time and a locale—
we come upon

> Beyond . . . on a convex . . .
>
> attingent squeezed light,
>
> what-is touches what-is[26]

For many years, I have thought of reading (particularly of the kind
of poetry that Wolsak writes) as an instance of qi gong, of being in
channeled proximity to energy patterns (as Olson had suggested in his
invocation of "field"), as a kind of transferred-being-proximate expe-
rience of the healing or energizing power of words (which, we often
refer to as "being touching"). "Attingent" turns out to be an archaic
word meaning "touching; in contact." The poem, particularly of the
variety, as here, that we often refer to as "experimental," thus consti-
tutes a kind of laboratory, a site where "what-is touches what-is."

Wolsak has observed that "thoughts have mass,"[27] and her poems, in
their placement on the page and in their necessary fragmentation, prox-
imity and brushing against each other, incorporate that inclination into
substance, space, and dwelling that Levinas and Hegel are tracking:

> . . go with me,
>
> disquisit · hour of terse·
>
> touch and sight
>
> transhumance,
>
> fever themselves[28]

The poem occurs in that momentary slippage in which spirit, by a
kind of self-opposition, becomes a way of knowing (though in Wolsak's

work, that perhaps Germanic dream of completeness and totalization—"*the* living truth"—does not occur nor is it even wished for). Wolsak's poems then, in their tentativeness on the page, in their shifting and truncated residence in the word and phrase, link questing to questioning, much in the manner that Levinas thinks of philosophical writing: "The question mark of every question comes from the question: What does being signify?"[29] For me, questioning itself lies at the heart of a credible relationship to "spirit." Inherently, with respect to "spirit," one engages in a nonreciprocal relationship, with an invisibility that is at most a breath. While we can begin to stack up an array of approximations for the spiritual, for an engagement with "spirit"—being, consciousness, the invisible, that which cannot be apprehended or comprehended, thinking—each of these terms points toward an erratic and unsteady process, a flaring into awareness and its disappearance, rather than offering anything resembling a conventional definition.

This in turn draws us into what I have called a "discourse of the cosmos," the complex poetics of the other, large and small. It is this poetics of the other that may be the essential term/concept for my exploration of a new poetry of "spirit" and "spiritual" experience and Lissa Wolsak's work is particularly exemplary here. Her poetry, as with that of others writing in this vein, explores being and time toward an Otherness of/in language and manifests that exploration in a form that does not negate (or fully digest) that Other-ness. Consider, as an example of this dialectical relationship/residence in an othered language:

mock·   cup-nest

manacle

proliferati   mystico-nuclear

          mimicry[30]

Or, from Wolsak's *Pen Chants*,

and after,

istle, finnochio, ixia

"rich in apples"

they, for emissive

lips cooled forth

chilled persimmon sheathes,

disinterest in the speech of

ill-lit, rigor-like

ink flows on top of milk[31]

When Wolsak begins "Figmental" with these lines

Let this put me   another way...

as a way of waking[32]

I feel that we are precisely in that unmastered/unmasterable relation-
ship to language that is at the heart of what it means today to write a
poetry of "spiritual" experience.[33] Note this parallel to Wolsak's sense
that at the moment of composition one is being written/ridden ("Let
this put me   another way"): Blaser, in writing about Jack Spicer's writing
methods, points toward a similarly unwilled or unmasterable way of
proceeding throughout a series or book or ongoing poetic project,
noting that the poet could ideally work "in that long form without
looking back and without thought of the previous poem, so that the
poet could be *led by what was composing*" (emphasis mine).[34]

Perhaps poets have a peculiarly active awareness of the sacred and/
or philosophical understanding that language is not something to
master; language is an other-ness with which one develops an intimate,
complex, ever-unfolding relationship. The poet's is a complex relation-
ship to will, time, language, and coherence. Indeed, habitual coherence
is suspended or avoided in favor of a heuristic relationship with a realm
that is merely an invisible potential that *may* be actualized by means of
a peculiarly developed placement and selection of language. I recall
again Wolsak's line, "Let this put me   another way." Language, as
exemplified in the body of Wolsak's poetry makes manifest another
instance of the possible—an instance particular as well to its moment,
to the historical nature of its relationship to a manifestation or (human)
awareness of being.

Wolsak, in her essay *An Heuristic Prolusion*, points toward just such an engaged tentativeness. Her remarks stammer toward an almost simultaneous statement and an ethical withdrawal (or moving on):

> Consciousness breaks with its own imaginative skeleton to exist inside and outside the manner of things . . . in anti-totalitarian postulates[.] . . . To find axis, or, an orbital angular moment, in rejection of its own centrality, always already disturbing its own refinement.[35]

That ethics of perpetual disturbance—of a kind of deliberate antimastery—is Wolsak's method as belief. Her methodology leads to this sort of page from *Pen Chants*:

o, thoughtic sleeves,

enclued side-swipes . .

moteing gyro-vague and

part-time wooer . . . kyriist,

fib-snout and booze-bonding

perfecto-distingo at San Marco . . ,

do not rescind space

pangless between atoms . .

but at the shadows of

species and ideas

for the love of

the covering animal[36]

In presenting the unrepresentable, this poetry seeks and creates a "next"—not in a developmental, progressive, or evolutionary sense, but as a testament and bearing witness to a current (and thus historically specific) momentary relationship to being. The poem, in its formal adventurousness, becomes that perhaps adequately complex "twin" for the unrepresentable. Blaser attests that, "Alongside the modern experience of the materiality of language, there is also afoot a materiality of soul."[37] Wolsak's poetry is one of the most exciting, engaging contemporary instances of that materiality of the soul. In it, we find a language for the ethical un-mastering of method, as well as a sense of reverence or wonder for the radical otherness of language itself.

I have deliberately focused on a key strand of Wolsak's thinking in the passages I have been reading in this essay: an attentional (attingent?) beam that illuminates *being*. The ethical nature of her writing—a kind of ethics of poetic composition—becomes most apparent when the reader begins to realize just how many passages of her poems open up to such reading, dwelling, conjecturing, and etymological diving. As one is schooled in such a mode of reading (which, I believe, is virtually identical to the mode of writing that makes such poems), we become schooled in an essential grasp for what we are as creatures suspended in the solutions of *being* and *time*.

Notes

1. Wolsak, *Squeezed Light*, 144.
2. Blaser, *The Fire: Collected Essays of Robin Blaser*, 134.
3. Levinas, *Otherwise Than Being or Beyond Essence*, 42, 46.
4. Wolsak, *Squeezed Light*, 3.
5. Wolsak, *Squeezed Light*, 6.
6. Wolsak, *Squeezed Light*, xxi.
7. Wolsak, *Squeezed Light*, 253.
8. See three previous pieces of my writing on Wolsak's *Squeezed Light* (portions of which have been revised, extracted, and incorporated in the current essay for *Quo Anima*): Hank Lazer, "Squeezed Light: Collected Poems 1994-2005," *Rain Taxi Online Edition* (2010), http://www.raintaxi.com/squeezed-light-collected-poems-1994-2005/; Lazer, "Lissa Wolsak's *Squeezed Light: Collected Poems 1994-2005*: A Defence of Being," *Golden Handcuffs Review* 1, no. 14 (2011): 238–242, http://goldenhandcuffsreview.com/ghi4content/Lazer. pdf; Lazer, "Lissa Wolsak's *Squeezed Light: Collected Poems 1994-2005*: Thinking of Spirit and Spiritual," *The Poetic Front*, 4, no. 1 (2011): The Lissa Wolsak Issue, http://journals .sfu.ca/poeticfront/index.php/pf.
9. Levinas, *God, Death, and Time*; Blaser, *The Fire: Collected Essays of Robin Blaser*. Note: while I do believe that the passages from Levinas and Blaser help develop a more nuanced reading of Wolsak's poetry, I am not, in a traditional sense, claiming that their work influenced Wolsak's writing. Though indeed she has read and is familiar with quite a bit of Levinas's writing, in recent e-mails (two e-mails on October 10, 2012), Wolsak indicates, "but for the record, just sayin' (as they say) so that you know: I don't consider Robin Blaser an influence at all, even while I recognize his great beauty . . . I have not read but a few of his poems."
10. Levinas, *God, Death, and Time*, 167.
11. Levinas, *God, Death, and Time*, 160.
12. Blaser, *The Fire*, 40.
13. I make this argument well aware of the Catholicism of Peter O'Leary and Fanny Howe, as well as the deeply sounded Christian riffs and phrases in John Taggart's work

(Taggart being the son of a minister). Nonetheless, I would argue that the deeper residence or engagement of the poem itself constitutes an a-institutional domain.

14. Blaser, *The Fire*, 39.
15. Blaser, *The Fire*, 56.
16. Blaser, *The Fire*, 29.
17. Blaser, *The Fire*, 119.
18. Wolsak, *Squeezed Light*, 189.
19. Wolsak, *Squeezed Light*, 122.
20. Wolsak, *Squeezed Light*, 257.
21. Levinas, *God, Death, and Time*, 80.
22. Wolsak, *Squeezed Light*, 189.
23. Blaser, *The Fire*, 54.
24. Blaser, *The Fire*, 48.
25. Wolsak, *Squeezed Light*, 194.
26. Wolsak, *Squeezed Light*, 201.
27. Wolsak, *Squeezed Light*, 244.
28. Wolsak, *Squeezed Light*, 74.
29. Levinas, *God, Death, and Time*, 58.
30. Wolsak, *Squeezed Light*, 61.
31. Wolsak, *Squeezed Light*, 113.
32. Wolsak, *Squeezed Light*, 159.
33. Such a writing of "spiritual" experience resonates and rhymes with Mallarmé's "The Book A Spiritual Instrument." I offer that if language is the house of being, the book is a similarly large home.
34. Blaser, *The Fire*, 119.
35. Wolsak, *Squeezed Light*, 144-145.
36. Wolsak, *Squeezed Light*, 136.
37. Wolsak, *Squeezed Light*, 41.

Bibliography

Blaser, Robin. *The Fire: Collected Essays of Robin Blaser*. Edited by Miriam Nichols. Berkeley: University of California Press, 2006.

Levinas, Emmanuel. *God, Death, and Time*. Translated by Bettina Bergo. Stanford: Stanford University Press, 2000.

Levinas, Emmanuel. *Otherwise Than Being or Beyond Essence*. Translated by Alphonso Lingis. Pittsburgh: Duquesne University Press, 1998.

Wolsak, Lissa. *Squeezed Light: Collected Poems 1994–2005*. Barrytown, NY: Station Hill, 2010.

An In-Feeling in Jean Valentine
Absence, Gaps, and Empathic Readership
Sara Nolan

> out towards strangeness
>
> you
> a breath on coal
> —Valentine, "Home"[1]

Poet Jean Valentine, now in her seventies, ends her *Collected Poems* with emblematic *transience*, a gap that lets "strangeness" resonate: the reader, in open space, is left with "you"—or is it me? or even a universalized self?—reduced to a "breath." This ending is a false one. It is instead an invitation. I imagine the "breath" (emotional, personal, and impersonal) as she writes it here, as an exhale, which travels out, because I see her trajectory as moving away from the physical world. But it could just as easily be an inhale, marking Valentine's authorial stance of receptivity, and so making it the perfect place to begin to puzzle out what connects us to reading, to one another, and to the heart of Valentine's poetry.

My commitment in this essay is to empathic discourse as the most appropriate means for putting words to empathic readership. Empathy is a process of intersubjective *resonance*; so empathic discourse will necessarily be led by feeling, and supported by, rather than led by, analytical progression. And because empathy by definition occurs between an "I" and a "you," I will use those pronouns here. Empathy *is* intimate; in mimicry and faithfulness to this fact, its academic treatment must be as well.

Empathic readership means that we agree, consciously or unconsciously, to establish a resonance, an "I feel what / as you feel" with text. We see in the text a resemblance, but a resemblance with something "I" cannot (quite) name. (Even as it is part of the materiality of the text, we agree not to objectify it.) And because Valentine's *absence* is the angel wrestling its way into form, we must make space for that absence to surface in our way of reading, in our willingness to feel-into, or gain an "in-feeling" for, the gaps. Empathy is experienced in the medium of poetic texts in particular through processes of recognition in response both to the content and the texture of the lines (specifically and as the components of delineated verse). The diction and syntax, the self-reflexive/conscious selection and placement of words, erect subject-spaces for other-hood and hold a place for absence. The virtual space of text is an *as-if* space, or in Valentine's text, space within space, the absence. The reader can read *as if* s/he too were predicated on absence. This process cannot be purely intellectualized, and analysis, at a certain point, breaks down, as one cannot give the anatomy of emptiness.

Looking at absence in Valentine's work, or gap at the heart of presence in the body of persons (readers) and in the body of her texts, I will offer and model an experiential approach to empathic readership. I hope this will demonstrate the value of such personal engagement of the reader as a legitimate, if unusual, form of academic inquiry. To do so, we will enter through the numerous "gates in the dark" that Valentine hospitably leaves ajar in her poems to feel their implications.

At first, "the spiritual" was supposed to define the scope of this essay. But that term is slippery and bound to the ineffable. When working with the implicitly spiritual, about which she tells me emphatically that she has "nothing to say," Valentine translates it into *absence*. In her poems, absence is visceral, syntactically negotiated, complex, and invitational. By engaging with absence the reader—like the writer—comes into contact with something at the heart of her own being.

I. The Heart of Being: Bodily Presence & Innermost Art

We can situate to the centrality of absence with a quote from the Zen teacher Gabriel Moran: "The self enfolds, infolds, and unfolds all of reality, history, time and space. The center of the human being is a hole, a zero, an empty nothing, through which the entire universe flows in and flows forth, transformed and recreated."[2] To practice zazen, Moran's tradition, "is to be at the heart of the convergence and emergence of all times and beings."[3] Although Moran is describing the ontology of "a self" (to the universe) in general, to talk about empathy, we must apply this to *relationship*. When we make the gesture of relating to one another, or to "another" as is held in the body of a text, we are relating to that thing, that hole, where "nothing joins" (Valentine), but from which all arises. And when we read, the same thing happens. Here, the "hole" at the center will be important to how we read and register both poem and other. We can also compare this description of the self with a description critic Philippe Lacoue-LaBarthe offers of the poetry of Paul Celan, whom Valentine finds particularly compelling: "We must think the innermost of the art, a kind of spacing and hiatus at this very innermost. A secret gap . . . the place of poetry, the place where poetry takes place each time, is the placeless place of the innermost gap" and Lacoue-LaBarthe quotes Celan: "O this empty erring hospitable middle."[4] What you'll see in Valentine's work[5] is that this place of gap is paradoxically palpable: it is the wrestling of (content with its) form. As her work over time becomes more and more spare, the gap has increasing muscle, as in these lines from "The House and the World":

But then
the other world
was going to be given:

the cello part
carrying us the whole time

the earth   the scarred hip

tipped groin

the flying whitehorn hedge

the cup (20)

In this poem, the "me" and "you" that comprise the "us" are non-specific. We readers recognize the objects that appear, but we don't know why the space is so open. We have to explore it from within the text.

To read honestly and to be empathic, in the unflinching way I argue that Valentine writes, it is critical that we center ourselves in our own bodies in real time. It is integral to empathy that we *actually* feel ourselves, no matter how alien that practice might seem in the room of this essay. In an interview, Valentine remarks that for her it is "hard to know where the mind leaves off and the body begins."[6] Her work is built on this blurred boundary, and so in "Home" we get the intimate melding of the physical and the conceptual:

Home   not words but / I know it on my lips (274)

And:

steps go beside you   the sun
crossing a line   sun kinds to you   sun you. (274)

In these lines, she blurs a boundary with light. We cannot avoid the inclusivity of the second-person pronoun. The subject "you" invites every reader equally. The resonance has been set in motion. If we are to be empathic readers and to fully engage with Valentine's work, let's go there, to the blurred boundary—where body and mind, self and other, "I" and "you" coextend. Since this is as much a spiritual as an academic concern, one must also take a minute to feel for this self-sense and "innermost" place together. At a certain point, as Moran suggests, presence is replaced by absence. Let us shift our attention towards text. Valentine begins a translation of an Osip Mandelstam poem, "Toward the empty earth / falling, one step faltering" (145). Valentine reveals to us an empty ground. Slipping, faltering, the inner filled with absence. At first it seems that (you) reader and text are separate. But side-by-side while reading, words can recede away, from you and your thoughts. Hold the possibility that the writing is not only an *object*, but possesses an innermost identity just as you do. This innermost place is distinct from the otherness of *other* objects, retracted from them to an otherness within. To read empathically, you will need to sustain the tension and resonance between your innermost self and the innermost point of the text; feel for both points at once.

In the poem "Sanctuary"—significant that this is our word for the innermost place in a holy structure where sacred objects are kept—the following lines possess substantial visual density, as a physical body; nonetheless, their progression tracks the breaking up of identity to make way for an intersubjective experience:

> Drown out. Not make a house, out of my own words. To be quiet in another throat; other eyes; listen for what it is like there. What word. What silence. Allowing. Uncertain: to drift, in the restlessness... Repose. To run like water— (148)

This speaker is seeking in words, but also beyond the house of words and its (present) protection, that mysterious phenomenon of "another." Like her, we will also seek and hold the tension of listening. It is not always pleasant, this communion of mutual absences.

II. Empathic Readership

When we connect with the innermost gap of the poem, via the innermost gap of ourselves, we have become the poem's intended reader, its intimate "other"—akin to what poet Osip Mandelstam calls its necessary "conversation partner" or poet Paul Celan's estranged, metaphysical "altogether other."[7] Moving inward, we are simultaneously moving, like Valentine, "out towards strangeness" (275).

The connection is an empathic process. Valentine's formal decisions favor emptiness ("the hole"), primarily through elipticism, and her perceptions favor empathy. The presence of a gap or space of "not-ness" as what makes you *not* me is also what allows for transmission. We see this in "The Basket House," which charts the simultaneity of closeness and distance, where the other

> nurses me
> in the emptiness,
> holds me the way
> paper made out of a tree
> holds a deer.
>
> And he holds me near:
> he pulls the cord
> out from me, into him,
> length over length. (21)

The "other" is figured compulsively in Valentine's work, and her poems seek to apprehend difference, charting that field where the other can "become available to be understood" without necessarily fulfilling any obligation to be understandable. Our point of contact may be but slight:

> Our brush with each other
>
> —two animal souls
> without cave
> image
> or
> word (258)

Valentine allows strangeness to remain close without translating it into something familiar, and she allows vacancy to be participatory, almost material. When she asks in "A Bit of Rice," "What will be left here when you die?," her answers excavate rather than provide:

> Not the rice
> not the tea
> left *somewhere* when the monk
> knocked over the cup
> not
> not (235)

Line composition and line breaks replace the guidance of (conventional) punctuation, which would normally serve to anchor the reader on stable ground.

The vacancy leaves its residue. In the lines above, otherness hinges on, and is represented by, the adverb "not." Elsewhere, the connection between self and other is figured on such a deep level that the extrication of one subjectivity from another can seem surgical and painful:

> you are becoming gone
>
> to me   but
> the cut-out hurts
>
> where you were
> behind my eye. (34)

Her poems chart something uncanny about all of us: other-less, we are rendered unstable, "cut out"—but of what? We are pointedly called into relation, with you-me references, while also being told we are "gone." The space of the poem and the self-other dynamics both aggravate and soothe. As readers, we must look to empathy for consolation.

Empathy is figured explicitly in the following short burst of a poem, "Flower," wherein self and other come into intimate contact; whatever each is, is here transactional, nearly interchangeable:

> You, I, steadying
> in our in-borne, out-borne sparks
> of empathy, the flower
> of Earth: wet red fireworks-flower. (214)

A mere comma, as typographical mark and cue to inhale, falls between "You, I" indicating a *slight* breath, and preventing these pronouns and selves from merging: "You" and "I," kept apart in our close-farness by punctuation only. Empathy is predicated as "the flower / of Earth: wet red fireworks-flower" and marks a stabilizing transit between the two selves. Thus, each is steady only in its continual movement or communing.

Similarly, a "firework" is what it is *because of* kinesis or explosion— becoming hundreds of disparate points of light. This poem affirms the absence of a fixed self or in any single self, but doesn't fall apart into abstraction. Empathy is blazing and organic, an eye-catching, and "I-catching," growing thing of the earth, but one liable to explode into—or reveal that it is comprised of—fading singularities.

Valentine uses the "gap" in her work as aesthetic strategy reflective of a spiritualized consciousness. By that, I mean a consciousness aware of itself, an *apperceptive* consciousness[8] predicated on and around a formative gap. In this process, "the other" and otherness is registered in her conscious field, and as a consequence, her awareness is "magnetized and configured to a pattern not of [her] own design."[9] In the role of poet, however, Valentine gives a presence to this awareness by how she shapes her lines. As she writes in "Go Clear":

> I swam   out of the streaming ikon eyes
>   who loved me: not-me (12)

Here, the self is evanescent; the destination of its movement is demonstrated in a gap in the line. The *other* is the context, the "eyes" that set the frame. In the view of this other, the one "loved," the "me" is both made object and freed.

Valentine is both compelled and vexed by this ideated *other* towards whom her work and consciousness—her work *as* her consciousness—extends. She has expressed her semantically palpable wish for (poetic) "movement into other and otherness": her "in-feeling" (here a literal translation of "einfühlung," the German equivalent of our word "empathy"[10]) not only for a particular "other," but for the context/cradle of "otherness" in which we live out our individual selves?[11]

We can see this principle in action in "The Rally," a political poem, in which the speaker, vexed by her own role, is present on behalf of a black man. As she tells us right away, "His tongue has been cut by a razor / the tops of his ears have been cut off" (23). Her empathy allows her to sit squarely with the ugly, material truth—and then to be implicated. The dissolution that follows the directness of these opening lines is as much a consequence of the predatory nature of injustice as it is a spiritual testimony:

My clothes   my bag
my money   my papers
                                        It's
the young man

My palms
my soles
              It's
the young man (23)

His literal absence—his body parts cut off—is due to human cruelty. In empathy, Valentine becomes absent too; she becomes him by gently excavating her own body, divesting herself of her things and of herself as embodied thing: "My palms / my soles." At the close, he becomes present again as "your silent invisible body here at the door / your glance" (23). The poem itself is this door at which the presence hovers; pronouns are the vehicles through which empathy travels. This "your" could just as easily now have "the reader" as its implied antecedent as "the man." We—(the bodies of us) as readers—and the young man are interchangeable. But so are we and the implicated "me."

In other poems, the transitions may happen more gently (see below), mapping self and other together and recalling Celan's line, "I am I when I am you."[12] The violence of "The Rally" at first seems a far cry from blurred boundaries of a dream, or a theorist playing with subjectivities. But Valentine's empathic writership invites the reader to become engaged in this risky openness to all experience and not to instinctively slam shut the gates against the dark.

As noted earlier, in Valentine's poems, the breath is a key vehicle between self and other. The breaths transit us to the very edge and innermost of ourselves—it's one way we ascertain and confront the blurred boundary—directly to the gap between inside and out. Valentine uses the breath not only as measurement of poetic line, but as imagistic and metaphoric conduits or containers for the other. Thus in the short poem "How I've Hurt You" Valentine writes, "I dream I *am* you / full of fear and dread / with me in your arms / : my cloth love / holding your breath" (15). The gap that begins the line is snagged or capped by the colon, like a sudden catching in the throat when one is just drifting off to sleep.

And likewise, in "To the Bardo," where she writes of getting through to C., who has been sick, she allows a pause before the exchange:

You know how in dreams you are everyone:
awake too you are everyone:
I am listening   breathing your ashy breath. (25)

In closely reading Valentine, we *breathe her breath*. We cannot help it. It is an empathic chain—her listening, her writing, our reading. In this strange "third space" it is possible to explore the effects of this kind of shared breathing on the bodily-housed consciousness in which we exist as readers. For *that* is where words and, more largely, poetry itself, can open into what Valentine calls "their third / star darkness" (257). She marvels, "We didn't know / we were so close / to the world's mouth" (184). We can further explore the empty space, the gap that Valentine lays bare between

"listening   breathing."

Inhalation and exhalation thus cyclically delineate and enmesh identity. And you can hear it resonating in the poems as in the world. In "Radio: Poetry Reading, NPR," the speaker tells another poet, whose voice comes over the radio thirty-years after her death: I "got across the kitchen to / get next to you / breath and breath / two horses" (255). Valentine looks synaesthetically with her ears, saying of herself, "I was made for this: listening" (243). She listens as much for what isn't here as what is, as much to what comes from "inside" herself as what comes from various sources—not all of them human—"outside." By the quality of her attention, Valentine looks to lay bare the innermost secrets and the absences (and truths) they scab over, even as she is contained within them: "so many secrets / held you in their glass" (10).

Valentine says in an interview, "And I think mine is . . . to get past the secrets, to try to get to, for the lack of a better word, the truths. What is being kept secret, what is not being said."[13] These absences and truths—or truth-as-absence—poke through, sometimes roughly, but only once one has cultivated a reverence for *other*:

> If there was a hole through you
> and a hole through me
> they'd take the same
> peg or needle
> and thread us both
> through the first station
> and there we'd lean
> and listen and listen . . . (195)

Perhaps because of these intrinsic vacancies, what is present is heightened. We, as readers, can be witnesses, if we just listen well enough. What gains her attention retains its mysterious subjecthood. Her understanding, even where partial, is generous and resolute.

The experience of reading Valentine, entering the strangeness of the poems, both has and awakens in us an erratic pulse: our reading selves first merge with the text, then retreat and diverge, then merge again. This mimics the way one nervous system attunes to another, as happens for a hysterical child who will only be calmed by being met with calmness. In this process Valentine is also listening for you, reader—for "your heart / lapping against the birth door of my ear"

(205). *Otherness* is key to her hearing—it is what is listened for. It is the gap in the self, but through which the self comes to be.

III. Tensions: This-side, Other-side

Valentine's poems are full of transactions from above and below, this world and another. The vertiginous ground is a yearning from which articulation arises; this is so despite what she calls "the fucking reticence of this world" (8) in "I Came to You," a poem that seems to chastise an absent "Lord" for his belatedness. Note that she then abnegates: "no, not the *world*, not *reticence*, oh" (8). This "Lord" as distanced other is being summoned to come to those people "sad on the ground" (8). "God" and "Lord" are words that for Valentine seem to symbolize absence at its most mystical remove, so much so that they strain the limits of even metaphysical worlds.

Although Valentine is somewhat catholic (little "c") in her affinities (occasionally God is called for) and not identified as Buddhist-per-se, the influence of the Zen Koan/"no mind" tradition shows in her knack for leaving dissonance (even intersubjective) unresolved, and this constitutes another kind of textual tension. As scholar Joseph Campbell remarks, in Zen "life and experience of life are antecedent to meaning."[4] The experience can be conjured by the analogy of an Escher staircase built of language, wherein one is forced first to climb entirely inside language as vehicle, and then, only upon abandoning it altogether coming to see both worlds at once. In other words, the very terms we use to attend to such an experience necessarily disintegrate even as we use them.

Tension between self and the other organizes the terrain of Valentine's poems. Even when "set" in a recognizable world, this terrain is often governed by strange metaphysics in which "air rises up out of air" and people are encased in one another like Russian dolls, or swim out into space as if gravity were optional. There are enough familiar nouns that we recognize these poem-places as potentially inhabitable: rallies, cups, knees, milk, fedoras, prisons, candles, pills, straws. Yet the poem-places retain a sensibility of what is there only through the strangeness of being gone, not of themselves:

: the dead don't go away
: you   "   "   "   (260)

The most accessible—and least theoretical—way to connect to absence in these poems is by noting the *many* dead beings, "all my dead friends," who make appearances from elsewhere. The poems are "basket houses" (19) for these absent presences, holding "the emptiness / where the other one holds me / nurses me / in the emptiness" (19). Sometimes the speaker is literally weighed down by death, as in "Door in the Mountain" where the speaker runs "hard through a valley" looking for a door "in": "never ate so many stars // I was carrying a dead deer / tied on to my neck and shoulders," but "People are not wanting / to let me in" (24–25).

Her poems are pocked with exits, as in "The Drinker": "heading out through the / chimney   the body-hole" (258). It is easy for things and people to disappear in her word-world: "Into love / the size of a silver dollar / [the soul] disappeared / to a pencil point then / nothing" (22). As poet, her work is to leave that "nothing" open. Her words themselves often seem to have as little traction as we mortals do, all prone to vanishing:

this minute
vanishing   I
befriended with it (22).

Thus, presence and the body can also be easily stepped into or out of:

left my soul   not "mine"
"my" clothes   off
I left the edges of "my" face
"my" hands (23)

Standing outside of easy theologies, Valentine's allegiances are instead to a presence—whether measurable and palpable or not—that swallows the self, "the other thing holds us in its mouth" (261). But the swallowed self keeps talking, from the displaced center:

My whole life I was swimming listening
beside the daylight world like a dolphin beside a boat

—no, swallowed up, young, like Jonah (243)

Already absent "her whole life" from *this world* (could we call it "occupational otherness"?), Valentine writes this absence back into the center of "things" from behind the whale's smile, "from the other side" (243), as if playing a game of telephone with bones instead of old aluminum cans. In this process, her poem "Poetry" is figured as:

the string I followed blind
to leaf by thick golden leaf
to your stem
milky
poem without words
world electric with you (268)

A poem without words, devoid of the features that make it itself, is made alive through empathy, here figured as some variety of plant life. Its "milky" stem is a Braille-like irritant, leaking. But nonetheless, "blind," the poet is in-feeling her way to "Poetry" which vivifies and maybe even coextends with "world."

In another poem, Valentine writes of "My ink-stained hand / his paint-smudged hand / gone where / nothing joins" (249). Between "gone" and "where" is the lacuna that presses up against the poet's consciousness, the gap that signifies just such difficult cartography as the poem (blindly) glyphs. It is hard to know just where we are. Valentine is a friend of antitheses, so we rest first with the pair of hands, each made dirty by materials of their respective art. These hands, joined only by parataxis, an ironic kind of conjunction, are our last touch-point of what feels to be a material world before they (and maybe we?) are "gone."

But the very nature of absence means that the participle "gone" cannot be delimited by an adverb—unless we think of absence as a state open to description and modifications. And look at the complexities that the sparse language leaves us with: Are these "hands" now joining "nothing" or are they themselves in a place of irreconcilable separateness, of two-ness? The poem sits in a sea of unanswerable questions about its meaning. So too does the following poem:

Once in the nights
I raced through fast
snow to drink life
from a shoe

> what I thought
> was wrong with me   with you
> was not wrong
>   now
> gates in the dark at thy name hinge (10–11)

"Once in the nights" is beautiful, perfect, and intact. Hurrying into the piece, we immediately trip over a grammatical contradiction, "[o]nce in the nights," an adverbial phrase which attempts to express both an aorist (completed) and iterative (repeated) action at once. But is this event a singularity or repetition? Both the energy bound in this contradiction and the rush of the speaker into the scene flood the poem with the flavor and textured nature of a recurrent dream—literally, a dream that "runs back" or "runs again." The dream—and, here, the poem's action—comes stamped with the flavor of a singular event that is uncannily familiar on a deeper cellular and mnemonic level. The stated purpose, "to drink life from a shoe," welds the thirsty speaker—who is "thirsty for experience," as another poem explains—to an absurd projective.

Whatever its means, the effect on the speaker is curative. After an interlude, signified by blank space, and with no necessary repentance in the Christian sense, a simple but profound correction of perception occurs: "What I thought / was wrong with me with you / was not wrong." As reader prone to draw lines between actions, the sequence feels causal (drinking from the shoe purified the speaker's self-concept), but could also be simply contiguous or coincidental. The truth of suffering from the Buddhist viewpoint is that *nothing* is wrong with us but our fundamental tendency towards misperception; what we *think* is wrong with ourselves, we experience and enact as such. This poem absolves other and self simultaneously.

One reading of the last line, "now // gates in the dark at thy name hinge" (10–11), is to understand "thy name" as some kind of joint, or the presence of language itself as a hinging gate. No one is named; pronouns dominate, and yet the salvific presence of *naming* is close at hand. A hinging gate is theoretically neither one that is open nor closed, but hanging, suspended, capable of swinging. Like language, it can reveal some or all of what is other. Like a semi-permeable membrane, it lets some things in and others out. The lone image of the swinging gates—Zen teacher Suzuki speaks of the *mind* as a swinging door—is what we too are left hinging from as readers. I leave this poem haunted by creaking because in the dark, deprived of visual orientation, we need an auditory cue to help us find our opening. To see the gate in the dark, one must be able to hear it.

IV. Inconclusivity

In "Eleventh Brother," Valentine writes:

Outsider   seedword
until I die
I will be open to you as an egg
speechless red. (10)

An egg, however, is *not* open; it is meant to encase, to protect. So what is this pledge Valentine makes?

The title, "Eleventh Brother," alludes to the Grimm's fairy tale in which the twelve brothers must be sacrificed by a painful contract when their mother births a daughter; when the red flag is raised to announce that the newborn is a girl, the brothers flee, leaving behind their home in the castle and the twelve coffins filled with shavings that await them. In the course of the tale, discovered by their sister who means to rectify the awful contract, they are transformed into birds, and fly off.

"Eleventh Brother," which hearkens the penultimate, as well as the darkest hour, begins mid-transformation: "one arm still a swan's wing" (10). The becoming is unfinished; the cause unnamed. The speaker is also mid-loss:

. . . love—before
I knew it was mine—
turned into a wild
swan   and flew
across the rough water (10)

In the fairy tale, the "outsider" status marks fatal danger for the brothers, but it is the only way they can survive. Their sister, whose presence ("red egg"?) signals their fated absence in death, ignores the story written for them, and comes to reconcile their separation. Valentine too shirks the original story, the kind of grammar that fixates relationships in linear and logical ways; hers is intended for a conversation partner, a "seedword" ringed in strange, and strangely free, space, a hole through which, to recall Moran, the entire universe might stream. The only true "outsider" to this experience is her reader, but if we feel as she feels, we will not remain long in that position. She flies to us; one arm already a swan's wing. Our absence from the predicament of the poem is her vanishing point. She is open to us to be judged, to be witnessed.

While we ponder what that might mean, to be opened to in that way, we may need simply to keep reading, as committed to the openness of empathic reading as Valentine is in the way she listens or writes. Hence we get this in "Single Mother":

—the baby birds'
huge mouths
huger than themselves
—and God making
words
words (272)

These baby birds are continuously hungry: all they can do is open to what comes from another. Their hunger for sustenance is bigger than they are, but the gap made by their mouths is not to be filled with sustenance; "God," adjacent and perhaps akin to the empty space that follows, offers (merely) words, material enough to render the situation visible, but too immaterial to sate the need.

Having tried on this poetic hunger for what is absent in any text and even here in this essay, we may be too ready to rest near the open beak of such a fragile, winged creature, barely alive, a new presence to life. These babies exist on the precipice of their own absences. Words are not the worms these creatures need to survive. The "Single Mother" of this poem has nothing; I argue this is what she can offer her babies. Words will point to the gap, but they will never fill it.

Valentine's work seems to insist that the mystical space must be left open. She uses language in a way that neither congeals that space nor tries to stuff the gaps of the unknown. The instinct to feel and connect remains. Ultimately, hers is a spirituality (a word she does not use herself) that guides towards the edge of understanding, moving *towards* the blank spaces and absences in which the poems themselves germinate. Perhaps precisely because her words maintain their relationship with a yearning for something more than what we can ever consciously apprehend, the poems are hospitable to otherness, and take great care to leave it intact— even as they hold it wholly, even if in pieces, in their laps.

Notes

1. Valentine, *Door in the Mountain*, 275.
2. Gen-Un-Ken-Roshi, "Why Did Bodhidharma Come from the West?"
3. Gen-Un-Ken-Roshi, "Why Did Bodhidharma Come from the West?"
4. LaPorte, "Readings of Paul Celan," 222-27.
5. All poetic line references are cited from Valentine's *Door in the Mountain: New and Collected Poems, 1965-2003* and page numbers are hereafter cited in the body of the essay.
6. Sagan, "3 Questions for Jean Valentine."
7. Valentine is explicit about the influence these two poets have had on her. She has translated poems of Mandelstam as well as written poems *to* him.
8. See Marianne Sawicki's refined work on Phenomenology of Edith Stein—especially in *Body, Text, Science,* to which the scope of this essay and its fledgling theory of empathy can do no justice.
9. Sawicki discusses one facet of empathy as the "imaginative capture of the other through taking the other's place.... The feeling of empathy registers entirely within one's own consciousness, but it registers there in a way that announces a foreign life.... My awareness is magnetized and configured to a pattern not of my own design." Marianne Sawicki, *Body Text and Science: The Literacy of Investigative Practices and the Phenomenology of Edith Stein* (Norwall, MA: Kluwer Academic Publishers, 1997), 96.
10. This term "empathy" has a rich history of use rooted in aesthetics and art appreciation, and later in philosophy and psychology. For in-depth discussion of empathy in these other contexts, see: Susan Keen (Narrotology), Carol Jeffers (Aesthetics), Vittorio Gallese (Neuroscience/Neuresthetics). Each of these authors trace the lineage of this term and its significance to these various fields. For this paper, the older understanding of empathy as a means of projecting self into object of art (see Vischer, etc.) was most illuminating, as empathy is so rarely used to signify this in current discourse, and Valentine renders humans in/as/through art—though Keen's in-depth work on narrative fuses this principle of aesthetics with ethical implications of reading fiction.
11. Valentine, "The Hallowing of the Everyday," 29.
12. Celan, "In Praise of Remoteness," 43.
13. Grubin, "A Conversation: Jean Valentine & Eve Grubin."
14. Campbell, *Myths to Live By.*

Bibliography

Campbell, Joseph. *Myths to Live By*. San Ansalmo, CA: The Joseph Campbell Foundation, 2011.

Celan, Paul. "In Praise of Remoteness." In *Paul Celan: Selections*, edited by Pierre Jorris. Berkeley: University of California Press, 2005.

Gen-Un-Ken-Roshi, Samy. "Why Did Bodhidharma Come from the West?" *thezensite*, http://www.thezensite.com/ZenTeachings/Teishos /WhyDidBodhidharmaCome.htm.

Grubin, Eve. 2009. "A Conversation: Jean Valentine & Eve Grubin." *Poetry Society of America*, September 4, 2009. http://www.poetrysociety.org/psa /poetry/crossroads/interviews/2009-09-04_2/.

Hollander, Benjamin, Ed. *Translating Tradition: Paul Celan in France*. San Francisco: ACTS 8/9, 1988.

LaPorte, Roger. "Readings of Paul Celan," translated by Norma Cole. In *Translating Tradition: Paul Celan in France*, edited by Benjamin Hollander, 222–227. San Francisco: ACTS, 1988.

Sagan, Miriam. "3 Questions for Jean Valentine." *Miriam's Well: Poetry, Land Art, and Beyond* (blog). October 13, 2010. https://miriamswell.wordpress .com/2010/10/13/3-questions-for-jean-valentine/.

Sawicki, Marianne. "Personal Connections: The Phenomenology of Edith Stein." From lectures delivered at St. John's University in New York on October 15, 1998, and at the Carmelite Monastery in Baltimore on November 13, 1998. *Hesburgh Libraries at the University of Notre Dame*. http:// www.library.nd.edu/colldev/subject_home_pages/catholic/personal_ connections.shtml.

Sawicki, Marianne. *Body Text and Science: The Literacy of Investigative Practices and the Phenomenology of Edith Stein*. Norwall, MA: Kluwer Academic Publishers, 1997.

Valentine, Jean. *Door in the Mountain: New and Collected Poems, 1965–2003*. Middleton: Wesleyan University Press, 2004.

Valentine, Jean. "The Hallowing of the Everyday." In *Acts of Mind: Conversations with Contemporary Poets*, edited by Richard Jackson, 27–31. Tuscaloosa: University of Alabama Press, 1983.

Refuge

poetic statement by Laura Moriarty

In a purely practical effort to get through a bad time in my life, I began sitting zazen January 31, 1993. It was the day of the Super Bowl. My first husband, Jerry Estrin, was four months into the cancer that would take him in June. I had decided to try sitting because vague knowledge from the '70s gave me the idea that meditation changed one's brain waves. I thought if I meditated this change might allow me to make it through this time of helping Jerry with chemo and hospital visits and watching him waste away while working at the Poetry Center to keep our insurance going. I had arranged to meet with Kit Robinson because I knew he sat zazen and thought he would give me a less religious version of sitting than our mutual friend Norman Fischer, who was, at the time, abbot of Green Gulch and San Francisco Zen Center. Norman was watching the Super Bowl with Jerry in our apartment on Nob Hill in San Francisco when I went to meet with Kit at his house in Berkeley. I remember Kit lending me a copy of *Zen Mind, Beginner's Mind* by Suzuki Roshi but he denies it. In any case, when I returned I had the book with me but hid it from Norman. The Cowboys played the Buffalo Bills that day, with the Cowboys taking it. Michael Jackson performed at half time.

That ten-month period in my life, in our lives, was full of anguish and the sitting helped me get through it in ways it is difficult to describe. I think it allowed me to feel more emotional pain, to keep up with the pain as it was happening, rather than going numb or trying not to feel it in some other way. I sat blindly without any expectation. Reading

Zen Mind, Beginner's Mind also helped, suggesting that awkwardness and not knowing how to sit were the best ways to approach the activity. I told myself with amusement that I was a "natural." Jerry made fun of me, asking when I planned to levitate the Pentagon. I shot back that I did not malign Levinas or Surrealism and that I would thank him to have some respect for my delicate beliefs (that is how we spoke). I didn't yet really have any beliefs about sitting or about Buddhism. Later I thought I became a Buddhist from the first time I sat, like love at first sight. I tried to earn or deserve the feeling that I was a Buddhist, once sitting a day of sesshin, attending the San Francisco and the Berkeley Zen Centers regularly for a while, but I never thought I deserved it. I only thought that if I was dying I would ask for a Buddhist priest to come in so that meant I was a Buddhist. I still think so.

For my birthday in April that year Jerry engineered the purchase of a zafu and zabutan, the traditional mat and cushion used in zazen. He had Lyn Hejinian buy them from a place in Berkeley. I never knew how she got them to our house. Then, very weak but triumphant, he pulled them out of his closet on the day. Jerry, Norma Cole, and I went to Golden Gate Park and sat in the Arboretum in the drizzle. I was strangely happy—but by Jerry's forty-seventh birthday a month later things had gotten got much worse. Jerry was going to have a shunt put in for the chemo or maybe for blood transfusions. There were many emergency visits to the hospital. Before our eyes, he declined.

During Jerry's illness I kept writing, stopping finally, for several months, with his death. We worked together on the "Nudes" section of his book *Rome, A Mobile Home*, editing with a directness that came from our sense that there was little time left to complete the project. I began writing a book that I would call *The Case*. The title evoked for me the use of that phrase in Zen koans, particularly those by Dogen, founder of the Soto tradition in Japanese Zen. "Koan" means "the case," as in a "public case." My use of it relates also to my relentless reading of crime fiction and Jerry's reading of this genre, for the first time, at the end of his life. The phrase is also redolent of Ludwig Wittgenstien's "The world is everything that is the case," as well as Marcel Duchamp's *Boîte-en-valise*. These associations were ones I shared with Jerry. The main thing one can say about all of these considerations—evoking my life with Jerry, my connection with Buddhism—is that they come from an intense experience of death and of love. The book, *The Case*, works through these experiences and my investigation of my own spirituality and the language that came out of reading, sitting and grieving. In this passage from the Introduction to *The Case* I try to make that clear.

> One feels the cut. Existence leaves off from time to time. History is what we are left with. Reality is conflict. It is compromised. It is and is not the case. This writing is a performance. A display. It occupies a place on both sides of paradise. There are objects and we are among them. There is love and daily life and, strangely, faith.[1]

I had faith that the zazen would help though it seemed to allow for more suffering. The obvious disadvantage to my being as open as I was to this suffering was the pain itself, but because I felt that it would occur anyway, I kept on with it. I loved reading Dogen and Suzuki Roshi. I liked Buddhism's Four Noble Truths and especially liked that the first Noble Truth was the existence of suffering. When I would think about this dictum and then get to the last Noble Truth with its idea that sitting was a way to address this situation it always seemed completely great and unexpected like the cookies and tea that were served at the end of zazen when, after Jerry's death, I began sitting with others. Death and suffering were a normal part of life, not Jerry's or my particular tragedy. The cookies, the silence, the dharma talks, the facing the wall were all a pleasure and the sitting was a great solace, a refuge, as I eventually learned to call it.

Notes
1. Moriarty, *The Case*.

Bibliography
Estrin, Jerry. *Rome, A Noble Home.* New York: Roof Books, 1993.
Moriarty, Laura. *The Case.* New York: O Books, 1998.
Suzuki, Shunryu. *Zen Mind, Beginner's Mind.* Boston: Shambhala, 1970.

I Find Out Everything I Believe Through Writing

An Interview with Alice Notley

Claudia Keelan

CLAUDIA KEELAN: Reading you, I've come to see that you believe poverty is important. At the same time, I can't see that you share faith with the Franciscans, or have any allegiances to systems of thought or religious principles, do you? How did you come to believe that poverty is important?

ALICE NOTLEY: When I was young, I attached great importance to certain ethical statements as received, viz., "Blessed are the poor in spirit for theirs is the kingdom of heaven..." and everything else about poverty in New Testament Christianity. It bothered me a great deal that I was taught these things by people who didn't practice them (it still bothers me—look at the Christian billionaire President and his praying Christian cabinet: I just read that Condi Rice gets down on her knees to pray every night.... Blessed are the peacemakers, yeah). I am not a Christian, but I think the ethic of the Sermon on the Mount is a superior one. It got into my system. Poverty also suited my temperament from an early age on: I am inept and shy, and I hate to work for people doing things I don't understand. I preferred being on my own to having money and never got a summer job in Needles. Though I respected my parents' hard work and meditated constantly on why one might spend one's life selling auto parts: it required accepting cars and then auto parts, and I've never accepted cars. But I do accept the fact that my parents grew up very poor and this was a way not to be poor: I didn't think they should suffer.

I became a poet and fell in with Ted Berrigan, who believed that writing poetry was work enough and that he shouldn't have to do other work that wasn't connected to being a poet. Of course, *poet* is the world's most underpaid job, but it was years before I caught on that no one respected it anymore either and that hardly anyone really cared if there was poetry in the world or not and that was why it was underpaid. Still, I didn't want to work except for writing and a bit of teaching. I write every day. I read every day.

Living with Doug Oliver I began to think more about how being poor, one doesn't use, or take, what the truly poor—people in sub-Saharan Africa, say—ought to have. I don't feel entitled to more than anyone else's share of the world's money or goods. Although of course I automatically have that even not having much by our society's standards. I have an Episcopalian Franciscan friend, a monk who has become a priest, and who took the vows of poverty, chastity, and obedience. He told me that by far the hardest of the vows was poverty, since, for example, even in the monastery he automatically had health care and the people in his parish—Bushwick in Brooklyn—didn't. I feel clearer not having much; I don't feel part of the infernal and illusory machine which churns out jobs, objects, and the walls of the visible world.

CK: You sound like a Christian to me. If you listen to Bush, his politics (poetics) are more attached to the Apocalypse, which was an added book, by dumb old John of Patmos. If Bush is a Christian, then Jesus sure wasn't. But that bit in the Sermon on the Mount about how to pray, by "going into the closet and begin newly, not with vain repetitions as the heathen do." Certainly your poems follow this?

AN: My mother always talked about going into the closet to pray except she quoted Paul. I always liked the idea because it meant I didn't have to bow my head in public with everyone else: I detested public prayer, saluting the flag, and singing the school song. I recently attended a poetry reading where parts of the audience were supposed to respond with particular words at points in certain poems: it was quite amusing but I couldn't do it. I can't participate in a group.

I'm not a Christian because I don't believe in god and I detest the idea of the male religious leader and/or model. I am extremely hostile to all the major religions. However, my thinking has been influenced by Eckhart, the anonymous author of *The Cloud of Unknowing*, Buddhism to the extent I understand it (and given that I'm hostile to the Buddha), etc.

CK: I asked about your ideas of poverty and faith because your work, at least from *Désamère*, is filled with children who live in the aftermath of their father's, or a powerful male figure's decisions. The tyrant in *The Descent of Alette* is both a businessman and a father-figure, isn't he? The brother is also prominent, isn't he? And the narrator, or leading figure in *Désamère* and in *The Descent of Alette* is a woman who wants to—is the word *remedy*? The sins of the father?

AN: The chronology of the work is as follows: first *Alette*, then *Close to me & Closer*, then *Désamère*. The dominant male figure is that of the Tyrant, who is not at all the same as the father. The Tyrant is the military-industrial–intellectual-artistic complex; he is how the made objects of the world have found their shapes. The father in *Alette* is the owl; a human transmuted into a purer nature by his death, and so able to teach Alette how to combat the Tyrant. In *Désamère*, there is the Satanic figure in the prose section, who is the Human as people sentimentalize it. And there is Robert Desnos. The brother is always the victim, in *Alette* and elsewhere, being a soldier and having been turned into a killer despite his sensitivity.

CK: Your use of Desnos really interests me. He's somehow a channel, yes? Is it Eckhart's mysticism, his direct connection to the divine that influences you? Is that a stance you seek as a poet?

AN: *Désamère* was the first work I wrote after arriving in France—fall of 1992 I believe, into winter 1993. For some reason, the minute I left the United States I perceived the reality of the global warming crisis which had not penetrated my dim skull before. *Désamère* is my seeing that. I was very lonely and went to a zoo here almost every day, the menagerie of the Jardin des Plantes. It is one of the world's oldest zoos, very small, and I stared at the animals dreaming up *Désamère*. I bought and read every book I could find on global warming and the greenhouse effect. *Désamère* is my version of summing up the second half of the twentieth century (like all the big-fat-tome male novelists; DeLillo's *Underworld* comes to mind), bringing it into the global warming desert future, pinning it down into specific lives, using dead Desnos to tell the story. Yes, he is a channel. I wanted someone French, and the form of the third part is from him; the form of the first part is from Marie de France.

I'm not sure how to answer the Eckhart question. I suppose it is his connection to the divine. His heresy as perceived by the church was to make no difference between himself and god (though he didn't think he was doing this, but it was obvious to everyone that he was). I go with that. It is what I mean by being an atheist (which seems to me the only honorable thing to say one is right now). I like the ways he uses god and Christ, especially the latter, as metaphors for his experience—Christ is reborn in the individual soul each day. It sounds so grotesque in certain passages, and I get a kick out of that. I have a workshop I sometimes do where I lay out an Eckhart sermon, Lawrence's "The Ship of Death," and O'Hara's "Joe's Jacket" next to each other. Doug got a wonderful poem out of this workshop the first time I did it called, "The Soul as Crumpled Bedsheet," so now I do the workshop using Doug's poem too, which stands up.

CK: Emily Dickinson didn't see any difference between herself and god either; it seems to me the history of Protestantism—radical Protestantism—makes that case, i.e., to be Antinomian, to go without name or company, which is why both *Alette* and *Désamère* seem to be—well, descendants—of that kind of spiritual quest. I guess I'm trying to get you to make a connection between spiritual practice and poetics. I know you say in your short essay "Disobedience" that there can be "no doctrines"! But both those poems are epics. Could you talk about your take on the epic, on the "new" protagonist?

AN: I find out everything I believe through writing. Most of my significant experiences, and most of the things I "realize" are found out through the practice of poetry, specifically during the performance, the literal writing of it. My poems seem to have gotten longer as the so-called quest has become more detailed, more exact. *The Descent of Alette* was a conscious attempt to write a traditional epic, first of all—not a modernist one. But what I am finding out—well, in this case I had had an epiphany outside the poem, an incredibly negative one, about two things. One, I'd begun to know how monstrous my brother's actions had been in Vietnam in the context of that country (he didn't do anything very bad by "army standards") and of his own sensitivity (he was not what you'd call a natural sniper, if there is such a thing) and my own implication, as an American and his sister, in these actions. Second, that not one thing in the world, not one object and not one practice or habit had been invented, as far as I could tell, by a woman. *Alette* is about those facts, though most obviously the second one—but I wouldn't have chosen epic if I hadn't had to deal in some part of myself with the fact of that war. In the course of writing *Alette*, I mean in the story of *Alette*, there is the black lake and there is Alette's enlightenment, which is tied to her acquisition of natural "owl" powers. I became, after having written the poem, obsessed with the lake. *Close to me & Closer* is me wading into the lake, the black lake, the other side of which is infinity. *Désamère* confronts, again, the necessity for a political stance and tried to combine it with the knowledge of the lake—which in this case is not the lake but the desert. *Disobedience* idiomizes all these themes, uses a flip, of-these-times voice and material out of a life lived in Paris to pull everything together in a more overt way. I have two other manuscripts, "Reason and Other Women" and "Benediction" in which I continue the research.

CK: I'm intrigued by the detective in *Disobedience* and also by the notion of American-ness expressed in the first poem, "Change the Form in Dream," where you write: "the only / thing American really worth bringing is the sense / that you must accept me, exactly. / Not as your woman." What do you mean here? Do you consider yourself an expatriate writer, and if so, what does your exile serve?

AN: The detective arose gradually out of a dream process. I first had the dream of the detective looking for the woman in the back room: he wasn't recognizable. Then a couple of other dreams fed into the construction of this figure as a charter in the poem, including a dream of a childhood friend named Tommy Harward (now lives in Boulder City) whose name suggested the name Hardwood. But then I got to a point, simply writing, where the next words that came out of me, because they sounded right, were, "Oh sure I can, I'm Robert Mitchham." At that point I knew I'd be able to talk to him for a while in a poem. He became my friend.

I was recently looking at those lines ["the only / thing American..."] trying to remember exactly what I meant. They are addressed really to the French, not to Americans—to the place where I now live. I am saying that I am not a member of your French culture, but I will not be a member of American culture, here: I am an exact entity, exact person. I am insisting on my individuality as an exactness. But then I knew the poem would be read mostly by Americans and that the statement works in both directions.

Expatriate is a funny word; I don't know anyone here who uses it, except for certain magazine writers. I've never heard anyone say, "I'm an expatriate," though I know many people who have been here for years, are French citizens. I'm not talking about writers particularly. You become part of an international community, Anglophones in Paris. I suppose I'm an expatriate at the moment—I've been here now for ten years. I don't feel that I belong either here or there, but it has become more interesting for me to write from here. My viewpoint is made more complicated by my being here, and my response to poetic language is shiftier. Language seems more substantial and less precise, more about texture and presence and less about meaning in terms of individual words. The experience of speaking and hearing French has made all language mysterious to me again.

CK: The more I read of your work, the more aware I become of your interest in what you call "the forgotten possibility," which seems to be a figure more animal, more mineral, than human. Humans are always evolving into animals and plants in your imagery. Do you think that what we call progress is misguided, that we should in fact get closer to becoming animal? Is it an idea you got out of reading?

AN: I'll try to answer your question about the animal, but the answer seems so obvious I don't know where to begin. It doesn't come out of reading at all. We (my sons and I and then Doug) had a cat for fifteen years, named Wystan, who was very ugly, witty, and "good." He was a good being. If there is an afterlife, I would hope to see him in it (this sounds corny). Recently I dreamed I had three sons and one of them was a cat. But this doesn't get at any of it. I "know" that animals and plants and rocks are as important and knowledgeable as we are. I don't think they are anything like the descriptions of them biologists make. But most of the biologists I know love animals and use science as a way to hang out with animals. Theory of evolution drives me crazy because of its point toward "man"—and being dreamed up by a "man." How come man is carnivorous and apes aren't? Chimps are somewhat, but humans are obviously unmerciful, inferior, so aggressive. I love the wild eyes of wild animals and how they don't even bother with people. You can't make friends with them through the eye—have you ever looked at a duck's eyes? I finally had an experience of burrowing owls last summer in Needles and their eyes seemed to take me in, but they were doing their dance of trying to keep me away from their nest, which was somewhere on the high school lawn. I loved going through this with them. My Aunt Margaret said we were scaring them, but I don't think so. They were doing their job. Burrowing owls are in danger, as are most animals, desert tortoises, common frogs. . . . It's so unjust. I feel so stupid because I'm fifty-seven years old and I know very little about animals, and except for roaches and rats and mice—and coyotes—they're disappearing. They're so much less destructive than we are. Their ethics are generally better, and they're so mysterious.

CK: I guess what I was thinking about in the question was how writing, when you are really writing, you're becoming. Deleuze says: "writing is inseparable from becoming; in writing, one becomes woman, becomes animal or vegetable, becomes molecule, to the point of becoming imperceptible." Your writing seems dedicated to something like this...the whirling, morphic style of *Alette*, and her dismemberment, etc.

AN: What Deleuze says makes me nervous. I dislike it when men talk about becoming women in writing: I have heard other French men say such things. It means that they don't want to give up power to women. They would rather say they are them. One imagines many things in writing, but I'm not sure one becomes what one imagines. I am not Alette or Désamère: they are the ones who become. The dismemberment of Alette—the dismemberment of a woman—is something I've dreamed many times—still do—in many different ways: I know the dream well, it's terrifying. It's part of what's happened to me, on several levels.

CK: The fact of dismemberment—how did it occur to you, on what levels, and did writing *Alette* help?

AN: Now that I'm pinning it down, it seems that I wrote about dismemberment, in *Alette* first, and then proceeded to dream about it at key times. I don't remember how it occurred to me, since I wrote *Alette* out of what I was dreaming and "seeing" and I "saw" the dismemberment. Later someone reminded me that that was a traditional shamanic initiation: the body is taken apart and put back together with some new parts. And I had read that literature somewhat, particularly Eliade. But I wasn't thinking about it at all—shamanism, my reading—when I wrote that sequence in *Alette*: it was logical and I saw it. Since then I have had a number of dismemberment dreams, as if this is happening to me over and over. I or someone is being torn apart, sometimes eaten by people, sometimes stabbed repeatedly, sometimes attacked by birds. I have a number of poems, in my unpublished manuscripts, that refer to these dreams. In the dreams, the corpse is not given the grace of being put back together. After Doug's death, I had a feeling of being remade out of metal parts. I think the poet becomes more and more shamanic getting older, in the sense that so much happens to one, and there's nothing left but the poetry function, which is a healing, ecstatic function, as much as it is anything else.

CK: Since there seems to be a dearth of shamans everywhere I've ever been, that seems like good news to me . . . I'm hearing that you don't like—or maybe more accurately—don't purposely bring your reading to bear when you write poetry. Is that right? If it is, does your resistance to that kind of empiricism have a lot to do with the disobedience you've described? Do you think, unlike many writing now, that the poet can find the same or like-knowledge in writing as in reading?

AN: All of that and more. I haven't had to read the literary theoreticians/ philosophers because I don't teach except for workshops; I escaped having to read them in college, by virtue of my generational placement. I think they're mostly a factor in the university environment. I know what the conversation is like, from a perhaps minimal exposure; I haven't the slightest interest in what the theory people have to say. I tend to think of them as more men telling me what to think (I know that about three of them are women). And I, after all, am the poet. I also think of the French theoreticians as people writing for French society out of the French language: I have a sense that Americans misunderstand where they're coming from, how they're educated and what situations they're really speaking to. I do an enormous amount of reading long poems, a lot of reading about Australian aborigines, and ancient Sumer, reading of Sumerian literature, plus books about owls, snakes, etc. My reading for *Désamère* consisted of a few books about Robert Desnos, the lais of Marie de France (whom I used as a former model for the first section), and everything about global warming I could get my hands on.

CK: I want to switch gears for a while. I'm in Mississippi now, going to read for the *Mississippi Review* this afternoon. The editor of the magazine, Angela Ball, asked me about you as part of the second-generation New York School. I know you lived in New York with Ted, and your sons live there now. To what extent do you see your project in conversation with, say, Bernadette Mayer, Ashbery, Koch, O'Hara?

AN: I was probably part of the New York School until the mid-eighties and I remain of it, to some extent, through friendships and certain interests. In fact, I have a book of essays coming out from the University of Michigan Press called *Coming After*, which is largely about second-generation New York School people. I changed after Ted died, and then again after some other deaths in the late eighties, and I needed to become my own school, if you wish. I was obviously deeply affected poetically by Ted. I, in fact, learned to be a poet from him. But his sense of community was much wider than the New York scene and included such figures as Phil Whalen, and Bob [Robert] Creeley, Anselm Hollo, certainly Allen Ginsberg, all of whom became my friends too. And all of whom have some New York School characteristics, such as humor, which I myself seem incapable of having, no matter how I'm writing. I would define the New York School in terms of its relation to New York City, how those poets were or are affected by living in an international city which overwhelms one personally with its own story. In New York, you construct a personal story or character for your poetry in accordance with how the city's going, with what the city tells you to say. I sometimes think of *Alette* as my last New York poem, since the first section of the poem reflects so strongly the presence of the homeless people in the city in the late eighties. In *Mysteries of Small Houses*, I consciously tried to revive some of my New York School styles in order to reflect the times of my life I was commenting on. And certainly some of the verve is in the style of *Disobedience*.

CK: I felt your connection to the school in *Mysteries of Small Houses*—the sense of being in a present that has the past and future running right through it, like in O'Hara's "The Day Lady Died." I've always thought that the notion of time and its fluidity was one idea the poets of the New York School shared.

You talked about Ted helping you become a poet. . . . You've also talked about your resistance to men telling you what to do. . . . But your poems are full of owl-men and maintenance men and detectives who often give sound advice. Do you feel a split between your resistance and allegiance?

AN: Sometimes. But I have spent most of my adult life married, and am used to being in conversation with a golden partner—alas now not. I felt myself to be a sort of "school" with each of my husbands, actually. Although Ted taught me how to be a poet, I did become his equal and he had no problem with that. He had a particularly selfless love for poetry itself. And with Doug, I engaged in a sort of internationally based school of narrative poetry, no problems. I like to talk to men. I think I believe, or have believed, in dialogue, and one person speaking being formed out of the two present, the way when you talk to someone and you're enjoying it, you lose consciousness of individual self—are the conversation. If men and women were engaged with each other in this way habitually, in all levels of life, there wouldn't be problems of power.

Ted's favorite quotation from Whitehead was: "Everything that is going to happen is already happening." It is the basic belief behind *The Sonnets* and he applied it to his life as he was living it. He also used to teach Frank's poems such as "The Day Lady Died" as past time playing back in the present and rendered as present. With my sons, I am now editing Ted's *Collected Poems* for the University of California Press—a very big book.

CK: I'm curious as to how Ted taught you to be a poet.

AN: He was someone who was always being a poet, so I too became someone who related everything I saw in life to my poetry. He had a lot of books, so I read all of his books. And we showed each other our poems, and he suggested changes (later I helped him). He also talked about forms, reading further things to do. He quite literally taught me, though I never had him for a teacher at the Workshop. I hardly ever went to class in Iowa; I was sick of school by the time I got there. I feel as if I got my training from Ted after I graduated. I think I've said he was eleven years older than I was. He had already become this thing I wanted to be, but at great cost. He always said he couldn't have done it without pills—amphetamines—since he was a working-class guy from Providence; the pills had made his brain light up from the first time. I do believe that. I shared his predilections to a certain extent, but my brain had actually started working when I was a kid in Needles, and it didn't need that kind of stimulation. I was a liberated little girl and thought whatever I wished—somehow a possibility in the desert but not in Rhode Island where one behaves and thinks exactly as one's family always has and never ever leaves the state except to go to Massachusetts.

CK: In *Mysteries of Small Houses* there's reference to drugs a lot, and a sorrow about it in the later poems. Did you and Ted use drugs for vision in the shamanistic sense? Did it work? What's your take on it now?

AN: I don't think I ever did drugs for shamanistic purposes. I've had my most interesting visions without them. I view drugs now as mostly destructive, but not more so than anything else we're up to: I think I compare cares and pills in *Désamère*. I probably consider the average drug addict to be more "moral" at this moment than the President or any of his company. I'm interested in the idea of addiction. Americans are addicted to lots of things: power, righteousness, fear, money, possessions, as well as the usual alcohol, food, gambling, pills.

CK: At least one of addiction's appeals is changing one's sense of powerlessness to one of power. That propensity seems to be one you're protesting in many of your books, am I right?

AN: I think I listed power as one of the things Americans are addicted to. In terms of drugs, the classic paradigm is less power than it is control: the addict, as in Burrough's *Junkie*, takes total control over his or her life. Drugs are then both a regulating principle and schedule: your life makes sense! You always know what you're doing. And you can live a very long time in this way, as Herbert Huncke did (I think he was approaching eighty and still addicted when he died). As far as poetry goes, there is a lot of power-wielding in our world even though the territory is usually pretty small. A lot of poets are interested in power. I find it hard to say whether this is antipoetic or not. It isn't always cleanly outside the poem, either. Sometimes one is as good as the poem. I, of course, usually see all of this in terms of the male power bid; but there is also the mainstream poetry power bid, for example. This is the whatever-our-group-is power bid as well. There is also the sense that if one doesn't have any power, one can't do any good, can't even get published. As related to poetry, power is complicated.

CK: Earlier you wrote that "Everything that is going to happen is already happening" was Ted's favorite quote from Whitehead. Do you believe this too and how does it make you feel? I mean, you've been with Hepatitis C for thirty years and didn't know it, Ted died from it, also without knowing it, and your brother was a sniper in a shitty war despite his goodness, who later overdosed . . . and all the other things "already happening," both good *and bad*.

AN: I think I do believe this statement, but it's important that "what is happening" has a lot to do with what you personally have done and are doing. You can sometimes change what is happening. Ted used the statement; it was an amulet for self-recognition and actions (possible change). I got Hepatitis C from/with Ted—doing drugs—thirty years ago; he died of the disease without knowing that was what he had (I didn't know until last fall), but I was crossing forbidden boundaries—so in a sense I "knew." However, it is clear to me that I wouldn't know anything if I hadn't crossed forbidden boundaries, and knowledge is part of what is happening and the key to change. My brother was in a bad war, because men have believed in war for a long time; war has been happening for a long time. He had already gone to that war before he was born. Virtually every man I've been close to, including both my husbands, has done military service. He got a very bad war, because the military-industrial complex and twentieth century male politics were happening in their particular, very bad ways. So the big question is, how does one change what is happening? There are, I suppose, specific answers at specific points.

CK: That's a very good question. Your answer suggests that for you, changing what was happening involved knowing you were crossing forbidden boundaries, without fearing what the result or results would be. Has the achievement of knowledge always involved this dynamic?

AN: Not always directly. I've unfortunately learned so much from being near people who were dying, and then grieving for them later. But many of them had been "disobedient" and almost all the poets I know are disobedient—the vocation has that requirement somehow. No one wants you to be a poet; in being a poet one is disobeying society's wishes. But I've learned what I know from all the ways I've suffered, in disobedience and obedience, and that's the knowledge of my poetry. Society's interest is in having everyone who has disobeyed reform. I have only reformed superficially. I'm loyal to everything I've done and all the people I've been close to. I'm loyal to Mitch-ham, the seedy detective, who is my Will in *Disobedience*. Finally, ideas like "the will" seem seedy in themselves, so why not have a dilapidated, not terribly good actor, represent that? All ideas are pretty seedy, aren't they?

CK: Not the good ones, which I admit are few. The necessity of disobedience is a profound idea and has informed all the poetry, social movements, and even architecture that I love, structures where a new kind of "reform" is made all right, but a reform in service of the disobedience which opens categories to a further inclusiveness. Blake and his "without contraries there is not progression," Williams's *Spring and All*, the relationship of the civil rights museum's form in Memphis to King's notion of the "beloved community." All those structures "change what is happening" in conventional ideas of law, of beauty, of responsibility. I'm not thinking of "the idea" as Wallace Stevens did, as something that is conceived in an individual imagination and then foisted upon a reader in place of the world, but as something more related to the French use of the word—the *idée*, a plan, a suggestion, a dream—which participates with the world, not exclusive of it. You're right that ideas like "the will" seem seedy, or simply empty, but Mitch-ham's presentation of your Will in *Disobedience*, his pathos, is something I follow and therefore know more about how you view deterministic ideas such as "the will."

In *Disobedience*, where Mitch-ham is talking about "the slip" as transgression and Alice steps in and says, "I'm trying to be as clear as possible / as unfictional as possible / given that I have allowed 'fiction' in." What is your sense of the fictional? A lot of poets—I think of Stevens, [Robert] Duncan, Susan Howe, others—promote the inherent fictionality of the word/world. I don't feel that belief when I read you.

AN: A sense of our fictions is something I struggle with endlessly. I believe a fictional view of existence has been imposed on us: that time and will and history are the result of other people's fictions taking over whatever the "everything" may be. I don't believe any of the stories I've been handed: the scientific story, for example. And I'm not interested in what historical figures did: I don't think they did it like that. I believe the story my brother told me as I present it in *Mysteries of Small Houses*, but I omitted some events to make the events more streamlined and believable as art (can you feature that? More happened than even in the poem). I don't think my brother lived that so-called story as story. I think he lives it as shock and instances of—what—confrontation in chaos? But Mitch-ham is a total, blatant fiction, so I really enjoy his presence. In *Disobedience*, I posit, rather than story or narrative as reality, the "tableau." That is, the scene impregnated with event and time crisscrossing back and forth. This is based on my sense of how things "happen" to me and also on the way my dreams operate. My dreams don't contain long stories, they contain these tableaux. Doug's dreams, however, were stories, and we used to discuss this, particularly when I was writing *Disobedience*. There may be a large gender difference, based on prevalent social perceptions and how one is brought up to be in "the story."

CK: So then, I'm hearing you do believe we operate in, or struggle inside of, fiction imposed upon us—patriarchal fictions, scientific fictions, historical adaptations—but that sometimes something (awareness of the fiction, personal fear or love or desperation) breaks through and time becomes real momentarily? What your brother lived through, for example, and how he understood it, how he told you about it. A tableau suggests a series, a seriality, which given in individual conscience, would delineate the individual's preoccupations. The recurrence, for example, of the caves in *The Descent of Alette* and *Disobedience*, and the first woman who reappears as soul in *Disobedience*. Caves and reclaiming a first woman. . . . Fake male guides. Are you trying to write yourself out of the fictions when you write?

AN: Sometimes, but not always. This is very sticky. One thing I often think is that everyone operates as if she/he were in a novel. To this extent, I find the rise of the novel, the novel itself, something like a culprit (followed of course by the film). I think it would be a very good thing if the novel could be demolished, but not in a postmodern way where you just write another kind of novel. I love the narrative poem because it can create "extension" without all that psychological tyranny. In poetry, words themselves lead you out of time and the story: they stop you or they say "this part of the so-called story can be gotten through very quickly because the important thing, after all, is the poem." And why should anyone identify with a "character" in a poem? I don't believe one escapes time by being within certain moments: I think it really isn't there. The first mother in *Alette* doesn't really correspond to the Soul in *Disobedience*. The first mother is the first woman— Lucy the African skeleton; the Soul in *Disobedience* is the narrator's soul. She isn't damaged as the First Woman is; she's whole.

With regard to seriality, tableaux are not necessarily experienced as serial and connective. In *The Descent of Alette*, the caves don't make a linear story together, they may be parts of something but they aren't all of them. Their order isn't terribly important (I had a music professor in college who compared a certain kind of medieval music to string beads). My brother didn't necessarily tell me his "story" in order—he told me these things that happened. My memory of what he told me imposed a second order (I have a set of notes from the meeting); then a third order was imposed by the writing of the poem in *Mystery of Small Houses*. When you're asked to think of everything, it tends not to come "in order." People who practice storytelling (in bars or professionally) give an order to events so they can remember them. Time becomes a mnemonic trick.

CK: I suppose it's their "underness" that connects Lucy and the Soul for me. Both exist in fiction which would keep them in under, if Alette in the one case, or the Soul herself in *Disobedience*, didn't keep "retrieving" her. Perhaps Soul isn't broken, but she's definitely in conflict with the story she finds herself in.

Isn't the tableaux of your dreams cinematic in the same sense film is? At least "serious" film? The tableaux in *The Descent of Alette* also remind me of Spenser and *The Faerie Queen*.

AN: The First Man and the First Woman are standard figures in myth. The First Woman is that kind of First Woman. I read a lot of Native American myth before writing *The Descent of Alette*, and was quite influenced by it, particularly *Dine bahane*, a translation/rendering in English of the Navajo creation cycle, by Paul Zolbrod. In Navajo and Hopi mythology, there is an "emergence" of the first people through successive worlds—five in the Navajo story and four in the Hopi. My descending levels of reality in *The Descent of Alette* have more to do with this "emergence" reversed, than they do with, say, Dante. When I told my mother how *Alette* ends—how Alette kills the Tyrant—she said, that sounds just like an American Indian story.

As for the tableaux, they're not cinematic, they're dream-like. The caves in *The Descent of Alette*—and much of the material in *Disobedience*—come directly from either dreams or automatic (tranced) envisioning. The rule in *The Descent of Alette* was to take an element from a dream and then to "see" as quickly as possible whatever I "saw" with my eyes closed, to use it without judging it. That is, the initial element would trigger an automatic visionary sequence which would become a "cave." I've been studying my dreams for the past twenty years or more; much of my theorizing about time and tableaux is based on these dream studies. I've also thought about the traditional relating of myth to dream, that a myth is a dream become more wakeful and made useful to more than one person. I never think about film; I know there are a couple of films of the caves, but they are dreamed.

I've already mentioned that I read a lot of books by Mircea Eliade right before I wrote *Alette*. He says, over and over, that among indigenous peoples, when someone died, when something bad happens, the only thing to do is to sing the world back into creation: start over again at the very beginning. My books always seem to be about trying to find that beginning in order to start over. I think I should point out that in such cultures, one must think about time in an entirely different way. Eliade (who knows how much he knew?) speaks constantly of sacred and profane time. The Australian aboriginal life was geared almost exclusively toward sacred time; there were sacred stories always going on—one lived them and they were embedded in the landscape (as Shiprock, in New Mexico, is one of the monsters killed by the Twins in the Navajo cycle.)

I haven't read much Spenser; it's gorgeous but a bit too late for my purposes. Happy New Year, Claudia! (We are starting over again.)

Notes

Keelan and Notley, "A Conversation: September 2002–December 2003."
See Gilles Deleuze, "Literature and Life."

Devotional Practice

Writing and Meditation

poetic statement by Laynie Browne

> "Let us do good deeds and engage in aloneness—sitting in a loft with books, myrtle, ink, pen, paper, and tablet, to combine the letters and draw the divine mind into us."
> —from *The Essential Kabbalah*[1]

Approach

> "One day we shall be able to read between the words, read the blank spaces through which we come to the words."
> —Edmond Jabes[2]

> "The hour jumped out of the clock, stood facing it, and ordered it to work properly."
> —Celan[3]

Meditation is a devotional practice. Though I did not begin with this understanding articulated in such a manner, it becomes more and more clear to me as time passes that writing poetry can also be a devotional practice. The word devotional, as I am using it here need not suggest one particular religious orientation, but rather, as Nick Dorsky so aptly writes in his book *Devotional Cinema*, "It is the opening or the interruption that allows us to experience what is hidden, and to accept with our hearts our given situation. When film does this, when it subverts our absorption in the temporal and reveals the depths of our own reality, it opens us to a fuller sense of ourselves and our world. It is alive as a devotional form."[4]

Alive, as a devotional practice, writing can take many forms—from the moving meditation of community and the incantatory use of sound, to the rhythmic repetition of mantras and memorization of verses, and finally the iconographic substance of letters themselves—here a connection is inherent if we choose to look for it. And this is not to prescribe to anyone how or why to approach writing. Instead, take this essay as one possible lens through which you might view not just the process of writing, but the entire process, the medium of being in the world and experiencing questions, which can only be answered through your existence. Writing, like meditation, can be a form of investigation, a way to approach the unapproachable, and the invisible.

So how to describe this devotional vantage, where writing can be a form of meditation? To begin, it is my hope that the practices of writing and meditation will continue to make immediate the questions of who we are and why we are here. These are questions that will never be answered in any static moment. The practice of inquiry which asks, *who are you now*—is never done but it hopefully opens or unlocks the present. These are practices of opening the mind and perception in general with the aim of not becoming fixed in ways which obliterate freedom. Additionally, writing and meditation require us to exit the world of constant motion long enough perhaps to comment upon the world of constant motion. Or, as Patanjali put it in his compilation of the yoga sutras in roughly 200 CE, "Yoga is the cessation of the fluctuations of the mind."[5] Yoga, meaning union, or to yoke the individual soul with the universal.

Before beginning a yoga practice I had come to think of meditation as a means of relaxation, or health benefit. In finding teachers in the yogic tradition I began to see meditation as potentially something more. I was still thinking of practice as something that could benefit me. "I" was practicing. But what was the purpose of meditation? Beyond the intent of the "I."? And what is the purpose of writing, beyond the intent of the writer?

This is the white space—the opening where understanding and listening can occur—the quiet between tones in music. The exhalation that mirrors the inhalation. But meditation is also beyond the duality of such metaphors. Meditation is not sleep, nor regular waking consciousness.

Poetry also occupies such an indeterminate space, one with borders, which are difficult to delineate. Call it reading without books. Although we live in a world of "this" and "that" we also perceive a reality in which such categories don't apply. Norman Fischer writes in an essay on Zen meditation and the artistic impulse: "There is the sense that in the useless and unmade space and time of actual living there is a subtle endlessness and namelessness that is delightfully available to everyone at all times."[6]

Silence is underrated. At how many countless gatherings of writers have I stood, well aware that even among avid talkers, a large group can have each person standing, virtually alone in a crowd of busy minds. What if all of the busy minds were to sit together? What kind of telepathic writing could be produced? Which quarrels might end and egos fall momentarily away? Meditation clears the room of the useless revelry in your mind, so to speak, and moves hopefully in the direction of an intimate dialogue, the kind we all wish we could find more time within. Writing is a similar pursuit, an attempt to enter that other stream of time, the one there all along although we often miss it.

Meditation, like writing, exists in the realm of possibility first. In the beginning, and possibly for a long time afterwards, you don't know where you are going. This is especially true for poetry, which does not seek to describe an event or experience that has already occurred, but rather is intended to be the experience itself, in the present, as it is written, and again, as it is read. Art here is unfixed in the sense of what is being asked. We are all being asked not merely to receive, but to participate. This participatory model insists that art is dynamic, which I see as hopeful in the sense that it belongs potentially to everyone. For instance, my four-year-old son, this morning lying on the couch under a blanket while I finished my asana practice said, "Mommy, the candles are talking to each other." Meditation is a practice of a particular type of attentiveness, whereby certain things fall out of focus leaving space for others to emerge. The "candles talking" is one such possible state.

Jewish Meditation

Many people have never heard of Jewish meditation. For this reason I'd like to say a few words about the tradition here. The Jewish mystical path maintains an emphasis on passionate attachment—in Hebrew, "devekut," and can be characterized by a strong connection to the physical body and the physical world. The Jewish path is generally not monastic. There is not a modeled emphasis on celibacy or isolation.

Many of the techniques employed in Jewish meditation, such as mantra meditation, contemplation, chanting, and visualization are somewhat universal. The practice of joyfulness is key. The central prayer in Jewish liturgy, the Amidah, a silent standing prayer, was originally designed to be a meditative exercise. The practice of prayer is one of reorienting and realigning the self. It is a meditation of remembering and affirming one's relationship within the whole of existence.

Meditation—whether it be through silence, song, or other means, is a preparation for the practice of Tikkun Olam, or repair of the world. Thus, the discipline is not in retreat but in action and in relation to others. While action is inherent in other paths as well, this is the intimate and messy, the argumentative and the daily assertion that it is better to leap and be incorrect than to maintain a cool demeanor, from a distance. Detachment is the opposite of what is being asked.

So why is it that Jewish meditation is relatively unknown? There are many historical reasons. Much was lost of the flourishing of Jewish mystical teachings in the Middle Ages due to extreme persecution. The oral tradition, out of necessity, became hidden. And much later, immigrants to the United States in particular were interested in assimilation. The Holocaust also created a devastating loss of mystical teachings. Rabbi Avram Davis writes "During the Second World War, just a little over fifty years ago, 30 to 40 percent of the Jewish people were killed. This fact is well known. But what is pertinent here is that 80 percent, perhaps as much as 90 percent of the traditional community was destroyed. . . . The destruction of these foundations of transmission resulted in widespread ignorance regarding the Kabbalah, Jewish spirituality and contemplative practice."[7] The recovery of the practice has been slow but interest is emerging. In the last few decades many books have been written on the subject, texts which remain are being translated, teachers are teaching and training others in the tradition.

Two Visions of Community:

1. My Essay on Community
The blank page will never desert me.

2. Community: A Meditation
Imagine that you are sitting in an urban setting and watching so many persons pass by.
This is watching the thoughts.
Notice them, and let them proceed.
Your thoughts are pedestrians, strangers perhaps to your task at hand.
See them. Greet them. But do not follow.
As the thoughts thin out, settle more deeply.
Notice that you are being perfectly supported by the earth—that this occurs continuously.
Your spine is rising in opposition to the horizontal plane upon which you rest.
You are a vertical mast. And shed some light.
Now imagine that the dark room is filled with other persons sitting.
See each illuminated spine.
A grove.
Now extend your vision beyond the room and see all of the illuminated spines walking, running, working, sleeping.
Extend the vision as far as you can.

Contemplation (or *Textual Ecstasy*)

> "Twenty-two elemental letters. God engraved them, carved them, weighed them, permuted them, and transposed them, forming with them everything formed and everything destined to be formed."
> —from *The Essential Kabbalah*[8]

> "Everything in the world began with a yes."
> —Clarice Lispector[9]

The world was created through divine speech. And on a more mundane level, we all know the power of words to delight and to destroy.

This is not to suggest a simple moralistic view as to how poets should employ language. Rather, I mean to suggest, that we use language daily often without noting its power. And that the origins of the power of speech and writing are as old as writing is old. Take for example, this passage described in Kabbalah in which Hebrew letters are employed as focal points in a consciousness altering practice. "Their intrinsic value is proportional to their degree of incomprehensibility. The less comprehensible, the higher."[10] This seems particularly relevant to innovative poetic practice. The intention here is not to create sense literally, nor to be nonsensical, but to liberate oneself from conventional notions of meaning and more importantly from limitations in our perception which we fall into by habit.

> Begin to combine letters, a few or many, permuting and revolving them rapidly until your mind warms up. Delight in how they move and in what you generate by revolving them. When you feel within that your mind is very, very warm from combining the letters, and that through the combinations you understand new things that you have not attained by human tradition nor discovered on your own through mental reflection, then you are ready to receive the abundant flow, and the abundance flows upon you, arousing you again and again...
>
> All this will happen after you fling the tablet from your hands and the pen from your fingers, or after they fall by themselves due to the intensity of your thoughts.[11]

When I first read this passage many things began to crystallize. Why is there so much pleasure in the arrangement of words? How does this connect to a meditative state? If the letters themselves can be a focus of contemplation, then so of course can a word, a sentence, a paragraph, a book. In working with words we are working with a substance potentially primordial, something which contains all possibilities.

The twenty-two letters of the Hebrew alphabet are represented here as gateways to expanded awareness. What more incentive could a writer want, to try to see all language as connected to such a source, knowing that perhaps our ancestors have dropped their writing instruments by candlelight or flung them away in a fevered state? Rabbi Gershon

Winkler explains it like this, "To experience the so-called ordinary, mundane material existence as the carrier of the very mystery we expend so much of our life quest seeking in other more transcendent realms."[12]

From where do ideas come? We are constantly receiving from a source, which could be conscious, unconscious or beyond our understanding of mind. Are we receiving Spicer's radio waves, tuning into a frequency, recalling the words of other living or dead poets, being influenced by cultural icons, music, headlines, landscape? Bernadette Mayer once said to me that she was told her writing was influenced by Stein before she had ever read Stein. If we consider influence as a type of emanation, which is alive, and everywhere present, it isn't hard to see. On a mystical level, there is a collective consciousness of the species that is evolving, and we are all affected by it. No act, including the act of writing poetry—which can at times seem hidden and insular—is without a physical emanation, a reaction, a result in the universe. The result may be invisible, but remains actual. Just as the way one is changed by sitting is somewhat invisible, yet at the same time manifested.

Contemporary Poetic Practice

All language, all alphabets have potency. Immediately coming to mind along the lines of visual poetry and meditative practice is Cecilia Vicuña's collection *Instan*. The way in which her hand-drawn word formations revolve about the page is an example of how text can become a vehicle for entering contemplative practice. I am interested in how the text operates on various levels here. One can enter her text by gazing at the design and enter again through the reading of the text, and enter again through relation of the words and letters to each other upon the page. One revolves the book to read, and so one is revolved. The text undulates, invites us towards the center or the perimeters of the page. And so we are pressed, turned, poured, or curved. A particular waking consciousness with which one moves about must be broken open and reforged in order to proceed. Her content, though difficult to quote without losing its essence, is related to the process described. An alchemy occurs. In an earlier poem, titled "Entering," she writes: "If the poem is temporal, an oral temple, form is a spatial temple."[13]

Here, reading requires a suspension, immersion and relocation. The mind is a part of this, the mind we all can agree upon. But there is another mind beyond mind. H.D. in *Notes on Thought and Vision* called it the "over-mind" or "jellyfish consciousness." "Into that over-mind, thoughts pass and are visible like fish swimming under clear water."[14]

And beyond "over-mind" is something else, unnamable.

In "fables of the beginning and remains of the origin," the third section of *Instan* in which poems appear in conventional print format and move between three languages (English, Spanish, and Quechua), Vicuña includes quotations from a number of thinkers also concerned with the nature of silence and time, a concentration akin to meditation—such as Lispector and Dickinson. She writes, "Silence / turns the page / the poem begins,"[15] and later, "A word is a non-place for the encounter to take 'place.' "[16]

Text can create not only a quiet mental residence, but also a resounding space, and a much longer investigation—one's life for instance—could be dedicated entirely to how sound and song live within poetry and contemplative practice. This applies to Vicuña's inspiring performances and performance of poetry in general. The spaces where readings occur are transformed by sound and presence. This makes them prime locations for the walking and talking meditation of community to be kindled and tended.

One such example of a space transformed by poetic enterprise is that of Norma Cole's installation "Collective Memory" in San Francisco, and a piece called "House of Hope." This piece is made up of 426 quotations, printed on white strips of polyester and sewn so as to be suspended from a cast-iron frame. The strips reach from near the ceiling almost to the floor. An observer can stand outside the piece and carefully read from the strips, lifting them one at a time but also can step inside this waterfall of text and remain hidden from view while continuing. On a broadside printed for the show, the first quotation reads:

The house is a metaphor of hope that is impossible to grasp physically. —*Montien Boonma.*[17]

The experience of being inside a house of text, or a house of time or light are synonymous in the sense that they all may be employed from a meditative stance. From this vantage there is no object or subject to which a meditation cannot be directed because one isn't trying to contact anything that doesn't exist internally or permeate everything. For instance, imagine a fish attempting to contact water. No matter which way it swims, it remains within the medium it seeks. We can think of language as a similar container. One so present we may not realize we reside within it, and therefore miss many aspects of how it directs our perceptions. The "House of Hope" is a delicate and palpable reminder of how easy it is to forget the space within the center where it is possible to reside. It is also an inspiration in its suggestion that the limits of how and where to practice exist solely within the limits of one's imagination, and that of our dedication. Regardless of our personal circumstances, regardless of bleak headlines, there is a choice to be made in each moment. Who will the poet become?

Nothingness

"If you want to know what nothingness really looks like, concentrate on what you see behind your head."
—Rabbi Aryeh Kaplan[18]

"the no rock rests / you gotta believe in it or it wont work / it isnt exactly astral and it isnt exactly imaginative its just that you can climb unto the rock and sit down."
—Hannah Weiner[19]

". . . most meaningful subjects in life are invisible. Time can't be seen. Love is invisible. God, come to think of it, is invisible."
—Sparrow[20]

In Hebrew it is called *Ayin*. In practice, we return to blankness. As writers, the blank page, again and again. This is the place of creation and humility. The emptiness in the center of a vessel or womb. Gestational darkness, below ground, the unknown. And yet the blank page is not nothingness, any more than space or darkness, which are all things. Yet what the blank page and these images allude to may point us closer to nothingness. Everything worthy of contemplation or poetic investigation is, on some level, beyond the understanding of mind.

> ...If a thing exists only insofar as another would agree, there is a poverty of
> being...
> —Lissa Wolsak[21]

And so let us gladly disagree. And please write your own meadows and send them to everyone. And then there will be more meadows in which to exist. Or more schools, more transport, more shelter, and aid. Write into existence all that is lacking. As a first attempt.

Thinking shall not stop you from entering.

Beyond forgetfulness, beyond void, oblivion and non-existence, beyond stupor or sleep, beyond the mind as we understand it as a limited aspect of consciousness, and beyond unconsciousness as well. Beyond intellect and beyond reason is a contemplative state which can be brought into being through verse.

> My mind swings this way and that
> Mira says: I am Yours
> I will proclaim this, with Your permission,
> To the beat of a drum.
> —Mirabai[22]

Because we cannot describe such a place though, does not mean that we do not inhabit it. Imagining what has no image is also a way to envision the future. If we cannot imagine it—it cannot come into being. Writing—into existence—is one route to mapping the future. But it requires an endurance of blankness, an admission of not knowing. And in no uncertain terms. A dedication to seeing what is not yet visible. This is a devotional practice. It both is, and is not, a practical exercise. In the mind of production-oriented citizens, it may hardly seem worth mentioning. Yet in the realm of the poetic we may move beyond "sense" in order to forge new initiatives to meaning.

Fanny Howe, in her collection *Gone*, writes:

> The holes in our haloes
> widen the higher we die[23]

Howe's lines speak to me of a breaking open, required for reanimation, or realignment in keeping with where we wish to evolve, especially if we consider writing as an emanation of consciousness. The process may be invisible, and yet for this the practice is no less meaningful.

Notes

1. Matt, *The Essential Kabbalah*, 108.
2. Jabes, *The Book of Shares*, 7.
3. Celan, *Collected Prose*, 12.
4. Dorsky, *Devotional*, 16.
5. Iyengar, *Light on the Yoga*, 46.
6. Fischer. "Do You Want to Make Something Out of It?, 133.
7. Davis, *The Way of The Flame*, 15–16.
8. Matt, *The Essential Kabbalah*, 102.
9. Lispector, *The Hour of The Star*, 11.
10. Matt, 106.
11. Matt, 103–104.
12. Winkler, *Magic of the Ordinary*, xxii.
13. Vicuña, *Unraveling Words*, 4.
14. H.D. *Notes on Thought & Vision*, 19.
15. Vicuña, *Instan*, from part 3, "fables of the beginning and remains of the origin." Text does not include page numbers.
16. Vicuña, *Instan*.
17. Cole, "House of Hope."
18. Kaplan, *Jewish Meditation*, 85.
19. Weiner, *We Speak Silent*, 51.
20. Sparrow, "kite soup & minus 54 other recipes," 28.
21. Wolsak, *An Heuristic Prolusion*, 9.
22. Mirabai, *The Devotional Poems of Mirabai*, 75.
23. Howe, *Gone*, 18.

Bibliography

Celan, Paul. *Collected Prose*. Translated by Rosmarie Waldrop. Rhinebeck, NY: Sheep Meadow Press, 1986.

Cole, Norma. "House of Hope." (Installation Exhibit). In *Poetry and Its Arts: Bay Area Interactions 1954–2004*, San Francisco: California Historical Society, 2004.

Davis, Avram. *The Way of The Flame*. Woodstock, VT: Jewish Lights Publishing, 1999.

Dorsky, Nathaniel. *Devotional Cinema*. Berkeley: Tuumba Press, 2003.

Fischer, Norman. "Do You Want to Make Something Out of It?: Zen Meditation and the Artistic Impulse." In *Success: A Poem*. San Diego, CA: Singing Horse Press, 2000.

H.D. *Notes on Thought & Vision & The Wise Sappho*. San Francisco: City Lights Books, 1982.

Howe, Fanny, *Gone*. Berkeley: University of California Press, 2003.

Iyengar, B.K.S. *Light on the Yoga Sutras of Patanjali*. San Francisco: The Aquarian Press, 1993.

Jabes, Edmond. *The Book of Shares*. Translated by Rosmarie Waldrop. Chicago: University of Chicago Press, 1989.

Kaplan, Aryeh. *Jewish Meditation*. New York: Schocken Books, 1985.

Lispector, Clarice. *The Hour of The Star*. Translated by Giovanni Pontiero. New York: New Directions, 1986.

Matt, Daniel C. *The Essential Kabbalah*. New York: Harper Collins, 1983.

Mirabai. *The Devotional Poems of Mirabai*. Translated by A.J. Alston. Delhi: Motilal Banarsidass, 1980.

Sparrow. "kite soup & minus 54 other recipes." *Ascent*, Winter 2005.

Vicuña, Cecilia. *Instan*. Berkeley: Kelsey Street Press, 2002.

Vicuña, Cecilia. *Unraveling Words & the Weaving of Water*. Translated by Eliot Weinberger and Suzanne Jill Levine. Minneapolis: Graywolf Press, 1992.

Weiner, Hannah. *We Speak Silent*. New York City: Roof Books. 1996.

Winkler, Gershon. *Magic of the Ordinary*. Berkeley: North Atlantic Books, 2003.

Wolsak, Melissa. *An Heuristic Prolusion*. Vancouver: Friends of Runcible Mountain, 2000.

part ii.

the memory of the journey unraveling

Becoming Animal in Leslie Scalapino's
The Tango
Faith Barrett

In *The Tango*,[1] Leslie Scalapino juxtaposes her photographs of Tibetan monks and her textual queries about the relationship between language and community with visual artist Marina Adams's abstract collages of found materials. Offering multiple layers of visual imagery and textual inquiry, *The Tango* examines both the violent repression of religious communities by the state and the relationship between language and suffering; simultaneously, it offers a meditation on the practices of a spiritual community. While Scalapino's language is densely laden with theoretical meaning—the text pursues a series of questions about the relationship between language and subjectivity—it also offers readers a luxuriant array of aesthetic pleasures. Phrases recur in a formal pattern that is at once intellectually insistent and hauntingly musical. Lavishly produced and often in ravishing color, the photographs in *The Tango* point toward the enduring beauty of monastic practices even as the parallel texts underline the threat of state suppression of religion. In analogous fashion, even as the fractured language of the text suggests the impossibility of sustaining communication, its insistent repetition underlines the possibilities that language offers for sustaining community.

As the volume's title suggests, Scalapino's project focuses on the dynamic relationship between partners: the dance partners in the Argentine tango, the debating pairs of monks in the Sera monastery, and the pairing of her own photographs and texts with Marina Adam's pieces. Yet not all of the pairings the text establishes are collaborative: the text returns again and again to the relationship between an observing witness and a suffering victim and to the relationship between the Chinese military and Tibetan monks. Moreover, the layering of recurring images onto one another produces pairings of jarringly different terms, with the Tibetan monastic debates juxtaposed with the Argentine tango, for example, or the gaze of a western tourist at the Sera monastery juxtaposed with the gaze of an American in the US watching a dog get hit by a car. Combining images of monks with images of dancers, and images of witnesses and victims with images of aggressors and victims, Scalapino layers binaries onto one another in order to unsettle their oppositions. While some writers might arrive at this undoing of binaries through their readings of poststructuralist philosophy or avant-garde poetry, Leslie Scalapino, as I will go on to suggest, comes to this commitment by way of Buddhism.[2]

Among the array of paired and recurring images in the poem, three animal figures feature prominently, foregrounding the strong connections between animal and human experience. Section two of the poem introduces the image of an injured dog, hit by a car, and this becomes one of the text's central figures for suffering. Section one introduces the phrase "military wolves" to evoke the violent suppression of Tibetan religious culture by the Chinese government, and this phrase is developed more fully in sections two and three. Finally section two also introduces the image of an elephant's head and face, a description that is interwoven with images of human faces and bodies, and that will recur with variations throughout the rest of the poem. While the images of the collective of aggressive wolves and the solitary suffering dog read as a pair of opposites, the image of the elephant hovers between these poles, unsettling this opposition and underlining the interconnectedness of aggression and pain.

In contrast to the text's intent focus on the limitations and consolations of language, these three animal figures point to the extralinguistic realm of animal being even as they also point to the ways that animals use their bodies to communicate. It is no accident then that Scalapino chooses to focus on three animal species that live in social communities.

Readers frequently note the comparative absence of affect in the language of Scalapino's poetry; in *The Tango*, descriptions of animals' bodies and movements seem to suggest possibilities for both animal and human affect.[3] Still more importantly, however, Scalapino's attention to animal being foregrounds the Buddhist commitments that underpin this text's lines of inquiry: attending both to the suffering of animals and to the violence perpetrated by humans against other humans, *The Tango* offers a meditation on the inevitability of suffering for all sentient life, the first of Buddhism's four noble truths. *The Tango* thus also underlines the interconnectedness of animal and human suffering.

Ultimately Scalapino's text links these three discrete animal figures through an exploration of the tango, a dance form that relies on gesture and movement to convey emotion. Moreover, by choosing to focus on the tango, Scalapino highlights a cultural form that uses ritualized dance movements to express both political resistance and national identity. Closely linking the tango and the ritualized debates of the Sera monastery, Scalapino's text considers how suffering can engender a cyclical pattern of violence and further suffering; at the same time, however, *The Tango* foregrounds alternative responses to suffering, including not only the Argentine tango and the rituals of the Tibetan monastic debate but also by extension broader cultural possibilities for dialogue and attention, practices that might allow individuals to perceive and respond to the suffering of others, both animal and human.

In order to contextualize my analysis of these layered animal and human figures, I want to begin by offering a brief history of the Sera monastery and the tradition of monastic debates in Tibet. By choosing to situate the project at the Sera monastery, Scalapino focuses on centuries-old spiritual practices that have, since the 1950s, been disrupted and threatened by Chinese repression. Traditionally monasteries were the seat of higher learning in Tibet, and the Sera monastery was particularly revered for its long history of educating Buddhist scholars. During the 1959 revolt in Lhasa, the monastery was severely damaged by Chinese forces and hundreds of monks were killed.[4] After the Fourteenth Dalai Lama sought political asylum in India, a new monastery was established there, and many Tibetan monks and nuns fled to India at that time.[5] Following the Chinese invasion, one tenth of the Tibetan population was forced into labor camps; about one sixth of the Tibetan population died as a result of the violence of the invasion and the widespread famine that resulted from the Chinese redistribution of agricultural goods.[6] The Chinese military systematically destroyed Tibetan monasteries throughout the region, and a second wave of widespread anti-Tibetan violence would follow with the Cultural Revolution of the 1960s. At the time of the 1959 uprising, there were some five to six thousand monks at the Sera monastery in Tibet; following the protests in Tibet in 2008 and the ensuing violent suppression, the number of monks there today is estimated at about five hundred. Since the majority of Tibetan monks fled into exile in 1959, the monks who continue teaching in Tibet are relatively few in number and are under increasingly close scrutiny by the Chinese.[7]

The Sera monastery is particularly known for its oral debates, the main method used to train Tibetan monks in the teachings of Buddhism. In these highly ritualized proceedings, younger scholars, formally dressed in their red robes, test out their knowledge, guided by senior scholars and a watching audience of monks. The dialogue is designed to teach not only the tenets of Buddhism but also critical thinking skills.[8] Thus, while training in Tibetan Buddhism begins with rote memorization, monks participating in formal debate must demonstrate not only doctrinal knowledge but also an ability to think on their feet, to respond perceptively to the argumentative strategies being used by the questioner. With both defender and questioner using anger, sarcasm, humor, and guile for persuasive purposes, debates are highly performative. The practice is also physically dynamic, as participants shout questions and responses energetically while standing amidst the circle of onlookers, and monks in the audience express agreement, disagreement, or impatience with the proceedings. The tradition includes a series of ritualized gestures, with the questioner using handclaps both to punctuate his questions and to urge the defender to respond more quickly; other hand movements are used to challenge one's opponent and to indicate the stages of the dialogue. Drawing on his own experience of training with Tibetan monks in India, Georges Dreyfus argues that Tibetan monastic debates are *"dialectical practices* aimed at reaching greater understanding and developing crucial intellectual habits, such as a spirit of inquiry and critical acumen."[9] Scalapino takes her title "The Tango" from this dialectical exchange of both words and gestures between defender and questioner. Outside observers are able to observe and photograph the debates, as she did. Scalapino makes her outsider status formally evident in the photographs by frequently focusing on the backs of a gathered circle of monks.

The book design of *The Tango*, which is an oversized volume twenty pages in length, reiterates the idea of dialogic pairings on multiple levels. That design includes a double fold of paper for each of the volume's glossy pages, an element that reminds the readers of the inseparability of the tango partners each time they turn the page. In the first eight pages, each page is divided into two vertical columns with Scalapino's color photographs of the monks on the left and Scalapino's text on the right; image and text are thus set in dialogue.[10] Page nine of the text introduces the first of Marina Adams's visual compositions. From this mid-point onward, Scalapino's text and photographic images are set in conversation with Adams's abstract images. The formal principle of two vertical columns is abandoned on pages eleven through fourteen. Each of these pages has instead four quadrants, and this is the only section of the book (apart from its last page) where images sometimes appear on the right-hand side of the page. This change in layout seems to suggest a more cacophonous group exchange instead of a two-person dialogue; the shift to multiple quadrants on the page echoes visually the dynamic of the debates in which monks who are onlookers shout out encouragement or dismay in response to the main participants in the debate. Moreover, the images included on pages eleven and twelve include no color, a startling change in view of the lavish color on the preceding pages. Though color is reintroduced in Adams's collages on pages thirteen and sixteen, Scalapino's photographs of the monks appear in black and white only after page ten. Both the removal of color from the photographs and the change in layout on the page build a dramatic arc into the text. That dramatic arc is resolved on the text's final page which places a square of Scalapino's text wholly inside the frame of a brightly-colored collage by Adams, the only time a piece of the text is so framed. The closing passage of the text describes the young Dalai Lama's escape from Tibet into Indian exile, thereby aligning the narrative arc of the text with the arc of the book design.

It is no accident, I will argue, that color is removed from the photographic images shortly after Scalapino, in the text, introduces the image of the injured dog, just at the midpoint of the volume. Scalapino opens the second section of the poem by layering onto the description of the dog's injury a description of the photographic images of monks' backs that fill this book. Section two also introduces the first of Marina Adams's images, in this case a painting on found materials, an image that suggests a flower and vine botanical motif even as it also suggests the dappled or spotted pattern of an animal's fur. The flowing triangular patterns in Adams's image are echoed by the two colored photographs of a monk or monks on the facing page, which show the back of a monk, draped in loosely flowing red robes, his hands behind him clasping prayer beads, his head and feet cropped out of the image, his robes dappled by the shade trees that surround him. The Adams image echoes this pattern of leaf-shaped shadows and light. Read in relation to Scalapino's biography, image and text remind readers of Scalapino's own back pain, a chronic condition that would have made her visit to the Tibetan monastery particularly arduous. Layering the dog's injury onto the backs of the monks onto her own presence as visitor, Scalapino underlines the inescapability of suffering in cyclic existence and thus the interconnectedness of human and animal forms of being. In the Buddhist worldview, a being is condemned to a continuous cycle of suffering, death, and rebirth until he or she begins to cultivate a higher awareness of his or her spiritual state. Unlike animals, human beings are privileged to have this gift of awareness, which offers them the possibility of eventual release from cyclic existence. Yet this cycle of death and rebirth also strongly connects human beings to the animal realm.

In section two of the text, Scalapino offers repeated descriptions of the injured dog and of the monks seated or standing at the debates, ringing changes on each new iteration. As Elisabeth Frost and others have noted, Scalapino's work is shaped by its commitment to what Joseph Conte calls "serial form," recurring discrete units of text that serve as an alternative to narrative or linear structures.[11] Frost astutely describes Scalapino's reliance on serial structures: "for Scalapino, serial form is inseparable from a poetics that documents minute acts of seeing."[12] Thus for Scalapino, a poetics of serialism would seem to correspond to a spiritual practice of attending carefully to the experience of others, a practice that is demonstrated in the acutely observed descriptions of the injured dog or the groups of monks. The section opens with a passage that layers description of the monks onto a description of the dog:

> *Before*, saw dog's end back crushed from hurtling car.
> its head curled to see walks anyway from greenery—here
>   the men's delicate backs' cages move the present only
> as if there were sleeping, but the backs move
>   'emerge' is one level the men's backs curling
>   or straightening   (9)

Throughout section two, reiterative variations of these two descriptions link the fragility of the dog's body to the fragility of the monks' bodies and their very way of existence, surrounded as they are by the occupying forces of the Chinese government. The phrase "delicate backs' cages" links the skeletons of animal and human, even as it also reminds readers of the ways that the witness or observer is excluded from the suffering victim's experience. The dog's suffering is evoked through the haunting detail of its continuing movement even after its grave injury: "its head curled to see walks anyway from greenery" (9). The reiterated narrative of its injury and continuing movement also evokes the painful cycle of suffering, death, and rebirth which is the foundation of Tibetan Buddhism. The image of the dog's looking back—"the back / that's curled to see still walking"—suggests the animal's mute awareness of its own suffering (9).

Moreover, the reiterated images—both textual and photographic—of monks standing and sitting and (in the text only) lying on the ground juxtapose the living tradition of the monastic debates at Sera with the reality of the Chinese government's increasingly restrictive control over the monasteries and the history of the violent repression of the Tibetan monastic culture. Like the volume's many photographs of monks' backs, reiterated textual references to the "delicate backs' cages" underline

Scalapino's position as tourist-outsider at the monastery. The phrase "the men's curled backs lying beside their hands" suggests both the patterns of gesture and figure in Scalapino's photographs of living monks debating and also the corpses of monks piled inside the monastery compounds after Chinese attacks (9). Thus the phrase "delicate backs" seems to layer, hauntingly, images of dead and living monks onto one another, a layering that is echoed in the text's many references to "dying and living" (9). Again and again the text evokes both the brevity and impermanence of human existence: "only being child until dying—everyone— is their / delicate back dies sometime / theirs one" (10). Here the paradoxical shifts from singular to plural back to singular suggest both the essential solitude of the human condition and our essential connectedness to forms of community. Serial reiteration lends this text its hauntingly lovely music even as that same repetition also underlines the inescapability of death, the impermanence of all living things. Serial structures in the text also echo formally the repeated words and phrases that are integral to the ritual of Tibetan monastic debates.

When color is removed from Scalapino's photographs and Adams's images on pages eleven and twelve, this dramatic change works to foreground the precarious position of Tibetan monastic culture: photographs in ravishing color that seemed to show a vital living tradition being practiced in a contemporary moment now seem to be cast into a documentary past. The replacement of the two vertical columns of image and text with the four-quadrant layout suggests, potentially, a breakdown in dialogue, a movement towards not just cacophony but perhaps also chaos. Adams here replaces her colored botanical patterns with black, white, and grey blotches that seem most suggestive of animal fur. Moreover, just before color is removed from the images, Scalapino strongly foregrounds color in the text. When she reintroduces the figure of the "military wolves" in section two, she adds a verb to the phrase: "military wolves rose" (10). By linking the "wolves" to the word "rose" which is sometimes used as a color and sometimes used as verb in the text as a whole, the text connects the perpetrators of violence to the color-word that is elsewhere strongly linked to the monks: the Sera monastery is named for the wild roses that surround it, and in the first several pages of *The Tango*, Scalapino's color photographs strongly emphasize the deep rose hue of the monks' traditional robes. Moreover, throughout the text, she links the verb "rose" with the natural beauty of the monastery's setting, often evoked through the phrase "moon rose"; this phrase and its related variants also seem to evoke the extraordinary resilience of the Tibetan monks in the face of Chinese repression. After the removal of color, section two also offers a more fully articulated account of this repression: "were killed practicing in the monasteries—shipped / to labor, dying, trains shipping them, ringed in by barbed / wire haul on dam sites tunnels exhaustion famine in lines" (11). The text's alternating pattern of evoking the injured dog and then the "military wolves" suggests the interconnectedness of violence and suffering in cyclic existence: the senseless injuring of the dog is layered onto the senselessness of the aggression perpetrated against the monks.

Throughout the text then, resonant paradoxes are suggested through paired layers of opposing images: of an injured dog and aggressive wolves, of dead and living monks, of a religious culture that is vital and yet also being obliterated. Reading Scalapino's work for its relationship to Tibetan and Zen Buddhism, Jason Lagapa identifies negation or cancellation as a central method of her poetics, suggesting that Scalapino echoes in her work the Buddhist precept that language fails in its attempt to represent enlightenment. Lagapa reads Scalapino's "repetitive, ironic, and self-canceling utterances"[13] as evidence of her critique of the limits of subjectivity. While noting the connections between Scalapino's poetics and that of other contemporary experimental writers, Lagapa contends that Scalapino arrives at her radical critique of the limits of self through her engagement with Buddhism. Central to Buddhist thought is the idea that the self is nothing more than an illusion: while some western philosophers represent the self as enduring or at least sustaining, Buddhism regards the construct of the self as a fiction each individual must overcome in her quest to recognize both the impermanence and the interconnectedness of all living things.[14] In analogous fashion, the tradition of the Tibetan monastic debates privileges the dialectical processes of communal inquiry over the teachings of any individual leader. Though Lagapa does not discuss *The Tango*, his account of Scalapino's poetics is particularly helpful in considering the correspondences between the rhetorical operations of this text and the tradition of monastic debate: "Scalapino's writing illustrates how knowledge is produced *through* a serial process of negations and contradictions that opens up the field of inquiry from one term to another."[15] By wedding serial repetition to practices of self-reflexive negation or cancellation in *The Tango*, Scalapino echoes both formally and rhetorically the ritual of the debates which rely on the recitation of memorized teachings as well as skillful use of reversals and negations to outmaneuver one's opponent.

Scalapino's balanced use of the three animal figures is one textual instance of this strategy of reversal and cancellation. In the midst of section two's serial juxtaposition of the injured dog and the "military wolves," the text introduces a third and final animal figure. The elephant image is the most ambiguous and hermetic of the three:

> moving is floating ears—elephants—a trunk and
>   face floating on one's ears
>   either charging or floating on grass, at once
>   man's chest: as trunk floating on ears of elephant's—
> he's that, coming. Ears on 'trunk recoiled or forward.'   (10)

The image presents the animals' bodies as moving with almost balletic grace; moreover, the description focuses with particular intensity on the animal's face, its ears, and trunk. The passage reads like a zoologist's clinical account of an animal's behavior, suggesting that the phrase "trunk recoiled or forward" might allow the human observer to begin to interpret the animal's mood or intentions. In the passage as a whole, however, those intentions remain unreadable: the animal is "either charging or floating," a phrase that suggests both the possibility of an aggressive attack and also the extraordinarily graceful movements of these enormous animals. The passage also reminds us of how performative displays of aggression—which may or may not do harm to other animals—are sometimes used in the animal world in order for an individual animal to establish its position in a hierarchical community. Thus in its description of the animal's face, its posture of either hovering or launching itself forward, the passage also echoes the monks' movements, gestures, and language in the ritual of the debate, a ritual whose tone can turn swiftly from playful humor to biting anger; the parallel between monks and elephants is further supported by the emphasis the photographs place on the monks' flowing and draped ceremonial robes, a detail that suggests the texture and movement of the skin of an elephant.[16] The description of the elephants seems also to suggest the outsider's position looking in on an inscrutable ancient ritual culture and its social hierarchies—either the social hierarchy among the elephants or the hierarchy of learning within the monastery. The ambiguity of the animal's intentions reiterates the fundamental duality of animal being: that animals are capable of suffering, like the injured dog, but also capable of acts of aggression, like the "military wolves." The text suggests that humans share with animals this divided capacity not only to experience but also to inflict suffering. Underlining the powerful connections between the animal and human worlds, the description creates a hybrid being: part elephant, part human.

Having established the careful balance of the three animal figures in section two, the start of section three swerves unexpectedly to a radically different cultural setting, unsettling again the layered pairs of images that preceded it. This section opens with a parenthetical tribute to the tangos of the Argentine composer and musician Astor Piazzola:

(Astor Piazzola's tangos: the tango is relentless. The embrace
—a couple?—entwining goes and goes. It skips, jumps
ahead of a horizon—itself—resuming. The tango is a
hopscotch 'ahead' of them, a couple, it's for convenience of
maneuver, it's for intense love.)   (15)

In this passage, Scalapino at last makes explicit the comparison between the debates and the dance form that had previously been suggested only by the title of her work. The passage evokes both Piazzola's music and the dance steps that accompany and shape it. The description of the tango dancers' ritualized sequence of steps and movements—"The embrace / —a couple?—entwining goes and goes"—suggests the dramatic gestures and movements of the debaters, underlining the extent to which both cultural rituals rely on gesture and movement rather than

language to communicate. Layering the tango onto the debates, Scala-
pino also forces the question of the similarities and differences between
the two cultural practices. Born in the working-class dancehalls of
Buenos Aires in the late nineteenth century, the tango was exported
to Europe at the beginning of the twentieth century, subsequently
becoming a global dance craze throughout Europe and then the western
hemisphere. When it "returned" to Argentina, the dance form had
gained new cultural credibility; it was subsequently taken up by middle-
and upper-class Argentines who had previously viewed it as too crude
or rough. During the rule of Juan Péron, the tango became a powerful
symbol of Argentine national pride. The tango involves ritualized
expression of anger, dominance, desire, and power, all of which can
be expressed through gesture and movement without recourse to lan-
guage; while the Tibetan debates involve gesture and movement as well
as language, the juxtaposition of the two cultural forms underlines
their position as cultural alternatives to acts of physical violence and
aggression.[17] Moreover, the juxtaposition of the tango with the debates
also obliquely reminds readers that the "export" of Tibetan Buddhism
to the west has in part enabled this spiritual practice to endure. At the
same time, however, the juxtaposition of the two cultural forms under-
lines the morally ambivalent position of the western tourist whose
consumption of cultural practices from the developing world changes
those practices even as it enables their survival.

Yet while *The Tango* unsettles the position of western tourist, it also
underlines the extraordinarily compelling power and beauty of the
cultural practices that that tourist observes. The project of *The Tango*
suggests that these cultural practices make possible sustained and sus-
taining models for community, even though these practices reenact
and are partially shaped by structures of "social dominance," in the
phrasing of the text (15). Shortly after the parenthetical description of
Piazzola's music, section three reintroduces the description of the
elephants, again emphasizing the movements of the animal's trunk
and ears and again interweaving the description of the elephants with
a description of a man's body:

> elephants' ears floating in grass.—recoiled or
> forward trunk.—moves.—on ears lying in air.—trunk as
> man's chest.—coming.—'there'.
>
>   it is never isolated   (15)

Closely following the description of the tango music, the animals' ears assume particular prominence in this recurrence, suggesting not only the physical movements but also the sounds and the listening, which are essential to elephant communication. Layered onto the description of the tango and also the debates, the hybrid animal-human's movements take on the quality of ritual expressivity, even as the meaning of this ritual remains inscrutable to the outside observer. Underlining the close relationship between animal and human experience, the passage closes by reiterating the importance of social community: "it is never isolated."

In its final recurrence in the text, this interweaving of elephant and human movements is linked explicitly to the rituals of the tango:

>   ears. a recoiled or forward trunk is floating on the
> ears.
>   a man's trunk, coming.
> a man is the tango. is relentless.
> gentleness. It is *speaking—there*. repeats 'just' space. (19)

Here the word "gentleness" replaces the syllabic count of the unstated word "elephants," and "relentless" and "gentleness" are juxtaposed as binaries. Yet by layering in quick succession the movements of the debates, of the tango, of elephant behavior, and of human behavior, the passage suggests that both humans and animals might be able to overcome the limits of this opposition, might be capable of rituals both relentless and gentle, might be able to create a "'just' space," where dominance might be expressed not through physical violence but through gesture and ritual. Pointing self-consciously towards its own serial movement, as well as the repetition of ritualized phrasing in the debates, the text implies that in the human world, language will also play a crucial role in this practice: "It is *speaking—there*. repeats 'just' space."

Scalapino seeks to offer with this project an opening into the "'just' space" of the monastery, a place where the language of inquiry is made possible (19). This text tries to hold that space open by observing the tradition of Buddhist debate and by pursuing its own fractured inquiry into the possibilities that language offers for sustaining community. In pursuing these lines of inquiry, the text counter-balances three animal figures, each of which underlines both the interconnectedness of violence and suffering and the interconnectedness of animal and human forms of being. In *The Tango*, attending to the animal offers a model for attending to the suffering of others; it also offers the model of elephants' complex social and communicative behavior as a contrast to the massive scale and enormous strength of their bodies. That behavior is then balanced against the animal's capacity for aggression. Scalapino offers these animal figures as exercises in attending to their extralinguistic world.

But *The Tango* also offers readers the immediate pleasures of language, evoking a haunting lyricism through its reiterated and negated pairs of images. Showing us a poetic language fractured by skepticism and self-consciousness, Scalapino also offers a photographic counter-narrative of Buddhist scholarly debate. *The Tango*'s array of textual and visual pleasures serves as a monument to the traditions of Tibetan monasticism, traditions now threatened with imminent destruction. The pleasures of this project result from the extraordinary connections that spring up between the two columns, between the two artists, between the different pairings of partners in this remarkable dialogue. Ultimately, *The Tango* offers the fragmented and elusive pleasures of language—both the language of poetry and the language of spiritual community—as a form of redemption from the human experience of isolation and suffering.

Notes

My thanks to Madera Allan, Celia Barnes, Sara Gross Ceballos, and Elizabeth Robinson who provided helpful responses to an earlier version of this essay.

1. Scalapino and Adams, *The Tango*.
2. Frost, "Interview with Leslie Scalapino," 22. In a 1996 interview with Elisabeth Frost, Scalapino emphasizes that her interest in Buddhism was formative for her thinking and preceded her reading of Stein and other writers of the avant-garde.

3. Frost, "Interview with Leslie Scalapino," 2. Frost notes that "Scalapino's language often suppresses affect and remains provocatively flat."

4. For a history of the relations between China and Tibet in the twentieth century, see Goldstein, *A History of Modern Tibet* and Smith Jr., *China's Tibet*. For cultural background on Tibetan Buddhism, see Kapstein, *The Tibetans*; Dreyfus, *Sound of Two Hands*; and Powers, *Introduction to Tibetan Buddhism*.

5. The monastery established by the Dalai Lama and his followers in India is also known by the name "Sera." In the essay that follows, however, when I refer to the "Sera monastery," I mean the monastery in Tibet, which Scalapino visited.

6. Powers, *Introduction to Tibetan Buddhism*, 181.

7. Human Rights Watch, "China: Tibetan Monasteries." A Human Rights Watch report from March of 2012 notes that while the Chinese government had begun in the 1980s to return at least nominal control of the monasteries to Tibetan monks, a new policy, begun in January of 2012, will place Chinese government officials in charge of all monasteries.

8. For a detailed account of Tibetan monastic training in general and the ritual of the debates in particular, see Dreyfus, *Sound of Two Hands*.

9. Dreyfus, *Sound of Two Hands*, 200.

10. While the pages of the volume are not numbered, for the reader's convenience, I have numbered them one through twenty, beginning with the first page of Scalapino's text. All references are cited from Scalapino and Adams's *The Tango* and are hereafter cited in the body of the essay.

11. See Conte, *Unending Design*, and Frost, "Interview with Leslie Scalapino," 3, as well as Lagapa, "Something from Nothing," 40.

12. Frost, "Interview with Leslie Scalapino," 3.

13. Lagapa, "Something from Nothing," 31.

14. Frost, "Interview with Leslie Scalapino," 6. In her interview with Frost, Scalapino comments on her poetry's critique of self: "My writing is fabrication of self, of subjectivity (which itself is seen to be 'cultural abstraction'), yet in it the 'self' is not separable from its own illusion."

15. Lagapa, "Something from Nothing," 40.

16. I am grateful to Madera Allan for her analysis of this detail in the photographs.

17. For an analysis of the tango as a ritualized expression of national pride and political resistance in Argentina, see Savigliano, *Tango and the Political Economy of Passion*.

Bibliography

Conte, Joseph M. *Unending Design: The Forms of Postmodern Poetry*. Ithaca, NY: Cornell University Press, 1991.

Dreyfus, George B. J. *The Sound of Two Hands Clapping: The Education of a Tibetan Buddhist Monk*. Berkeley: University of California Press, 2003.

Frost, Elisabeth. "Interview with Leslie Scalapino." *Contemporary Literature* 37, no. 1 (1996): 1–23.

Goldstein, Melvyn. *A History of Modern Tibet, 1913–1951: The Demise of the Lamaist State*. Berkeley: University of California Press, 1989.

Human Rights Watch. "China: Tibetan Monasteries Placed Under Direct
Rule." Accessed April 12, 2012. http://www.hrw.org/news/2012/03/16/
china-tibetan-monasteries-placed-under-direct-rule.

Kapstein, Matthew T. *The Tibetans*. Oxford: Blackwell Publishing, 2006.

Lagapa, Jason. "Something from Nothing: The Disontological Poetics of
Leslie Scalapino." *Contemporary Literature* 47, no. 1 (2006): 30–61.

Powers, John. *Introduction to Tibetan Buddhism*. Ithaca, NY: Snow Lion Press, 1995.

Savigliano, Marta E. *Tango and the Political Economy of Passion*. Boulder, CO: West-
view Press, 1995.

Scalapino, Leslie and Marina Adams. *The Tango*. New York: Granary Books,
2001.

Smith, Warren Jr. *China's Tibet? Autonomy or Assimilation*. New York: Rowman and
Littlefield, 2008.

This Wondrous World We Feel

Pam Rehm's Larger Nature

Peter O'Leary

1. The poet Pam Rehm

Pam Rehm, a poet likely unfamiliar to most, is the author of nine collections of poetry. She was born in 1967 in New Cumberland, Pennsylvania; if the landscapes of central Pennsylvania—its woods and streams, its rolling hills and its seasons—don't directly appear in her recent work (in which the natural world has largely been replaced by the inhabited world of the city), the place nevertheless continues to affect her work, in which there is a strong, even nostalgic longing for a harmonious co-existence with the natural world, in which the looming wilderness exerts a constant presence, and in which animals stand as emblems of the good.

Rehm studied with poet John Taggart at Shippensburg University; under his tutelage, Rehm encountered the poetry of the Black Mountain, Projectivist, and, more largely, New American lineages. She extended her studies at Brown University, where she worked with Keith and Rosmarie Waldrop, and where she became associated with a group of young experimental poets who would begin to publish themselves in the early 1990s in two landmark journals from the period: *o-blek* and *apex of the M*, the latter of which she co-edited with her husband Lew Daly (and two others, Alan Gilbert and Kristen Prevellet) after relocating to Buffalo, where Daly pursued doctoral studies in the Poetics program at SUNY-Buffalo, which at the time was a locus of inventive publishing activity and poetic thinking, especially among its students, many of whom have gone on to make important contributions to American poetry, including Benjamin Friedlander, Peter Gizzi, Juliana Spahr, Jena Osman, and Elizabeth Willis, to name only a few.

These details describe the context from which her work arises but don't begin to explain its compelling draw to her readers. Though Rehm lacks a large audience for her work, the audience she has is unusually dedicated. As Zach Barocas, a poet and admirer of Rehm's work, has it, Rehm is to her audience what the Velvet Underground was to the early days of rock and roll. Barocas is alluding to a comment allegedly made by Brian Eno about the band's first record, in which he claimed that while it only sold 30,000 copies (a pittance by rock standards), everyone who bought a copy went on to start a new band.[1] By this analogy, every member of Rehm's audience goes on to write a book of her own. Barocas is exaggerating, of course, but the comparison is useful in the sense that it describes the devotion with which her readers approach her work, and the sense that part of this devotion involves the impeccable craft and integrity with which her poems are made.[2] This aspect of her work is amplified by her personality, or at least what can be discerned of it in print: though her work is intensely inward and introspective, it isn't personal, at least not in the confessional sense. You have the feeling instead of being invited into the interior monologue of a modern-day anchorite. She rarely gives public readings of her poetry; though she has lived in Manhattan for the past several years, she has little involvement with the New York poetry scenes. Because she doesn't teach, she doesn't have the student followers that often accumulate around creative writers. The aura of her literary personality emanates almost entirely from her poetry. In a career spanning nearly three decades, she has published only one major work of prose, an essay, written in 1996 when she was twenty-nine, called "Beyond Impatience: On Motherhood and Poetry," collected in an anthology about poetics and motherhood.[3]

Rehm's work from the beginning, as seen in her first booklet, *Pollux*, published by Leave Books in Buffalo in 1992, involves itself in forms of privacy. Modes of private discourse exert themselves in her poems

but there is also a questioning of the capacity for language to protect
one's privacy, even as it draws the reader into intimate considerations:

> since Ponder
> examines itself
> you come as you are
>
> a token
>
> But how does inquiry welcome a stranger?[4]

Rehm's questioning is not significantly different twenty years later in
one of her most recent books, *The Larger Nature*, published by Flood Edi-
tions in Chicago in 2011. In one poem, she asserts, "Renunciation /
is an evolved form / of desire." In the next poem, she asks, "How do
you make / embodiment dear // if you fear / its hold on your life?"[5]
Rehm's work manifests throughout the tensions of seeking revelation
despite the difficulties of locating desires and needs in the body and
the larger self. She doesn't leap from desire to renunciation; rather, it
changes slowly to one from the other, over time, something toward
which she has an unsurprisingly vexed relationship. In "Beyond Impa-
tience," she writes, "[A]ll I complain about is not having any time to
myself, and yet if my husband says, 'Okay, now's your free time,' I can't
manage to do anything in it.... I've... learned how to take a day and
curse it the whole way to bed."[6]

2. Renunciation and Rue

Though her work erupts at times with joy and though it is pervaded
by passionate convictions about the crowning glories of the natural world
and the intimate intensities of family life, Rehm is at heart a rueful poet.
Rue is regret. It's one of the small feelings. It seems oriented by hesita-
tions and failures. The word "rue" comes from an Anglo-Saxon root,
hreowan, to be sorry for. It includes a quality of repentance. But Rehm's
isn't a poetry of hesitations or second guesses; rather, it's a poetry of the
Fall—aware of and witness to the world's rottenness in which Fallenness
is its most elementary fact. But is that all? It would make for a poetry of
unremitting gloom. Rehm's poetry's ruefulness is keyed less to sorrow

than to irritation and complaint. This might seem to be a put-down but it's not. It's as much a potential source of great poetry as religious ecstasy or romantic love. T.S. Eliot, like Rehm, was a poet of irritation and complaint. He transformed these into a poetic virtue that nearly circumscribes what modern poetry is. Lorine Niedecker, one of Rehm's heroes, made of plainspoken rue an evangelical, Midwestern truth. Those are only two examples. There are many more. The repeated sighs of regret in Shakespeare's sonnets. The magnified rue of Emily Dickinson's dares to death. One of Rehm's best poems, "City," captures the feelings of rue, irritation, and complaint, with a morbid clarity:

> I've seen each day
> distantly
>
> Awoke to the sound
> of cars parking
>
> I've looked down littered alleys
>
> The rivers on either side
> of me
>
> I've had enough
> of this tenuous
>
> intimacy
>
> Take a look or ignore it
>
> Always unsure
>
> From which direction
> the sun rose[7]

The poem presents four related observations in a sequence, until the declaration, "I've had enough / of this tenuous // intimacy." Here, she inverts the thrust of Whitman's hymns to Manhattan. That's the complaint. The irritation comes in the next line: "Take a look or ignore it," as much a dismissal as an injunction. The poem resolves itself ingeniously in confusion: where is the sun rising? No matter; she's had enough. You can read "City" as a stoic poem; its ruefulness leads the reader through sorrow and repentance to renunciation, an evolved form of desire.

But that isn't to say all her work wants to turn its back on the world or to sigh with regret about it. All along, she's cultivated a rich sense of being in the world her poetry enables. "I love to hold onto something," she writes in the poem, "Indebted." "Sew it to myself // The holes in my fingers / These patterns dress me."[8] In *The Larger Nature*, Rehm intensifies this cultivation, insisting, along with her native feeling of ruefulness, on the power and worth of forging new connections in this life and with this world.

Can repentance be joyful? St. John Climacus, a Christian mystic of the seventh century, calls repentance a renewal of baptism. He wrote, "[T]he fount of tears after baptism has become greater than baptism, though this be a bold saying."[9] In the same light, he predicted, "When our soul departs from life, we shall not be accused because we have not worked miracles, or have not been theologians, or have not seen visions, but we shall all certainly have to account before God because we have not wept unceasingly for our sins."[10] Vladimir Lossky, the great Russian Orthodox theologian, commenting on this prediction, assures us, "These charismatic tears, which are the consummation of repentance are at the same time the first-fruits of infinite joy. . . . Tears purify our nature, for repentance is not merely our effort, our anguish, but is also the resplendent gift of the Holy Spirit, penetrating and transforming our hearts."[11]

The first-fruits of infinite joy. That's how Rehm's new poetry reads to me. Here is a poet for whom repentance is a creative reality; namely, the poetry flows forth from her response to the experience of God's gracious love and forgiveness. In her poem, "One to Another," she puts it this way:

Surely living evokes
a majestic spirit

Illumined
the soul is an exquisite organ

Receptive
imagination does not require power

Sown in bones and flesh
Raised in flaming mysticalness

Your vision will alight
the fire to create

a continual source
of sustenance.[12]

3. Rehm's Blake, Rehm's Milton

The publication in 2011 of *The Larger Nature* affords readers an oppor-
tunity to taste these first-fruits of infinite joy, especially in the poem
"The Depths of the World," a sequence that runs for fifteen pages,
rather long for a poem of Rehm's. A note in the back of the book informs
us, "The epigraph to 'The Depths of the World' is . . . from *The
Waves.* . . . The poem itself takes its words from William Blake's *Milton*."[13]
The epigraph is worth quoting in full; it resonates with Rehmian
intensity: "I hold a stalk in my hand. I am the stalk. My roots go down
to the depths of the world, through earth dry with brick, and damp
earth, through veins of lead and silver. I am all fibre. All tremors shake
me, and the weight of the earth is pressed to my ribs."[14] In the novel,
Louis, the outsider, is speaking (this is near its beginning; he's the one
who might have been modeled on T.S. Eliot); he could be paraphrasing
Blake. Rehm's poem begins:

Come into my nerves
invisible
atonement

Murmured deep
in solemn
words
          woven

through
          living form

Mark well
my solitude and woe
passed over [15]

Rehm's poem begins as a summons: her verb is imperative. Atonement is a resonant word in Rehm's vocabulary. The word stands for the expiation of sin by Christ through his acts of obedience and suffering at the crucifixion. This is how Blake uses the word in his poem; by extension, it means at root the same for Rehm. Great art has been made from atonement; likewise from suffering and obedience. How are these things—atonement, suffering, and obedience—bound? Emily Dickinson insisted, "Gethsemane— / Is but a Province—in the Being's Centre—": that is, there are as many Calvarys as there are people. "Our Lord—indeed—made Compound Witness— / And yet— / There's newer—nearer Crucifixion / Than That—."[16] When Rehm coaxes atonement into her poem and commands that it "Mark well / my solitude and woe / passed over," she's bearing compound witness to the way obedience and suffering are bound in her. But she's also bearing witness to atonement's creative vitality, "woven // through / living form." She's extending its meaning, taking Blake's use of it and pushing it into her present. Atonement appears later in her poem as a color, shining "with fires intoxicating."[17]

Not only does Rehm's poem "take its words" from *Milton*, it gets the order of these words from Blake's poem, too. Here are the opening fifteen lines of "Milton, Book the First," from which Rehm excerpts the first six words of her poem (which I've highlighted):

Daughters of Beulah! Muses who inspire the Poets Song
Record the journey of immortal Milton thro' your Realms
Of Terror & mild moony lustre, in soft sexual delusions
Of varied beauty, to delight the wanderer and repose
His bursting thirst & freezing hunger! **Come into my** hand
By your mild power; descending down the **Nerves** of my right arm
From out the Portals of my Brain, where by your ministry
The Eternal Great Humanity Divine. planted his Paradise,
And in it caus'd the Spectres of the Dead to take sweet forms
In likeness of himself. Tell also of the False Tongue! vegetated
Beneath your land of shadows: of its sacrifices. and
Its offerings; even till Jesus, the image of the **Invisible** God
Became its prey; a curse, an offering. and an **atonement**,
For Death Eternal in the heavens of Albion, & before the Gates
Of Jerusalem his Emanation, in the heavens beneath Beulah[18]

The opening stanza to Rehm's poem is essentially two Objectivist-like pulsations in Blake's opening invocation to the muses who guide his poetry. Beulah is Blake's earthly paradise, the ideal created place from which all poetry emerges. The Daughters of Beulah enable his poetry by way of an electrical inspiration, surging from his brain to his hand through his right arm, the hand he used to etch his poems in metal. Rehm's focus on the nerves is telling: her understanding of poetry is neurochemical—hormones transmitting poetic signals invisibly. Atonement is an endocrine.

Rehm's technique is borrowed here from two sources: Tom Phillips's *A Humument* and Ronald Johnson's *Radi os*. Phillips's work, in which he endlessly and repeatedly alters pages from a Victorian novel written by William Hurrell Mallock, treating each page as both strophe and work of art with words connected amid images by bubbles and cords, provides the visual cues to the way Rehm chooses her words from Blake in clusters and nodes. Johnson's work is an antecedent of more complex reverberations: his poem is composed through the excision of most of the words from the first four books of Milton's *Paradise Lost*. In the introductory note to that book, he invokes Blake specifically, writing that *Radi os* "is the book Blake gave me (as Milton entered Blake's left foot—the first foot, that is, to exit Eden), his eyes wide open through my hand. *To etch* is 'to cut away,' and each page, as in Blake's concept of a book, is a single picture."[19] Johnson's is as much a spiritual as a practical example. Blake's relationship to Milton is reiterated in Johnson's reading of the same; Blake has given Johnson permission to read Milton's poem with a felt-tipped marker in hand, eliminating words. Rehm reiterates Blake's relationship to Milton, but this time directly with Blake. Milton, as for Blake, is for Rehm a character through whom her poem is amplified.

Erasure poems have become something of a fad of late. And fads tend toward dilution. For all the clever erasures out there, not a single one surpasses the intelligence and surprise in Phillips's and Johnson's poems. But Rehm's poem isn't a faddish essay in the form. Instead, it's a re-envisioning of *Milton* through reading and reinvention, a poetry written with a pencil in hand to identify necessities and to indicate resonances. Consider the second phrase in "The Depths of the World," whose syntax leads it to qualify atonement: "Murmured deep / in solemn / words /

woven / through / living form."[20] The texture of the metaphors in this phrase is luxurious and rich, as is the music (the "m's" leading into the "w's" and back to "m" in "form"). The first half of the phrase comes from three lines in Blake in which Milton's creative and moral quandary is presented. Milton was an immortal in Heaven but he was unhappy there; nevertheless "he obey'd, he **murmur'd** not."[21] Instead, in torment, he watched his "Sixfold Emanation" (the projection of the feminine principle within him) scatter "thro' the **deep**."[22] Next, something unexpected happens in Blake's poem: Milton's distress over the loss of his Emanation down from Heaven into creation shifts into a desire for action. He wants himself to leave Heaven and plunge back down into creation. At that moment, a Bard's prophetic song rings out from the eternal tables at which he sits (the Bard is something of an archetype for Blake himself in this poem), "Terrific among the Sons of Albion **in** chorus **solemn** & loud."[23] The beginning of the Bard's speech provides the remainder of the words that open Rehm's poem (highlighting mine):

Mark well my **words**! they are of your eternal salvation:

Three Classes are Created by the Hammer of Los, & **Woven**
By Enitharmons Looms when Albion was slain upon his Mountains
And in his Tent, **thro** envy of **Living Form**, even of the Divine
    Vision
And of the Sports of Wisdom in the Human Imagination
Which is the Divine Body of the Lord Jesus. blessed for ever.
Mark well my words. they are of your eternal salvation!

Urizen lay in darkness & **solitude**, in chains of the mind lock'd up
Los siezd his Hammer & Tongs; he labourd at his resolute Anvil
Among indefinite Druid rocks & snows of doubt & reasoning.

Refusing all Definite Form, the Abstract Horror roofd. stony hard
And a first Age **passed over** & a State of dismal **woe**![24]

Rehm's editorial innovations here are subtle: she resists Blake's spelling and orthography, and switches the position of "woe," placing it before "passed over" in her poem, providing her with an inverted, Blakean adjectival phrase, "woe passed over," and also with a lovely musical prolongation of the "o" sound from "woe" to "over."

Let's pause for a moment to listen to Rehm's quiet, rueful poem against Blake's cataclysmic, druidic roar. Blake's poem, of course, is epic and dynamically wrought from the archetypal narrative he'd been summoning into his prophetic works the previous several years, most especially "The Four Zoas," the uncompleted poem he worked on by his own account for three years (though not continuously), beginning in 1797 but coming into full force in 1800. Here is what Blake wrote to Thomas Butts about its composition:

> But none can know the Spiritual Acts of my three years' Slumber on the banks of the Ocean, unless he has seen them in the Spirit, or unless he should read My long Poem descriptive of those Acts; for I have in these three years composed an immense number of verses on One Grand Theme, Similar to Homer's Iliad or Milton's Paradise Lost, the Persons & Machinery intirely new to the Inhabitants of Earth (some of the Persons Excepted).[25]

From this vast quarry of his imagination, Blake mined material for two subsequent poems, *Milton* and *Jerusalem*.[26] In *Milton*, Blake sought in part to correct errors Milton had embraced in his own work, allowing his creation—the eternal poet Milton plummeting down from Eternity into the Mundane Shell—the opportunity to atone for the sin of the real Milton's errors in Blake's poem itself. But it's also at root a poem about the transmission of literary power, characterized at the moment when Milton, having plunged through creation, drifting silently by the slumbering Satan, descends to Blake's garden in Felpham and enters his left foot, giving Blake a glimpse of "the nether regions of the Imagination," which he then "As a bright sandal formd immortal of precious stones and gold: / I stooped down & bound it on to walk forward thro' Eternity."[27] This is the most ingenious depiction of literary lineage and visionary authority in English language literature. And it is seemingly as far from Rehm's "The Depths of the World" as one might imagine at least in terms of her intentions. But here I return again to one of the phrases that opens Rehm's poem—"Murmured deep / in solemn / words / woven / through / living form"[28]—to notice the way her poem with great subtlety receives, revives, and transforms Blake's envisioning of the living form.

4. Living Forms

Zoa is a Greek plural found in Revelation that Blake took as an English singular in his poetry and which he pluralized as Zoas. You can find it, for instance, in Revelation 4:6, "And round the throne, on each side of the throne, are four living creatures (*zoa*), full of eyes in front and behind." (The Authorized Version translates *zoa* as "beasts.") Blake's discovery of the Four Zoas is his most imaginative invention, whose forcefulness is reflected in the lexicogony of the word he invents to express it. He named them in terms of the "four fundamental aspects of Man: his body (Tharmas—west); his reason (Urizen—south); his emotions (Luvah—east); and his imagination (Urthona—north)"[29] These Zoas are the four rivers of the waters of life, they reflect aspects of the Divine, they emanate feminine portions, they warp into spectral presences, they battle each other in Time, they inform the totality of Blake's creative power.

Throughout his poetry, as in *Milton*, Blake refers to the Zoas as "living forms," typically capitalized. This phrase strikes me as a useful definition of the word archetype when used in the Jungian sense. Not static psychic entities, but living forms whose dynamism plunges them through the cosmos of the imagination where they exert magnetic, combative, fraught, and inventive destinies. Virginia Woolf's description of the depths of the world in the epigraph to Rehm's poem, "I am all fibre. All tremors shake me...,"[30] is a summoning of the qualities of a living form.

Like Blake, Rehm believes in living form. For her, it's something through poetry we can feel. "The Depths of the World" concludes: "In the still of night / a bird song / calls // enlarging and enlarging / until it touches us // This wondrous world / we feel."[31] But Rehm's citation of living form in her poem is as much a hesitation as it is a validation. "Murmured deep / in solemn / words / woven / through / living form."[32] Why murmured deep? Why so muffled? Why so solemn? For Rehm, contact with this living form is something intimate, something attuned to self-discovery. Elsewhere in the poem, she writes:

The twofold form
self-dividing

You
    putting on perfection

In natural religion
    bones never awake

the hand becomes rock
    or milky seed[33]

These lines show a quality of critique as well as aspiration—by putting on perfection you come closer to the living form of natural religion in which bones, as mere structure, never awaken. As the poem continues, it shifts mood:

Two, yet one
    Come then
        O beloved

Let us
    walk
        in the dust

against the great
consummation

and turn feeling
open
to hope itself [34]

Feeling open to hope itself emerges *against* the great consummation of internal energies, the worries that define the life of the one who seeks communion with the earth, whose life is informed by doubts: "Truth shakes the roots / Doubtfulness / takes refuge / in the prophetic."[35]

Taking refuge in the prophetic. What does this mean? Prophecy unnerves in its intermediation, unbalances in its proclamations. Prophecy is heavenly. It is an expression of living forms. François Jullien, in *Vital Nourishment*, writes about the difference between sources of vitality for the ego, which result from depleting expenditures of self, and heavenly sources of vitality, which demand nothing of the self. "A distinction must be made," he writes, "between, on the one hand, *stimulus [excitation]*, which is external, sporadic, and temporary, and which impinges constantly on my affective being, buffeting or consuming me, and, on the other hand, *incitement* [*incitation*], which is fundamental and which, stripped of my concepts and options, connects me completely to the ceaseless turmoil that keeps the world in motion."[36] *Incitement/incitation*: This is the energetic expression of a living form whose ceaseless turmoil, in connecting the poet to the depths of the world, turns feeling open to hope itself. It might also be taken as an expression of the kind of faith Rehm has in the world: she reserves belief for an incomparable love to be felt in the world: "Give and believe / all day."[37] There's a tone to her poetry that puts me in mind of something the Jesuit paleontologist and mystic, Pierre Teilhard de Chardin, wrote in his essay "How I Believe":

> If, as the result of some interior revolution, I were to lose in succession my faith in Christ, my faith in a personal God, and my faith in spirit, I feel that I should continue to believe invincibly in the world. The world (its value, its infallibility and its goodness)—that, when all is said and done, is the first, the last, and the only thing in which I believe. It is by this faith that I live. And it is to this faith, I feel, that at the moment of death, rising above all doubts, I shall surrender myself.[38]

5. Reading/Divining

Though derived from Blake's *Milton*, Rehm's poem isn't merely an excision of the master source. Though she advances largely by way of what might be called the typical procedures for making a poem by erasure—removing most of the words from the original and keeping those selected in the order they appear—she jumps around the first book of Blake's poem so that sections of her poems don't coordinate directly with *Milton*. For instance, the two sections on page 46 of Rehm's poem come from words taken from plate 6 of Blake's poem, the second section with words from earlier on the plate than those in the first. Put another way, Rehm isn't rigidly following the order of the appearance of Blake's words in her poem. In fact, she's reordering them. Or consider this section from page 45:

Created continually
two contraries turn

> a little narrow dark
> the great light fills
>
> The human shadow
> on the land
>
> is a vast dimension
>
> Born of sight
> where the lark mounts[39]

If you're reading along with Blake to locate the source of Rehm's words, you'll find the first four lines of this section have their origin in plate 5 of Blake's poem. For instance: "The Eye of Man **a little narrow orb** closd & **dark** / Scarcely beholding **the great light** conversing with the Void..."[40] The second half comes from plate 17, roughly five hundred lines later in the poem. For instance: "It is a cavernous Earth / Of labyrinthine intricacy, twenty-seven folds of opakeness / And finishes **where the lark mounts**..."[41] Rehm is not merely reading Blake's poem and excising it. She's divining from it, like a water witch with a dowser finding the fluid of inspiration coursing through the earth of Blake. Hers is a reading taking its refuge in something like prophecy. How so? Consider again the poem's conclusion:

> In the still of night
>   a bird song
>   calls
>
> enlarging and enlarging
>   until it touches us
>
> This wondrous world
>   we feel[42]

Most of these words come from plate 21 of *Milton*. This is the revolutionary moment in the poem when Milton enters Blake's left foot: the great scene that authorizes literary usage of the sort Rehm is conducting in her dowsing of Blake's own lines. Let's look at the context of this scene carefully because it's the way Rehm's prophetic, divining intelligence delves into Blake's poem that generates her own terrific work. In Blake's poem, once Milton, entering through Blake's foot, has been incorporated into his nervous system, Ololon, Milton's emanation, makes her extraordinary appearance. Originating as the name of a river in Eden, she is also a feminine principle embodying the entirety of the "truth underlying [Milton's] errors about woman."[43] She appears at the moment Milton seems to be plunging deeper into reality, into Ulro, a Blakean Hades of lifeless woe and suffering. Milton's descent is a cosmically catastrophic event that, because Milton is an Eternal, causes all the dynamic figures in Blake's imaginal mythos to pause. This includes Ololon, whose emanation is six-fold, thus giving her a choral voice, who has been wracked with lamentation by Milton's fall. Plate 21 records a scene of powerful pathos in Blake's poem. But where Blake's scene is bleak, Rehm's is exalted, laudatory. She pulls praise from the wreckage and agony Blake envisions. But she doesn't merely *pull*: she edits, arranges, adjusts, revises. Where Blake has "in the still night,"[44] Rehm has, "In the still of night."[45] Blake has "bird," "song," "call"[46] separated; Rehm binds them by grammar: "a bird song / calls."[47] Blake has "Enlarging and enlarging till" and below that, "touch'd;"[48] Rehm binds you, her reader, into her poem, "Enlarging and enlarging / until it touches us."[49] Blake has: "O no! how is this wondrous thing: / This World beneath, unseen before," and just below, "you also feel;"[50] Rehm summons Teilhardian surrender: "This wondrous world / we feel."[51] Each adjustment is a subtle discovery of something original, Rehm's own splendid envisioning of the depths of the world in which she believes.

6. The Incitement to Joy

Poetry is Rehm's incitement, the thing that connects her to the ceaseless turmoil that keeps the world in motion. In her poetry, Rehm occupies a state of habitual discernment, reading texts with a prophetic legibility she transforms into moments of joy and sorrow splendidly mixed. A poem, "Background Light," from *The Larger Nature*, begins: "Hold a blade of grass / up to your eyes / Contemplate / the ordinary field."[52] It continues: "Light is sown / and each day / the soul will flower / more and more" and includes the petition, "Give and forgive / Love in a mother's heart / is just a deep echo / of God."[53] In "Beyond Impatience," Rehm wrote, "A poem, for me, has always been what I do with what I feel, but not in a sentimental way. What I've come to realize is that when all else stops making sense, my own writing understands me; without it I lose part of my definition."[54] The deep echo of God is, in a sense, Rehm's recognition of that definition, of poetry—and by extension the world—understanding her. The poem allows her to be in this wondrous world she feels. This aspect of her work can be characterized, perhaps even without qualification, strange as it may be, by the work of an anonymous German mystic from the fourteenth century: "Listen. Look. Suffer and be still. Release yourself into the light. See with intellect. Learn with discretion. Suffer with joy. Rejoice with longing. Have desire with forbearance. Complain to no one. My child, be patient and release yourself, because no one can dig God out from the ground of your heart."[55] Rehm is one of our great living poets, creating poems like "The Depths of the World," in which the tradition lives, in which its forms take life.

Notes

1. Wikipedia, "Velvet Underground." A version of this anecdote appears in the first paragraph.
2. Observations drawn from a conversation between Zach Barocas and the author on July 29, 2012.
3. Rehm, "Beyond Impatience," 165–170.
4. Rehm, *Pollux*, n.p.
5. Rehm, *The Larger Nature*, 9–10.
6. Rehm, "Beyond Impatience," 166.
7. Rehm, *Small Works*, 16.
8. Rehm, *Small Works*, 37.
9. Climacus, *Ladder of Divine Ascent*, 137.
10. Lossky, *Mystical Theology*, 205.
11. Lossky, *Mystical Theology*, 205.
12. Rehm, *The Larger Nature*, 13.
13. Rehm, *The Larger Nature*, n.p.
14. Rehm, *The Larger Nature*, n.p.
15. Rehm, *The Larger Nature*, 43–44.
16. Dickinson, "One Crucifixion is recorded."
17. Rehm, *The Larger Nature*.
18. Blake, "Milton: a Poem in 2 Books," 95.
19. Johnson, "A Note and a Dedication," n.p.
20. Rehm, *The Larger Nature*, 43–44.
21. Blake, "Milton: a Poem in 2 Books," 95.
22. Blake, "Milton: a Poem in 2 Books," 95.

23. Blake, "Milton: a Poem in 2 Books," 96.
24. Blake, "Milton: a Poem in 2 Books," 96.
25. In Damon, *A Blake Dictionary*, 143.
26. Indeed, Damon suggests that in a subsequent letter to Butts, Blake was already writing about *Milton*, that one poem surged directly out of the work of the other. (See Damon, 276). There's no question, however, that Blake re-used a great deal of material from "The Four Zoas" for *Milton* and *Jerusalem*, including dozens of barely altered lines.
27. Blake, "Milton: a Poem in 2 Books," 114.
28. Rehm, *The Larger Nature*, 43–44.
29. Damon, 458.
30. Rehm, *The Larger Nature*.
31. Rehm, *The Larger Nature*, 57.
32. Rehm, *The Larger Nature*, 43–44.
33. Rehm, *The Larger Nature*, 52.
34. Rehm, *The Larger Nature*, 52-53.
35. Rehm, *The Larger Nature*, 49.
36. Jullien, *Vital Nourishment*, 44.
37. Rehm, *The Larger Nature*, 46.
38. Teilhard de Chardin, "How I Believe," 99.
39. Rehm, *The Larger Nature*, 45.
40. Blake, *The Larger Nature*, 98.
41. Blake, "Milton: a Poem in 2 Books," 110.
42. Rehm, *The Larger Nature*, 57.
43. Damon, *A Blake Dictionary*, 307.
44. Blake, "Milton: a Poem in 2 Books," 115.
45. Rehm, *The Larger Nature*, 57.
46. Blake, "Milton: a Poem in 2 Books," 115.
47. Rehm, *The Larger Nature*, 57.
48. Blake, "Milton: a Poem in 2 Books," 115.
49. Rehm, *The Larger Nature*, 57.
50. Blake, "Milton: a Poem in 2 Books," 115.
51. Rehm, *The Larger Nature*, 57.
52. Rehm, *The Larger Nature*, 60.
53. Rehm, *The Larger Nature*, 61.
54. Rehm, "Beyond Impatience," 168.
55. "The Silent Outcry," 141.

Bibliography

Blake, William. "Milton: a Poem in 2 Books." In *The Poetry and Prose of William Blake*, edited by David V. Erdman. New York: Doubleday, 1965.

Climacus, John. *The Ladder of Divine Ascent* (The Classics of Western Spirituality). Translated by Colm Luibheid and Norman Russell. Mahwah, NJ: Paulist Press, 1982).

Damon, S. Foster. *A Blake Dictionary*. Providence, RI: Brown University Press, 1965.

Dickinson, Emily. "One Crucifixion ís recorded—only—" #553. 1863 in The Complete Poems of Emily Dickinson. Edited by Thomas Johnson. Boston: Back Bay Books, 1976.

Johnson, Ronald. "A Note and a Dedication." In *Radi os*. Chicago: Flood Editions, 2005.

Jullien, François. *Vital Nourishment*. Translated by Arthur Goldhammer. New York: Zone Books, 2007.

Lossky, Vladimir. *A Mystical Theology of the Eastern Church*. Cambridge & London: James Clarke & Co., 1957.

Phillips, Tom. *A Humument: A Treated Victorian Novel*. New York: Thames & Hudson, 2005.

Rehm, Pam. "Beyond Impatience: On Motherhood and Poetry." In *The Grand Permission: New Writings on Poetics and Motherhood*, edited by Patricia Dienstfrey and Brenda Hillman, 165–170. Middleton: Wesleyan University Press, 2003.

Rehm, Pam. *The Larger Nature*. Chicago: Flood Editions, 2011.

Rehm, Pam. *Pollux*. Buffalo: Leave Books, 1992.

Rehm, Pam. *Small Works*. Chicago: Flood Editions, 2005.

"The Silent Outcry." In *The Essential Writings of Christian Mysticism*, edited by Bernard McGinn, 141–142. New York: Modern Library, 2006.

Teilhard de Chardin, Pierre. "How I Believe." In *Christianity and Evolution*. Translated by René Hague. San Diego, CA: Harcourt, Inc., 1971.

Wikipedia. "The Velvet Underground." Accessed August 24, 2016, http://en.wikipedia.org/wiki/The_Velvet_Underground.

Brenda Coultas
On the Transmigration of Things
Jaime Robles

In *The Body in Pain*, Elaine Scarry puts forth two interlocking theories. The first, that pain eliminates speech, and that the greater pain becomes the more it defies language and description, and thereby "undoes" the world for the human sufferer. For the most part, her theory discusses pain as it appears in its most extreme form: in war and in torture. Scarry seldom, however, talks about the battles that exist on psychological levels: the wars of class, sex or racial difference, although those are implicit in her argument. Nor does she emphasize the pain caused by mere existence, until she begins the second half of her book, in which she unfolds her second theory: that human imagination is an endlessly bountiful creator that works counter to the unspeakableness of pain.

Her most fascinating and difficult example of this proposal is her examination of the Judeo-Christian God, which, she posits, is the most radical creation of the human imagination, one whose function is a means not simply to soothe and banish pain but also—in contradiction to the human desire for a compassionate universe or deity—to threaten it. What the presence of God does, whether you believe him manufactured or manufacturer, is to define humankind in its mortality. And the implication—one that is undeniable—in Scarry's idea is that a sense of external divinity is an innate feature of the human imagination: that it is the deification of our fear of pain.

It's possible to miss that what Brenda Coultas writes about is pain, especially the pain caused by the psychological forms of class warfare, although it is clearer that mortality is a focus of her concern. For one thing, she presents the environment she inhabits with a droll self-deprecation that resolves into a deadpan sense of humor:

> A Bowery Bum asked "Can I talk to you for a minute?" He burped loudly in my ear. Later he asked me to look up at the sun where he had written his name, then to hug him. I did both. Why do I listen to Bowery Bums?[1]

The self that Coultas presents to the reader is that of the naïf, the innocent. Her stance allows her a certain objectivity vis-à-vis her perceived world: she is able to assume, in a poetic version, the perspective and methodology of a journalist or scientist. Innocence, posed as non-judgmental curiosity, is the state of mind necessary to her gathering of what she calls "evidence." She is the eternal observer: "That is what I do best, sit and look out windows."[2]

Through the detachment of assumed objectivity, she deflects the most devastating pain that humans undergo: making sense of human cruelty and of universal indifference. She buries it under a sympathetic irony for the absurdity of living in an economically unjust world.

*

In "The Bowery Project," which opens *The Handmade Museum*, Coultas examines a world that we in the U.S. conceptualize, and rightly so, as one of painful deprivation, bodily abuse, and spiritual degradation: the world of the homeless, represented by lower Manhattan's Bowery, where bums and junkies shamble and sleep in lean-tos made of old mattresses and cast-off plastic. These are the urban killing fields of poverty, racial and sexual prejudice.

Coultas enters this world as a collector: she is there to accumulate the "goods"—the best that is cast off in our material world. In the Bowery, though, there are reasons why things are abandoned, and she veers back and forth between desire and disgust for these material objects. A Gap T-shirt she finds on the street is the same as the one she sees in glossy ads of "real people":

"thought I could wear this one. Was damp with a liquid, got repulsed, dropped it."[3]

The airbrushed models in advertising photography are designated as "real"—a label proved ironic by the factual, and disgusting, physicality of poverty. It's not a far leap from the cast-off clothes and furniture in the street to the homeless, who have lost their connection, their use, and their beauty within the city they populate; they too are abandoned. Coultas, however, eschews moral judgment and clarifies her presence and her motivations by identifying with the drifting populations of the Bowery:

> The intention is not to romanticize the suffering or demonize the Bowery residents but rather to comment on poverty, class, suffering and my own dilemma and identifications as a teacher and poet one paycheck away from the street. It's the transparent medium I walk through with my own poverty.[4]

Coultas is pacing out what Scarry suggests is the motivation behind the great religious books of our collective history—which is to counter existential and physical pain through the imagination. She recognizes the religious analog that links her to the Bowery's life of pain, and within that she senses a form of power in which a battle is fought for existence. This is both a spiritual and a class struggle:

> Needless to say that for me, the Bowery has taken on a metaphysical weight as a passage and frame of mind as well as a power spot where ghosts and the nearly living compete for space with the cell phonies who have come to replace them.[5]

*

Scarry often comments about pain's lack of physicality in the world as being crucial to its unique power to obliterate speech:

> Though the capacity to experience physical pain is as primal a fact about the human being as is the capacity to hear, to touch, to desire, to fear, to hunger, it differs from these events, and from every other bodily and psychic event, by not having an object in the external world.[6]

And although the experience of pain may be entirely contained within the human body and therefore objectless, Coultas' poetry demonstrates that pain does leave physical markers. Tied into the imagination, these markers have both negative and positive aspects: they stimulate not only the creative act of writing in the poet but also evoke memories of pain within the reader. The compassion that rises within the reader in response to the writer's words is also a creative act.

Coultas explains her Bowery project as a kind of historical preservation, but her fascination with material objects is reminiscent of the Old Testament's focus on multiplicity: the primacy of Genesis with its creation of all the objects in the universe, in their vast numbers and unreachable scope, and the human drive for begetting all manner of things, especially generations of its own tribe, creates a metatext for our culture that prizes the effusion of material objects. For us, bounty is good. Coultas pursues the bounty of discards:

> I used to dream of yard sales, where I was the first person there and every collectable I ever desired was on the table, but I had to grab them before the others arrived. I trembled. I tremble before the good stuff.[7]

The oddity of the verb "tremble" and the adjective "good" serves to mark out the spiritual underpinnings of Coultas' fascination with material objects. One trembles before God, not before chairs that have escaped being broken or clothing free of stains. Or are they equal? Does her reaction—her trembling—suggest that there is something divine, or at least supernatural, in things—in particular, beautiful and valued things—that escape damage?

Much of Coultas' poetry is comprised of lists of objects, notated not only with a description, but also with the time, date, and place of discovery. Though her approach emulates investigative science, her expressed desire for "stuff" is charged and at times obsessional—she only stops collecting when she has no more room to stash the objects she wants. Failing physical space, objects collect in her writing. But where Coultas's lists swerve from the material profusions of the Old Testament, which also lists and notates in order to confirm historical accuracy, is in the decrepitude of the material world through which she travels, searching for "goods. Nonetheless, in either cases replication equals aliveness and vitality.

In "Some Might Say That All I've Done Is Stack Up a Heap of Objects" Coultas explains the metaphysics and the mission of her search:

> Some will say it's all been done before, and that others have done better but still I stack things up. I don't think about it, I put blinders on but hope that through accumulation they'll form a pattern out of chaos. I've stacked up twigs one by one, building a structure, weaving and shaping, forming a skeleton out of raw garbage transformed into beauty, maybe with something to say to any Bowery resident or reader of poetry. Please, I am intentionally writing this for you.[8]

Coultas' dumpster-diving resembles a form of spiritual practice, in which she mines the broken remnants of our consumer culture as if it were a source of riches, both redeemable and hideous, but capable finally of "alchemy": of transfiguring the lost into the saved. Her collecting allows for reshaping, which is an imaginative act that provides order in an inexplicable world. The act is, finally, one that soothes and overrides pain, and is generously shared. Its sense of community, or communal sharing, lauded if not practiced in Judeo-Christian religion.

*

Coultas juxtaposes the "reality" of middle-class America's commercial portrayals of itself as it aspires to wealth and fame to the "ghosts" that are the derelicts and detritus of the Bowery. She takes this a step farther in her second collection of poems, *The Marvelous Bones of Time*. The book opens with "The Abolition Journal," in which she draws parallels between Abraham Lincoln's life and her own:

> Lincoln looked out over the river and saw a slave state and he was born in one (Kentucky), like me, but was raised in a free state (Indiana), like me. We were white and so could cross the river.[9]

What she is seeking is some understanding of race, as it may have been perceived by her family; a burden often carried by those Americans who live on the borders of the South, even though racism was and remains endemic in most regions of the US. Tagged at the end of this passage is her self-reflexive understanding that her whiteness allows

her passage and freedom; the river she is allowed to cross because of
her race has spiritual links with black America, the other, subjugated,
race. It resonates with the gospel-singer's river Jordan, over which one
passes to reach the Holy Land, a land of saving grace. It is this insight
and self-awareness that prod her on to examine her family's history
for a connection to racial struggle.

Her search for her family's tie to abolitionism begins with discarded
objects, which are then set aside as inadequate, figured in a metonym
of the South, the tobacco leaf:

> I could follow these paths and find car bodies and dump sites
> deer bones and garbage
>
> I could mow a new path; still, it would not be evidence
> Even if the tobacco leaves all pointed north, it would not be
>   evidence.[10]

Thus Coultas begins her pursuit of history by abandoning material
"evidence" as a methodology for uncovering the unknown; personal
history, especially, cannot be found in physical signs. The world she
is seeking is interior and mental as well as chronological, its realm is
that of the remembered, and when attached to celebrated historic
figures, it becomes mythic.

Coultas attempts a more thorough escape from the material world
in "The Lonely Cemetery," the second half of the book, which is a series
of prose stories that she has collected from friends and strangers about
inexplicable events that suggest an afterlife, or, in the case of UFOs, a
life so alien as to be imperceptible within the physical abundance of the
planet's *oikos*. In the poem the collection is named after, Coultas does
something she seldom does in her writing, although it is a technique—or
rather a mindset—implicit in much of her interest in objects: she employs
a form of pathetic fallacy. She gives the cemetery humanity by infusing
it with her personal emotions: "There are cemeteries that are lonely and
there are cemeteries that wish to be alone so they send out ghosts."

In her late-night explorations, achieved on that most mysterious
and disembodied of territories, the computer, she tracks ghosts and
rounds up stories of the paranormal. No god per se exists in Coultas;

rather what she accumulates is evidence of the undefinable. She builds a private cemetery—the locale of bodies abandoned by life, beyond loss and pain—by populating her memory and her writing with ghosts, monsters, aliens, and stalkers—presences that exist, if they exist, in the borderlands of our consciousness.

As a child, she writes, the monsters she and her sisters were constantly seeking populated Coultas' imagination; she could name them but she could not capture them. Stalkers populated her young adulthood, and her current friends tell her stories of ghosts. None of these are terrifying creatures, however, but rather precious attributes of life's diversity, suggesting realms lying beyond ours. When creatures move from suggestion in the imagination into physical reality, they border on the miraculous.

> I dreamed of so many treasures buried in the earth or of just bones, all the bones buried by time, nature, or natives. Given eternity, we could find marvelous bones.[11]

Like ghost stories, the emotional nexus of Coultas's collected stories, or prose poems, is belief or disbelief. For most of us, belief can only be substantiated through manifestations of the physical—the seen being who is unrecognizable as human, the eerie and disconnected sensations that, nonetheless, can be read as proof of physical presence. By abandoning physical evidence, Coultas moves into pure belief. Belief is an unhampered emotion in Coultas' writing. She never urges us to believe the ghost stories that she relates, nor is it clear, with her droll sense of humor, that she believes them herself. Her tone is only just convincing. More often we recognize the pervasiveness of her belief by a sudden, sharp but fleeting, confession of pain, especially that caused by loss, which she reveals in her narratives. These moments stand as clear revelations of her sense of what it is to exist:

> When I think of death, I tell myself that I'm going to where my father is, and if he's there, that's a good place to be. I'm going to the place where all have gone before me, and that's what makes me human.[12]

> I got very upset at the thought that I could be a fictional character in the dream of a dog, but I feel pain and thus think I'm real.[13]

*

Coultas has maintained in several articles and interviews that she is interested in narrative as a communal activity: "I use narrative to connect, also I'm a sucker for a narrative riff and for beauty." It is the story rather than the attendant philosophies and psychologies that are her focus, which makes it difficult to derive a consistent theory about the "meaning" of her writing. Perhaps that's just as well. She tells her stories simply and cleanly; it is the movement of the tale from point A to point B that is primary, rather than decorations of language and device. The beauty within the stories is within each narrative as a recollection of a moment of life: one of those many "marvelous bones" that could be uncovered if eternity allowed us the time.

Her stories are not merely her own. The ghost stories of the several sections of "The Lonely Cemetery" are collections of what other people have told her, confirmations of her sense of community and connection. And, in good faith with that community, she notes in the section's epigraph: "Every word you are about to read is true or believed to be so." This impulse to collect harkens back not only to the dumpster diving of *The Handmade Museum*, but specifically to two poems in that first collection: "A Summary of a Public Experiment" and "Bowery Box Wishes." In the first, she describes how she set up "a table and a chair and put up a sign that read, 'Tell me a Bowery story.'" A friend films the stories, which are then retold by Coultas with her descriptions of the person and how the story was told. In the latter poem, which is a "film script for a home movie: 3 mins, b & w", she describes a box labeled "Bowery Wishes" that she leaves in a public place. She describes, as if it were a film, the many people who come by to drop their wishes in the box:

"Are you going to read them?" someone asked.

"No," I said. But I wasn't sure why, I had promised them nothing yet I felt that they had trusted me not to look, but maybe some of them hoped to be heard . . . what I felt was the need to protect them. So I did.[14]

What she suggests is that languages, especially personal stories, carry with them an obligation. Every story is a form of confession, even if they are unheard, and as such they carry the innocence of storyteller with them. Throughout her work, Coultas reverences not only those who suffer from poverty and prejudice but also the words they express as a salve to the wounds they bear. With humor and kindness she aspires to heal both the individual and the community through language.

Notes

1. Coultas, *The Handmade Museum*, 16.
2. Coultas, *The Handmade Museum*, 15.
3. Coultas, *The Handmade Museum*, 14.
4. Coultas. "Failure."
5. Coultas, "Failure."
6. Scarry, *The Body in Pain*, 161.
7. Coultas, *The Handmade Museum*, 16.
8. Coultas, *The Handmade Museum*, 16.
9. Coultas, *The Marvelous Bones of Time*, 17.
10. Coultas, *The Marvelous Bones of Time*, 15.
11. Coultas, *The Marvelous Bones of Time*, 88.
12. Coultas, *The Marvelous Bones of Time*, 80.
13. Coultas, *The Marvelous Bones of Time*, 91.
14. Coultas, *The Marvelous Bones of Time*, 35.

Bibliography

Coultas, Brenda. *The Handmade Museum*. Minneapolis: Coffeehouse Press, 2003.

Coultas, Brenda. *The Marvelous Bones of Time*. Minneapolis: Coffeehouse Press, 2007.

Coultas, Brenda. "Failure," *Narrativity*. San Francisco State. Issue 2. 2001. Accessed February 20, 2011. http://www.sfsu.edu/~newlit/narrativity/issue_two/coultas.html

Scarry, Elaine. *The Body in Pain: The Making and Unmaking of the World*. New York: Oxford University Press, 1985.

Wholly Spirit Culture

poetic statement by Tracie Morris

I grew up in the urban Northeast in Brooklyn, third generation, from southern (USA) family members. We were surrounded by, and incorporated into, the feel of the Black community (from the South, multi-lingual Caribbean and, to a certain extent, directly from Africa) like most urban folks. In my family, there were a couple of aspects of Black culture that we weren't directly involved with, however: We weren't involved with the Christian church and we didn't drink or do drugs, generally. I didn't think about how these two ideas were connected until I started writing this essay. We were surrounded by these elements but weren't a part of them.

What was interesting about not being avid churchgoers (and by "we" I mean my immediate and close extended family: mom, brother, maternal grandparents, aunts, uncles and some first cousins) is that we were infused with the sensibility of the Church (as many Black folks are) without being committed to believing what it believed. My grandmother liked church in a very non-denominational way. Catholic and Protestant effects were appreciated: from eating fish on Fridays and getting palms on Palm Sunday, to listening to Reverend Ike on the radio and believing in religiously-based prosperity consciousness. We observed Christmas and Easter culturally then (clothes and food) but we weren't compelled to *go* to church. My grandfather was not a believer, but also not an atheist. Nor did he, my grandmother, my mother, or the immediate relatives I saw drink or do drugs around me. A bit more on that in a second.

We would "peek our head in" and knew about "the church(es)" that suffused the Black atmosphere. We'd gone to various services and especially went to church for weddings and to show off our Easter bonnets and kiddie suits with knickers. Open-minded to holy rollers, street preachers, reform churches, and the "literal religious pillars" in brownstone Brooklyn environs. Being one step removed from a particular dogma, however, allowed us/me to think about the Black church conceptually, aesthetically, abstractly. We felt the sensibility of the Black Church (itself an amalgam of many spiritual traditions), its inhabitation, incorporation into the body revealed as the effect of "catching the spirit," being *touched* by simply reading the Bible without ecumenical mediation—just by the profundity of the language and its poetics. Its pacing, drama, incantatory power indicated something beyond words that moved me, moved through me throughout the streets, no matter what else was moving about the streets, too. Seeing the pervasiveness of heroin overdoses in the streets of Brooklyn steered me away from drugs as much as sobriety in my home did. And the Church demonstrated, regularly, that you didn't need an "outside agitator" (meaning outside of oneself) to get to some other place. What I mean is that the tangibility of spirit reaching into you, within a proscribed time frame, through invocation, evocation, cultural action, cultural sparks can be prompted by specific religious information but wasn't exclusively framed by religious belief.

This distinction between spiritual aesthetics and religious conversion may have laid the groundwork for my relationship to sound poetry—sounds unmoored from literal meaning but nevertheless meaning "full." In the great 1964 film *Nothing But a Man*, Ivan Dixon's character, Duff, stands in the doorway of a sanctified church, appreciating the choir and the power of the guest preacher from Birmingham, Alabama. I feel like Duff sometimes, standing at the church doorway, admiring. Raised on the sustenance of a good country meal, not knowing I'd be meeting my future.

That open door is an opening of the spirit. It wasn't a spiritual door, per se, but it was an opening. You can't go to a Black church, especially a sanctified/holy-roller (including Pentecostal) one, even just a peek in, without feeling, being felt. *Knowing* that there's something more. The fact that I wasn't raised around the obvious external ways to "get open" (drink, drugs) was likely paired with this concept of not needing something outside of myself to get higher. There was something all around, and it wasn't confined to a church, or for that matter, even a building.

My grandmother had luck beyond normal people. She contributed to the underground economy (the "numbers") and could intuit a "hit." She *always* hit, sooner rather than later. No great "by and by" when it came to that. (We didn't go that far in our cultural Christianity! No patient waiting, thanks to Garvey, Malcolm, Wells, Baker, Bethune, Powell, and King. More songs from the southern and South.)

Even when playing bingo or going to Atlantic City, I can see my grandmother making notes about numbers in her little books: it was its own divining, her nondenominational Bible code, an enduring color-coded Fibonacci sequence for pages and pages. Somehow those tiny digits translated into school clothes, perfume, groceries, a night on the town, Christmas toys. I saw this with my own eyes and believed in something beyond the self in ephemeral ways that manifest right here on earth.

I've talked a few times about the development of my own sound poems. It all started with walking down the street. Hearing the "character" talking to me, deep in my ear to the rhythm of my feet. The little girl stayed with me as I walked from the train station about fifteen minutes away. By the time I got home her riff was so ingrained that no other words, especially *my* mind's words, were allowed in. They were limiting: so I struck out with hers. A spirit I picked up on my travels that's been in my hip pocket ever since, "riding" me.

This sound, riffed sound, moving toward some other incantation is old school (Black preaching) and newer (Hip Hop cypher). The jazz riffs through words of Rakim and the collaborative dissonance of Eric B, don't just "move the crowd" because of the beat, but because they imply "testifying": the words *in service.*

"God is Great, God is Good, we want to thank him for our food" (we learned grace). Ivan Dixon got himself a *plate* from Abbey Lincoln. That sealed the deal. No matter what our cultural beliefs, we all got ourselves some of those fixin's. That holy roller opening led to more open doors, open windows, open floors.

The spirit moves in white brain matter, neurons, and *substantiae nigrae* connect hemispheres. This center fans out. The rhythm of Brooklyn walking connects to spiritual southern shouting as white noise, on the edges of hearing. Tectonic plates shift through the subway, train lines. The railroad my twelve-year-old grandfather rode in on. The unpredictability of the plate shifts syncopated with the movement of the tracks.

My grandpa was a farmer, believed the spirit to be in what we took in *every* day. He could intuit the living in them, the vibrant best roosting chickens, fruits, vegetables. Grandpa was akin to genius George Washington Carver's molecular dowsing of everyday plants. There's poetry in that—in sensing life. I discerned this non-concerted sound on other Brooklyn streets. It began to lead me back further and further to aged sounds of spirit, seasoned. As "cast" iron. The long memory part of the brain, the hippocampus, is one of the oldest parts and, over the many years of discovering more voices for sound poetry, I was trying to remember things I hadn't heard myself but had been heard by others.

The spirit moves: I had a framed picture of Mahalia Jackson in my house with no name ("I don't *think* that's Marion Anderson..." to myself) and later, while I was doing research on Black sounds, I heard her singing in a sound clip without a picture. I bought and framed the photo from a memorabilia store because I liked her face and have affection for 8x10 glossies. This was before I'd begun my sonic search. She'd been silently waiting in my house. Expecting me to catch up/catch back. She's near a picture of my high-stepping grandparents, posing for a photo before a hobnobbing evening. These two sides of my brain, a coin flip in my self: first uncategorized origins, then polish. Some sorting of sounds between. Sometimes I catch notes: it wasn't until after Mahalia was looking down at me, framed, in heaven, that I realized that hers was the sound I was searching for. Her picture and her voice of God became one, my grandparents beside, giving their best.

I think I'll say "unaccounted for coincidences" to hedge my bets on Gramma's numbers. Keep the hemispheres indie, happy, singing but bridged. Poetry is this open thing that doesn't like one side. Sometimes I just rant in my sounds, but the minute I read it again: no. I edit it down. Simmer. At times I'd try to control my sound poems to "make them" sound good in front of an audience of cognoscenti. Got golf claps. Gave up on that, working on getting soul-clap closer.

What's this echo under the sidewalk ringing against the subway girders below? At the opening of *Nothing but a Man*, we see Dixon and Yaphet Kotto on the railroad, as *free* men (neither chain, nor gang). I can feel these sounds and separate the obligatory baggage and some of the trauma, replacing it with my own assumptions, searchings, needs. *Picking up things I wasn't looking for and not sure I want to find, to lift out.* That's the job, the gig, the "hit," as the musicians say. That soul as music has to be a tune that's *carried.*

If this is the job, as the Black Christians say nowadays, "I'm blessed." Sign me up (with the spirit writing Harryette Mullen talks about). I'm still picking up tones from a religious instrument I don't play, but I like those sounds. Find myself tapping a foot to the higher calling culture of this supra-conscious glossolalia, noting it, intoning meanings behind the meaning, the door this *other* sensing opens. I give up assuming I'm the conductor, or the passenger, on those tracks. I'm only drilling a rivet into the rail, hoping the jackhammer doesn't make tinnitus. I like silence too. Looking up at the blue. When I die, please have a Black church lady sing the mess out of "His Eye was on the Sparrow" at the service. I put that in my will.

I like this job of keeping an eye out, an ear pricked, keeping the body primed by energy from above and below. In the recordings "Inner Visions" and "Music of My Mind," Stevie Wonder writes as someone seeing without sight. The renowned deaf Scottish percussionist, Evelyn Glennie, takes off her shoes to play so she can hear with her feet.

There is a sensing that expands beyond the mundane language associations of hearing, seeing, tasting, smells, that, as Susan Stewart notes in *Poetry and the Fate of the Senses*, affect their fate. Clear-hearted, unaided. The sounds that led me to being moved to utter some *thing* beyond my sense of what I *think* I know, going back to that familial place before *I* was from anyplace, *present* in deified disquiet, *joyful* noises.

from *Penury*

poem by Myung Mi Kim

Living Backwards

Cecilia Vicuña's Fleshly Language of Unsaying

Kythe Heller

"When a girl is born, her mother puts a spider in her hand, to teach her to weave. The memory of the journey unraveling."

"The poem is not speech, nor in the earth, nor on paper, but in the crossing and union of the three in the place that is not."
—Cecilia Vicuña

In the sacred Quechua language, the word for language is "thread." For a child in the Chilean Andes who is given a spider at birth, the spider's thread must seem to be a living part of one's own self, spooled out or withdrawn as the language in which the invisible world becomes visible, and vice versa, at a moment before the definition of self and other has been formed. This crucial space between presence and absence is depicted in Andean tradition as weaving, which is always accomplished with a doubled thread and represented by a couple making love. If the unraveling and weaving of the spider in the palm of one's hand is considered as a type of *quipu*, an Andean linguistic device made of knotted string, then this act of consecrating the body transmutes spider and child in such a way as to reorient "the sacred"[1] as a way of being simultaneously in language and in the world. Linguistic meaning here is not a self-contained situation but an emergent activity; it offers a doubled thread of receiving and response, a secret reciprocity strong enough to support the first radial lines between spider and child like the letters of an emergent alphabet.

Cecilia Vicuña is a poet and an artist whose distinctive practice and ethos begins (in her own words) with the act of weaving as "a continuous displacement, a field of *con* (togetherness)," and "the *quipu* that remembers nothing, an empty cord."[2] For Vicuña, whose work catches the woven echoes of several languages, this practice of continuous displacement is a form of apophasis ("speaking away") in which she weaves language through disappearance, or unsays what has been said before. It is language taken up and crucially charged with laying open and transforming the sociopolitical processes of power that construe meaning, especially in the formation of a language.

By engaging with *how* words come to mean, and with meanings (and peoples) that have been historically silenced, Vicuña's weaving is not merely a recursive practice, an image or metaphor of the structural violence imbedded in language. Rather, her work actively unravels the sociopolitical forces with which the sheer act of apprehending a word makes us complicit, and re-narrates the shifting mesh of relations among languages, peoples, and living matter, emerging as a mode of art-making suffused with the complexities of a witnessing presence. Maurice Merleau-Ponty describes this mode as "see(ing) more than one sees . . . where the invisible is *there* without being an object" in and through the structures of the world.[3] "An object is not an object," writes Vicuña. "It is the witness to a relationship."[4]

This emergent, complex, adaptive threadwork that passes through all of Vicuña's cultural production—poetry, film, installation, and pieces for live performance—is a form of spiritual *ascesis* (disciplined practice), by which I mean that it comprehensively resists and reinvents the way "the spiritual" has been used as a category in modern and contemporary thinking. For example, every image in Vicuña's new film *Kon Kon* is a word, as Jonathan Skinner observes in an essay published recently in *Rattapallax 21*: "the poet whispering to kantuta flowers (sacred to the Inca), a black flag (a plastic bag) hanging over a protest, red water swirling in a tide pool, birds foraging at the intertidal zone."[5] Yet every image is also an equation: we infer the relation between a dying sea and an oral tradition, between a double-flute's dissonance and the clash of industry and tradition, the absurd alignments of political cruelty and natural beauty. To experience *Kon Kon* is a double event we interpret and see simultaneously; it reveals the subtle equivalencies between documentary and divination, ocean and mother, human and hummingbird. As viewers, we interpret the tides as living metaphors, alert to their signs of synchronicity and dislocation.

Skinner writes insightfully about the most poignant image of the film, which features a laptop placed at the summit of El Mauco, on which is playing the endangered *Baile de los Chinos*. "The laptop's pearly white case," he notes, "recalls the seashells which, in the "oldest tradition of the Andes" are brought to the summit to honor the exchange of mountain and sea. Vicuña's metaphor equates the ghostly waves heard when seashell is pressed to ear—really the music of one's own circulation—with the sound that extinct, but still resonant, cultural forms make when we press them to our inner ear. To auscultate is to hear through a mediated technique of listening, one that doubles hearing, both inside and outside, amplifying the "torn sound" at the heart of creation."[6] Vicuña's art-making has always embraced this "torn sound," by the inextricable weaving of words with found objects and silences which communicate 'the sacred' as that which has been lost or discarded, yet is nevertheless precariously present.

What is a word? For Vicuña, this is a crucial question about the politics of language and the silencing of peoples, and she refuses to traffic in conventional definitions by writing (divining) across porous borders of language and medium. Like her book of poetry written in the form of spider webs (*Instan*) and like her installation performance limning the blood of the glaciers like a menstrual *quipu* (*La Sangre de los Glaciares*), *Kon Kon* is a reinvention of the word in film, a form of divination opening onto ancient and future possibilities of language. From the first images of the film, which Skinner describes as:

> Written in sand, or marked against the furling, oceanic horizon by vertical bits of detritus—words as knots, as language is weaving, the crossing of the horizontal and the vertical, the drawing of lines between constellations—to the last image of the dunes as knots, ground into tiny bones, to disappear into the sea, *Kon Kon* offers a treatise on the word, its power and its precariousness (a fragile kind of prayer), a manifesto on translation and on poetry as a place of exchange, activated only when we begin to listen.[7]

In *Precario/Precarious*, her "autobiography in debris," Vicuña fashions an assemblage of words and discarded materials, fragments of shells, feathers, twine, and sticks, which hover momentarily between appearance and disappearance. Vicuña says of these pieces, "We are made of throwaways and we will be thrown away."[8] Their histories, she suggests, like the histories of peoples in the Southern cone (Argentina, Chile, Uruguay), are therefore twice precarious: they emerge from prayer/garbage already aware that their lives may leave no trace. "Precarious," she writes, "is what is obtained by prayer (from the Latin *précis*). Uncertain. Exposed to hazards. Insecure. The word *oir* (to hear) was originally the same as the word *orar* (to pray). Reciprocity. By praying you reconnect."[9] Though the original *precarios* were intended to be evanescent, the first printed version of *Precario/Precarious* was published in New York by Tanam Press in 1983 with photographs documenting the sculptures. An important critical volume on her work was paired with a republication of this book in 1997, as *The Precarious / QUIPOem* (Wesleyan). In *Quipoem* as well as in recent work—*Instan* (Kelsey Street Press), *Cloud-Net* (Art in General), and the newly reissued early work *Sabor a Mi* (Chainlinks)—there is a dialectical (or beyond dialectical) tension between written text and visual art, between memory and erasure of peoples whose absence in the histories of Central and South America alter and stretch language to its full capacity as a mediator of the immanent. Crucial to this dialectic is Vicuña's lifelong human rights and eco-activism work. Presence and absence are not metaphysical categories for her but essential practices of solidarity with those known as the *desaparecidos*, or "the disappeared ones" from the political juntas of the 1970s.[10]

Yet in what ways does this performance of solidarity, this unraveling and re-weaving of languages and of peoples, interact in Vicuña's work with theology, mysticism, and what Fanny Howe calls a "theology of language"? How do these dimensions of Vicuña's apophatic imagination act formally to open up within and beyond the text to speak in new ways about actual human relations, and what kinds of implications does she propose for actual human interaction, between writer, reader, and literary/artistic/activist communities and beyond? Can language, she asks, teach us how to treat each other? In what ways does her work manifest sites of resistance, sites of evolution, realizations of new social and ecological experiments and relationships through radical re-narration?

On What Cannot Be Said—The Precarious

As an ongoing series of sculptural poems begun in Chile in 1966, Vicuña's *precarios* engage more than carefully woven fragments of words and other found refuse: their states of fragile transitoriness also introduce a different way of engaging with language. "There is something sacred," she says, "about something totally poor and totally denied."[11] The *precarios* address a response to what is physically present as well as what is absent, by valuing what has been lost or discarded; for Vicuña, "A word is a non-place for the encounter to take 'place.' "[12] Drawing from a capacious range of sources, Vicuña threads her words with those of others (ranging from found language to postmodern to ancient texts) into a collage of words and things conceived ("like the sacred Quechua language," she says) as a flexible formal weave which enacts the connectivity and dislocation crucial to her poetics. She has also continued to unweave words, dissecting their spines and renaming their phonemes, carving up their root words "so that their internal metaphors were exposed, so people would see words not just as abstractions but as something very concrete."[13] Within the re-imagined phoneme lies the wish for ways of thinking that we don't yet know about or have seemingly forgotten. For Vicuña, nothing could be more important or precious than this knowledge, however hidden. The sense of urgency, the spiritual dissatisfaction it reveals, continues to fuel her radical innovations.

> Opening words I arrived at no word.
> A moment of trance where transformation begins: silence to sound and back.
> An empty place within words where commingling occurs.

Though it has historically been through mystical texts that we have encountered this concern with language as a means of undoing conventional thinking, since modernism the most striking developments of such ideas have been made by poets like Vicuña. Some antecedents of contemporary poetry's dilemmas and formal strategies are to be found in the radical wings of mystical traditions. (Among Christian texts: the *Mystica Theologica* of Dionysius the Areopagite; works by Meister Eckhart and Marguerite Porete; and parallels in Zen, Tibetan Buddhist, Taoist, and Sufi texts). Like these mystics, Vicuña is dealing with language which "speaks of its own process: to name something which cannot be named."[14] Although she does not claim any of these mystical traditions as her own in a conventionally religious sense, her work is clearly propelled by a sense of the crisis in language. Her denial and defiance of conventional definitions resonates, whether deliberately or not, with the apophatic in its many historical articulations.

The body's presence in language is a persistent feature of her writing, as it is for many mystical writers, where the moment of greatest intimacy with the divine also has the most bodily detail. For Vicuña, everything we do mirrors and reflects us:

> The fingers entering the weave produce in the fibers
> a mirror image of its movement, a symmetry
> that reiterates[15]

For Vicuña, whose autobiography in debris is a body of text, meaning is woven and unraveling in the potential space we inhabit together, intersubjective space, the space between the fingers and the weave, and it is useless to describe "the sacred" here as an essence. Rather "the sacred" emerges variously out of the relationships we have and lose in this potential space between ourselves and our environment. We never see it all at once or in the same place twice, yet it becomes a common resource that can be drawn on in different ways to deal with the situation at hand.

> I prayed by making a quipu, offering the desire to remember.
> Desire is the offering, the body is nothing but a metaphor.[16]

A parallel process occurs in Plato's *Phaedrus*, where Desire is construed as the offspring of poverty and inspired resourcefulness, a pairing in which language is described as a weaving which twists back on itself, through itself, in the doomed effort to describe the form of the beautiful. Likewise, silence uncovers the precarious body of speech, by which I mean its ceaseless subversion of one's own normative language for experience. In silence the sensuous presence and imbedded particularities of the speaker become deeply suspect, vulnerable, unraveled—words quiver in silence, revealing their selves as concealments.

The idea that we do not know the created essences of things and therefore cannot know the essence of the divine—a problem which vexed early negative theologians like Gregory of Nyssa—was challenged by Dionysius the Areopagite, who used language to create a situation of dissimilar similarities. Language here is an "offering of desire," which sets the mind against itself by using paradox to open the reader to an experience through which language attains materiality. "Poor" and "Disappeared," for example, are not typically names we associate with divinity, and so are "dissimilar," yet this very dissimilarity aids in waking us to the inadequacies of language, unlike the more lullingly "similar" names we use, like "Beauty" and "Truth." The very materiality and unlikeliness of the dissimilar similarities makes it clear that the names do not literally describe the divine, and compel the reader to seek a deeper truth behind the name. Like the tension between the textual and the visual in Vicuña's woven *precarios*, the idea here is that the presence of the divine *in language and in the world* can be resonated in the paradox of naming that which cannot be named. Opening the mind from the familiar impasse between divine immanence and divine transcendence is like the first thread let out by the spider; it drifts across the span of a gap uncrossable by crawling. At the far end, when it sticks to an adhesive surface, the spider feels the thread catch and then carefully walks along it and strengthens it with a second thread. The thread that catches is neither the spider nor the caught surface it registers, but a form of recognition which the spider measures with its own body. It is also a biological description of the Platonic concept of Eros, that which carries something beyond itself.

Likewise, Socrates says he cannot talk about the Good, but he *can* talk about the sun, which weaves together vision with what vision sees. For Vicuña, whose work emerges from the weaving of text and context,

> The poverty of the thread
> was the limit
> and edge
> of the world
> was any
> moment.

As this stanza suggests, we as material beings are incomplete beings, with a poverty in which incompleteness is inherent moment to moment, in a weaving that is also an undoing. Like Vicuña, medieval theologians such as Thomas Aquinas were also interested in how the multiplication of speech can be its own apophasis "any moment," how one disputed question leads to the next and the next, so that all theological speech remains incomplete, a fact which mirrors us in our own cognitive incompleteness as human beings. In the work of art that is incomplete, however, human agency is newly implied: the incomplete, whatever its origin, is the reverse side of the act of making; the one suggests the other. The poem that is not finished but implies a new way of being has a particular power over our capacity to change.

> Word is thread and thread is language.
> Non-linear body.
> A line associated to other lines.
> The word is silence and sound.
> The thread, fullness and emptiness.[17]

Unsaying Multiplicity and Silence: Creative Etymology

Susan Sontag has described how, when separated by long silences, words weigh more; they become almost palpable. Or how, when one listens to the silence between words, one begins feeling more fully one's bodily presence in a given space.[18] For Vicuña, who has never accepted the separations of "culture," "politics," and "spirituality" into reified categories of modern and contemporary thinking, the heaviness of silence itself becomes a medium of artmaking, where the incompleteness of our speech in addressing atrocity and new forms of intimacy alike points to its own unraveling.

Her work speaks with a strong political emphasis, where the politics of language and memory are always at stake and particularly challenging of the vast silences around the massacre of the native populations of the Americas and our catastrophic ecological practices.[19] Vicuña's work is crucially committed to a formal strategy of creative etymology, of taking apart words to undo their power and the ways in which they are implicated in complex systems of power relations. She is concerned with the multiplicity and materiality of the roots of words, with hybrid languages and states of betweenness, with undoing the ordinary order of experience.

the eye
is the I?
cual
entre medio
es nues tro
lu gar?
a pond
res ponds
libar
the way
you
re spond
corazon
del aqui
why are
we here?
luz del
portal
mei
del migrar
changed
heart

"There will only be equality," she writes, "when there is reciprocity. The root of the word *respond* is to offer again, to receive something and to offer it back."[20] Beginning with "the *quipu* that remembers nothing," lack of memory becomes the engine of desire, absolutely unknowable and yet absolutely intimate with all that is emergent in response. "The contrast between the lack of memory and the heart of it," writes Juliet Lynd, "suggests that memory is in fact constructed on what cannot be articulated, on what is forgotten, on what once existed but cannot be faithfully remembered because it no longer exists except as memory."[21]

Likewise, in Dionysius the Areopagite, and later in Meister Eckhart, negating language becomes a way to elicit an encounter with God, for the soul must be free from egoic constructions in order for the light to be revealed in it. Our relation to "the sacred," for all three writers, is therefore often depicted as a call and response, a *response*-ability to the practice of language as a means of undoing the conventions of thought in which we describe our experience. The desire for reciprocity, for response, can be expressed then more accurately as a negative response, a No, another reality:

> The No
> The first precarious works were not documented, they existed only for the memories of a few citizens.
> History, as a fabric of inclusion and exclusion, did not embrace them.
> (The history of the north excludes that of the south, and the history of the south excludes itself, embracing only the north's reflections.)
> In the void between the two, the precarious and its non-documentation established their non-place as another reality.[22]

For Vicuña, the body is not only the basis of intelligibility; it is revealed and remembered as living presence in every act of language, as a means of re-inscribing human history. In a recent interview documented on YouTube, she describes the Indo-European root *–AR*, as a form of weaving that is also an undoing of false consciousness:

> All words exist from the waving ARM. The knowledge in the arm is deeper than the rational brain. In the ritual, something comes up (through your body) that is not commanded or controlled by you; if it were, people would know that it is fake. (How is it that you sing and a bird comes to sing with you?). Once you cease to be human in the sense of controlling, a deeper ART (AR-), a true ORDER comes, from WARP, (as in weaving). So our sense of order as commanding and dictatorial is not the origin of the word, it is WARP, a form of awareness and consciousness. So for the indigenous people, wisdom and ritual are not different; knowledge IS ritual, and you can only experience this if you allow yourself to go there.[23]

Vicuña has developed her practice of ritual poetics as a way of living backwards, a kind of physical mysticism in which "I look at things backwards, as they are going to look when I am gone. I have a very intense feeling that what we do is already the remains of what we are doing. The dead water, our poems. I try to bring an awareness of what we are leaving, so that by picking up things I am conscious of what has been thrown away, but is staying."[24]

The precarious works, which are made from debris that has been thrown away, bear an unlikeness to conventional Judeo-Christian ideas of sacredness, yet this very unlikeness presses further on questions that arise from the interaction of poetic language with a spiritual imagination.

Her work develops the practice of apophasis in public spaces, out in the open, with explicit political and social overtones which create a sense of urgency not dissimilar to Meister Eckhart's practice of radical public discourse. In his vernacular sermons, Eckhart takes negative theology outside the languages and elite institutions in which it was practiced, and makes it available for public use and discussion. By this public unsaying of the adequacy of the language to describe our experiences of the present, Eckhart offers a version of negative theology which is also immediately practical, concerned with the present, and towards making social change possible by undoing the ordinary language of experience. It maps out the disclosure of a participatory model for everyone, a map for progress democratic and spiritual, yet unlike Vicuña he does not go so far as to weave an apophatic *reality* of words and of things. The apophatic imagination in both Eckhart and Vicuña, however, deeply undermines the post-Enlightenment idea of the subject and emphasizes engagement with the sacred through an unlikeness expressed in cherishing the refused object, the negative value, the discarded person. While Eckhart tried to remove the private connotations of the mystic and presented himself as a translator, interpreter, and popularizer, Vicuña's concerns take this further, into translation, the politics of language, and the betweenness of languages and of peoples. Speaking of her book-length poem *Instan*, she writes:

> Instan, el libro de la palabra estrella, is the journey inside the word instan.
>
> It began as a night vision that landed on the page as a wave.
>
> Intrigued, I went to the dictionary. Instan is the third person plural of the infinitive "instar," meaning "to urge, press, reply." It first appears in Spanish in 1490, and is associated with political demands. In English it means "to stud with stars."
>
> For me it suggests a movement inward, towards the sta, the inner star "standing" in the verb "to be": estar.
>
> In English, it presses the instant. Yet the word did not wish to be just a door; it wanted to be a bridge between the two.

The poem was born as a cognate, un cognado potens in search of a middle ground, a language that would be readable or unreadable from both.

Acting as a riddle, each word gave birth to the next, opening up to reveal ancient or future meanings.[25]

Here Vicuña complicates the practice of unsaying, by showing us how what transpires in the spaces between people is not located in external reality nor in the inner subjective psychic world but emerges out of experiences in the potential space we inhabit together and which define for the moment the apparent reality of the world: from accounts of these experiences we see how easily fooled we are in thinking our concepts cover experience; often we find we are mistaken and that "reality exceeds our logic, overflows and surrounds it."[26]

A Perpetually Reinvented Language: Poetics, Politics and Community

Vicuña lives in and writes out of spaces of fragmentation and multiplicity, working within the space of what Joan Retallack refers to as the "poethical wager," "a dynamic present-tense poetics of human rights that might swerve minds out of intractable gridlocks."[27] Her model of a "perpetually reinvented language, constantly shifting to accommodate new concepts and information" shows a spiritual acsesis made visible, with the socio-political implication that the language could be made differently or made again, by anyone, like the spider whose web can only be seen because of the sunlight's reflection on its thread.[28]

A word is divine: internally divided.

Its inner division creates its ambiguity, the inner tension that makes growth and association possible.

She suggests that each one of her works acts as a hologram, where the smallest part contains the whole, each broken piece implying the larger order it recalls: "Debris, a past to come: what we say about ourselves."[29] Her language is invented from the possibilities of language itself, suggesting dimensions of Vicuña's imagination which open up within and beyond the text into actual human life. Various kinds of implications for apophatic human interaction emerge from this work, as all of her arts practices communicate variations of a unique and multivalent shape. Jorge Luis Borges's comment about the Argentinian artist Xul Solar could as easily apply to Vicuña, when he says: "Xul took on the task of reforming the universe, of proposing on this earth a different order."[30]

Vicuña's work is often concerned with this same edge, with the range of experience outside/inside of language, moments when we come up against the limits of language and enter a domain literally and figuratively beyond our grasp, where nouns give way to verbs in transition and continuity over time gives way to contiguity in space, moment to moment, where the "potential space can be looked upon as sacred to the individual in that it is here that the individual experiences creative living."[31]

Silence
        turns the page
            the poem begins.
                alba del habla, the dawn of speech.

alquimia   del   nombre   alchemy   of   names

                el   instan[32]

As she moves towards future possibilities, Vicuña is continually interested in "naming" as a system of kinship. To write, as Leslie Scalapino describes, as "continually undercutting the writing's own basis, unsustained by the continual constructing in it of its structure or sound even. [...] To risk even inertia 'to see what's there.' "[33] Writing has (at least) a doubled aspect for Vicuña, because "what's there" is neither speech nor written artifact, but rather a living being, changeable in form and therefore capable of reconstituting itself in time and place. Words, she says, want to speak. "The word," she writes, "creates the being or is created by it / in a mystery of which we only have the keys / to make it grow."[34]

Once we begin to uncover their etymologies, we find not only that our words are implicated in a violent system of power relations, but that in complex ways the languages and cosmologies of many peoples are deeply intertwined. Revealing these inner associations and re-connecting their etymological threads, suggests for Vicuña the fundamental cohesion between the name and that which is named. "Esperan silentes / y cantarinas / ... / agotadas por un instante / y vueltas a despertar"

(They wait, quiet / and singing / . . . / exhausted for a moment / then awakened again).[35] Metaphor, here, is not merely a figure of speech but rather an expression of kinship, the active unity between word and thing. Claude Levi-Strauss points out that "like phonemes, kinship terms are elements of meaning; like phonemes, they acquire meaning only if they are integrated into systems. 'Kinship systems,' like 'phonemic systems,' are built by the mind on the level of unconscious thought."[36] For Vicuña, re-membering or re-imagining phonemes becomes a way of engaging the mind to imagine new forms of human relation. She describes the poem *Instan*, for example, as born a cognate, *"un cognado potens* in search of a middle ground, a language that would be readable or unreadable from both. Acting as a riddle, each word (gives) birth to the next, opening up to reveal ancient or future meanings."[37] Her work suggests a number of innovative formal strategies by which this might happen, including several new forms of apophasis, such as the following:

1) narrating, re-narration, undoing "education" and guiding the reader away from certain conventional ways of describing experience, so that the work is not just about names or words, but requires a complete reworking of one's own normal language used to describe ordinary experience. (See *Quipoem*, "A Diary of Objects for the Resistance")

2) ecstasies of language, rhetorical possession, being seized by another power which flows through, as in her description of the Indo-European root of "arm." A kind of apophasis, where a new relation to speech happens. Here the names quiver in place because they reveal that they are concealments.

3) "precarious" images/words that serve as goads, like the debris that through dissimilarity or negation connects the reader to the *"précis,* prayer." (See, for example "Street Weavings," from the *Precarios* series.) And yet this language is not only negation, because it subverts itself ceaselessly, so that negation is only one of the ways it can be expressed.

4) structural apophasis, in which form mirrors the content of a text, whether that text functions as the performance of a conflict or a series of silences; apophasis here becomes a way to think with and through a text, holding multiplicities in the mind at once. (See the choreographic traces of *Instan* on the page.)

5) syntactic apophasis, or how language subverts itself at the micro-level within a word, a phrase, through double negations, etc., and the constant jarring between stretching and staying in the same place to keep the weave taut between languages, meanings, ways of knowing, etc. (*Instan*)

Conclusuin/No Conclusar

Of crucial concern here has been to sketch out the way Vicuña's work as a poet and an artist has laid bare a number of connections between mystical language and bodily inscriptions, on the one hand, and spiritual ascesis, on the other. For her, textual innovation is as attached to a new aesthetic language as to a way of becoming more human with and for each other. In mutual relation a different way of speaking and theorizing relational being is possible, involving an uncertainty, a precarious mode that offers evolving interpretations. It is as though Vicuña had fast-forwarded beyond the contemporary obsessions—with the status of the object, the relation of the poet to the reader, embodiment, the space/time relation, the environment, inner and outer, and the connection of the visual to the written. At once she moves readers away from their habit of compartmentalizing artistic production into separate media, to a more liberated and evolved era. She inhabits (im)possibility as a spiritual practice. Her ideal is coexistence in one space, in which the process of weaving through disappearance is taken up again to fuse with the flow of instants without separation between word and thing. With this approach, her practice recovers and recapitulates a religiosity which blurs the conventional borderlines between cultural traditions, the "real" and the "imaginary," between "art" and "life"—as the object is witness to and vital participant in the capacious and alive act of weaving itself.

Notes

1. Bataille, *Unfinished System of Nonknowledge*, 123. Bataille on "the sacred": "The word 'sacer' means both sacred and accursed. A sacred act must involve violence and rupture, breaking the boundary . . . for each being you have to find the place of sacrifice, the wound. A being can only be touched where it yields."
2. Vicuña, *The Precarious / QUIPOem*, 8.
3. Merleau-Ponty, *Phenomenology of Perception*, 244.
4. Vicuña, *The Precarious / QUIPOem*, 56.
5. Skinner, "Rajado: Word and Knot," 42.

6. Skinner, "Rajado: Word and Knot," 42.

7. Skinner, "Rajado: Word and Knot," 53.

8. Vicuña, *The Precarious / QUIPOem*, 79.

9. Vicuña, *The Precarious / QUIPOem*, 80.

10. Vicuña, *The Precarious / QUIPOem*. This phrase, as editor M. Catherine de Zegher reminds us in "Ouvrage: Knot a Not, Notes as Knots," "is the name given by the people of the southern cone (Chile, Uruguay, and Argentina) to men and women who were led away by the secret police from their homes or in the streets during the dictatorships of the seventies, because they were never seen again, and the military police denied having taken them in the first place. Only after years of struggle, human rights organizations were able to demonstrate that the people who had been 'disappeared' by the thousands not only did exist, but had been effectively tortured to death and/or murdered by the military regimes of the three countries."

11. Vicuña, *The Precarious / QUIPOem*, 87.

12. Vicuña, *The Precarious / QUIPOem*, 65

13. Vicuña, *The Precarious / QUIPOem*, 32

14. Vicuña, *The Precarious / QUIPOem*, 99.

15. Vicuña, "Word and Thread."

16. Vicuña, "Introduction."

17. Vicuña, *The Precarious / QUIPOem*, 77

18. Sontag, "The Aesthetics of Silence," 45.

19. More detailed information about Vicuña's crucial activist work is available on her website, www.ceciliavicuna.com, and in the introduction to her edited volume *Anthology of 500 Years of Latin American Poetry* (Oxford University Press), as well as in *The Precarious / QUIPOem* (Wesleyan/Kanaal Art Foundation).

20. Vicuña, *The Precarious / QUIPOem*, 79.

21. Lynd, "Precarious Resistance."

22. Vicuña, *Precarious/ QUIPoem*, 56.

23. Vicuña, *Precarious/ QUIPoem*. Editor M. Catherine de Zegher writes in "Ouvrage: Knot a Not, Notes as Knots": "Cecilia quotes that 'art' and 'order' derive both from the same root, *ar* (to fit together). The word *armus* (upper arm) comes from what the arms did. In this sense the Latin *ars* (art) was 'skill,' and the Latin *ordo* (order) from *ordiri* (to begin to weave) was 'a row of threads in a loom.'"

24. Vicuña, *Precarious/ QUIPoem*, 56.

25. Vicuña, *Instan*, 43.

26. James, *Varieties of Religious Experience*, 88.

27. Retallack, *Poethical Wager*, 24.

28. Vicuña, *Precarious/ QUIPoem*, 56

29. Vicuña, *Precarious/ QUIPoem*, 66.

30. Borges, *Labyrinths*, 47.

31. Winnicott, *Playing and Reality*, 77.

32. Vicuña, *Instan*, 43.

33. Scalapino, *Public World*, 85.

34. Vicuña, *PALABRARmas*, 21.

35. Vicuña, *PALABRARmas*, 23.

36. Levi-Strauss, *Structural Anthropology*, 45.

37. Vicuña, *The Precarious / QUIPOem*, 56.

Bibliography

Bataille, Georges. *The Unfinished System of Nonknowledge.* Edited by Stuart Kendall. Translated by Michelle Kendall and Stuart Kendall. Minneapolis: University of Minnesota Press, 2001.

Borges, Jorge Luis. *Labyrinths.* 1962. Reprinted with preface by William Gibson and edited by Donald A. Yates and James E. Irby. New York: New Directions, 2007.

James, William. *Varieties of Religious Experience.* 1902. Reprinted by CreateSpace Independent Publishing Platform, 2009.

Levi-Strauss, Claude. *Structural Anthropology.* New York: Basic Books, 1963.

Lynd, Juliet. "Precarious Resistance: Weaving Opposition in the Poetry of Cecilia Vicuña." *PMLA* 120, no. 5 (2005): 1588–1607. doi:10.1632/003081205X73434.

Merleau-Ponty, Maurice. *Phenomenology of Perception.* London: Routledge, 1962.

Retallack, Joan. *The Poethical Wager.* Berkeley: University of California Press, 2004.

Scalapino, Leslie. *The Public World / Syntactically Impermanence.* Middleton: Wesleyan University Press, 1999.

Skinner, Jonathan. "Rajado: Word and Knot in Cecilia Vicuña's Kon Kon." *Rattapallax 21* (2012), http://www.rattapallax.com/issues/.

Sontag, Susan. "The Aesthetics of Silence." In *The Susan Sontag Reader.* New York: Vintage, 1983.

Vicuña, Cecilia. *Instan.* Berkeley: Kelsey Street Press, 2002.

Vicuña, Cecilia. "Introduction." https://cecilia-vicuna.squarespace.com/introduction/

Vicuña, Cecilia. *Kon Kon.* Chile: 2010. Film/documentary poem. SD video, 54 min.

Vicuña, Cecilia. *PALABRARmas,* Buenos Aires: RIL Editores, 2005.

Vicuña, Cecilia. *The Precarious / QUIPOem: The Art and Poetry of Cecilia Vicuña.* Edited by M. Catherine de Zegher. Translated by Esther Allen. Kortrijk, Belgium: Wesleyan/Kanaal Art Foundation, 1997.

Vicuña, Cecilia. "Word and Thread." http://www.ceciliavicuna.com/poetry/.

Winnicott, D.W. *Playing and Reality.* 1971. Reprinted with preface by F. Robert Rodman. United Kingdom: Routledge Classics, 2005.

part iii.

continually dispersed along the web of the inter-relation

A Rangy Sense of Self

An Interview with Joanne Kyger

Andrew Schelling

The following interview took place in August and September, 2011, by email. Joanne Kyger was in Bolinas, California, and Andrew Schelling in Boulder, Colorado. The reference to Peter Berg (1937–2011) in the interview was occasioned by a series of memorials. One of the foundational activists and writers on bioregionalism & watershed awareness, Berg founded the Planet Drum Foundation. He died on July 28. The exchange late in the interview on Pai-chang and the fox is a reference to Case 2 in the Zen koan collection *Mumonkan*; various translations are available.[1]

—A.S.

Andrew Schelling: In your poetry you allow entry to animals—or I could say, "the animal realm"—more than any other poet I know. Animals and birds are familiars, though they are generally not domestic animals, and you do not use them as symbols or emblems. Deer, skunk, jay, hummingbird, and dozens of others including mice in the house and offshore mammals show up, and you often address them as people. One of your books, *Up My Coast*, is a poetic and projectivist recounting of tales collected by the unusual ethnographer and doctor, C. Hart Merriam. Those tales depict a time before the present world got established, when people were animals or animals people.

First, there were the First People
And the First People changed
into trees, plants, rocks, stars, hail and
Animals
and then Animals made Our People.

Joanne Kyger: *Up My Coast* was an attempt to write the history of part of this coast—"pre-invasion." I am fascinated by the First People, a way of speaking of ancient history. An animistic path. Where finally Animals create the people we are familiar with.

C. Hart Merriam's book, *The Dawn of the World: Myths and Weird Tales Told by the Mewan Indians of California,* published in 1910, was my source for *Up My Coast*—my adaptation of Coast Miwok people's creation stories. Coast Miwok territory included all of Marin County, where I live, up to Bodega Bay in Sonoma County where I lived before I moved here. I felt I needed to find a history of this area pre-"conquest." The stories, parts that remain from larger cycles of oral-tradition stories told only in the winter time rainy season, are the remaining history that I could find of the local people, who lived here before there was any such thing as "California." I always appreciated the fact that the Coast Miwok tribes have Coyote Man, the creator, coming to this shore by crossing the Pacific on a raft. The Bering Strait theory proposed by anthropologists who were unacquainted with celestial navigation always seemed very pat—that all "aboriginal" peoples crossed the land bridge and walked all the way down to Oaxaca, for example.

AS: How far back does this sensibility reach for you? Did the natural world engage you as child? Were animal stories part of your consciousness growing up? I wonder if either of your parents told you animal story-cycles. You might also say a word about why your selection of tales, which you made into poems, was distinctively Californian.

JK: I read the usual books as a child—for example the Dr. Doolittle books, where animals were able to talk, the Oz books where animals and humans conversed and had adventures together. I grew up with the Brownies and Girl Scouts who always engaged in outdoor activities, camps etc. Bird and tree identification were always of interest. From the ages of six to ten, I lived along the shores of Lake Michigan and found real magic and excitement in seasonal changes, the arrival of spring wild flowers—ordinary things but so different from the California life I knew.

Then, of course the Greek Myths in their simple Edith Hamilton retelling introduced the wonderful notion that birds could be harbingers of events to come. And that the "gods" were many and often able to turn into an animal of choice.

AS: Some of your poet friends—surely Lew Welch, and to some extent Gary Snyder—appear to be in search of (or have found) medicine animals. Welch's poem "Song of Tamalpais," with its wheeling turkey vultures is a good example. You could use that poem as an example of the search for spirit animals that Jaime de Angulo has written of so often—in Pit River or Achumawi the term would be *damaagome*: medicine animal or spirit power. This might be treading too close to something deeply personal, but do you have a spirit helper?

JK: I participated in several peyote ceremonies and in February of 1959, while taking it with some friends, I had a quite unpleasant experience of massed black energy intercut with animal faces. The fact that I was unwisely taking this trip in my apartment, which was over a bar in North Beach, and was not feeling well, added to a very unstable sense of "reality." This "black energy" resembled an animal, which I later named, hoping to focus it. A wild animal, which I paid attention to whenever I saw it, or saw mention of it. For years I was afraid of stepping over some edge into a loss of self, or schizophrenic duality. Living in Japan and seeing the guardian warriors outside the temple doors with their fierce animal-like expressions, I finally realized they were protectors. Fear creates a wall one can be afraid to pass by. If they scared you off, you didn't have enough courage or knowledge to enter further. I think I was fearful of the energy of the animal self, whatever I thought that was.

In 1967 I met Carlos Castenada and Michael Harner at Don Allen's one evening. I remember telling Castenada of this experience—seeing the demonic as a protector guardian energy—and him nodding his head wisely. Later I read his first book on the experiences with Don Juan with amazement and some degree of familiarity.

I was raised with phrases like, "don't act like an animal," and "you have manners like an animal"—one should rid themselves of "animal" nature—which was a debased sensibility towards the nonhuman world. Understanding that one does not have to "suppress" one's animal nature, in order to be civilized, is something I gained while living a less urban life, one in which there was no "cut-off" between human and non-human life. We shared the same air and small territory together.

AS: When I read your poetry, the first entry I find is to a deeply animistic world. There are also numerous references to figures from the Buddhist pantheon, a wry approach to impermanence, and sometimes a Buddhist "teaching" conveyed disarmingly, in colloquial speech.

Good Manners

The Bodhisattva waits
until everyone is finished
before he excuses himself

Under the surface-level aspects of the poem, I find a signal approach to the world—*ahimsa* or non-harming—to do as little hurt or violence as possible to any creature. In your poems the doors and windows of your house often let in small critters. One image I keep replaying is either you or Donald freeing some animal caught in the human house. Can you draw a line from the animist sensibility to the Buddhist?

JK: I'm not a big fan of letting critters live in the same room with me. And at this point I don't really care for "pets"—which has become for many the link between the human and the animal world—and in which wildness and freedom have been "domesticated" away. One is "using" an animal companion in a relationship of dependence and, often, emotional superiority.

Buddhist sensibility, as far as I understand it, has us all interconnected in a nonhierarchical lineage. It's okay to be born a worm. That's why one is respectful to the worm as it turns through the compost.

AS: Do you study up much on the nonhuman orders? Use field guides? Learn about your own watershed, or the drainage systems and eco-zones of other people?

JK: I was just reviewing again Peter Berg's term "bioregionalism"—in which one informs oneself of all the aspects—historical, cultural, natural—of one's "home." And of course, field guides are enormously handy and informative. So is just looking. That's why I so appreciate the reality of the "First People" who themselves turned into the sacred spots of the geography we experience today. In Japan, Shinto Shrines often encompass these spots. Two large old trees, tied together with a magical rope, indicate their history together, their marriage.

AS: Did you know Peter Berg personally? I'd also like to stretch the question a bit, and see if you could address the significance of bioregional thought—or practice—for your poetry.

JK: I met Peter Berg in the late '60s when he was part of the Digger organization in San Francisco's Haight-Ashbury. But I especially remember him as being part of the Reinhabitory Theater in their recreation of Northern California coyote stories. The theater did a cycle of stories in a canyon near Bolinas in May of 1977, and he was a memorable Lizard Man, who in his winning argument with Coyote over how "man" should be made, gave us five fingers "just like his own" instead of paws. This was, of course, a great gift to mankind.

Along with Raymond Dasmann, Peter also produced a great and useful word—"bioregion." A way to designate natural, watershed boundaries as opposed to sharp political lines. One became aware of the authenticity of the local with its attendant history and natural multiplicities. I became a detective of place, out of respect and an obligation to observe and inform myself of everything I could of the land west of the coast range.

AS: I suppose if we want to regard bioregion not just as a collection of helpful thoughts, but as a practice, then the key term would be Berg's notion of reinhabitation. Is that what you mean when you say you've become a detective of place? That this is a key practice for you? My own sense is that, for those of us who want to live according to the tenets of bioregional thought, the watershed world or our local ecology is coextensive with the spirit realm. Would you say this is close to your own perception?

And could you speak a bit to the region you investigate, "west of the coast range"? It is one of the richer areas in terms of biodiversity, and from pre-contact times until today has had about the greatest diversity of human languages and cultures in North America.

JK: If one thinks about the origins of the word "spirit" coming from "spiritus"—breath or "spirare"—to breath—then one understands that in a "bioregion" we all share the same air. So yes, there is a "coexistence" with the spirit realm. We share the same arena of breathing existence. And being attentive to that interconnected net is when one becomes a "detective" of place with all its history and animistic locations.

AS: I know you have made a long-standing practice of using notebooks or journals. Most of your poems of the past several decades are dated, which suggests a specific relationship to place and time. In a way this is exactly what naturalists do—birdwatchers, and mountaineers, and botanists. So the interest in the bioregion would link those other disciplined observers of the natural orders with the poet. Do you still write regularly in journals? Is it a daily practice or routine?

JK: I keep a daily notebook. Writing notations, short observations, names, etc.

Things I want to remember. Often I think of the page as a "document." The date, time, and place, putting it into an historic occasion—the first letter on a blank page, the note of the moment, unencumbered by a karmic dialogue—is a very pure act.

AS: Do you have a sense of journal writing being close to Buddhist practice? Many poets I can think of who draw on their journals for poetry have explicit ties to Buddhist discipline. Of your generation, Phil Whalen, Gary Snyder, yourself, Allen Ginsberg, have all published journals that are central to your output as writers. I also see younger writers, such as Shin Yu Pai, have extended the sense of the journal to a disciplined blog site.

JK: I think of notebook writing like a practice—I try and do it whether I have anything good or bad or interesting to say. And the chronology becomes the narrative, a history of a writing "self."

It is such an open form, anything can be included. It's very free.

AS: The one volume of journals you've published is *The Japan & India Journals*, which was retitled *Strange Big Moon* when North Atlantic Publishers reissued the book. Most of it was written while you lived in Japan. Were you aware at the time of the long rich tradition of *nikki* or journal writing as a genre there? Not only poets and literary women of the Heian Court—Lady Murasaki, Sei Shonagon, and some who are still "anonymous"—but Buddhist nuns, and then later poets like Matsuo Basho—pushed the journal to a high level of literary accomplishment. How much did their example spur you on? Or was it more a question of poet friends?

JK: I didn't become acquainted with Sei Shonagon and some of the "pillow book" writers of Japan's court until much after I had left Japan. I had kept journals, diaries, etc., since I was very young.

It was a matter of deciding what exactly it was that I wanted to write down during my stay in Japan. I was aware that both Whalen and Snyder kept daily journals. And Ginsberg of course. They gave it a sort of "literary permission." Like it was an authentic form in itself.

AS: Do you have journals other than *The Japan & India Journals* of the early sixties that you would consider editing and publishing?

JK: In 2007, *Lo and Behold: Household and Threshold on California's North Coast 1980–1992* was published. It contains a culling from notebook entries for those years, which make a kind of portrait of place, of a heightened sense of community. I found that to be a useful way to make a little history—taking incidents, phrases, "awakenings," and keeping them in their "notational" and chronological form. And yes, I do think about doing more of that. I have all my notebooks in their somewhat disheveled and traveled forms, and whenever I open them there is usually a flash of memory and recognition. I only wish I had written more down, but really that can become a dogged act.

AS: Let me ask about those "disheveled and traveled forms"—which anyone who keeps notebooks through the years can relate to. Is there anything particular you do for these notebooks, either when preparing to use them, or for organizing them later? For instance I learnt from Thoreau—who's sort of a patron saint of the North American notebook tradition—the almost obvious idea to create an index for each notebook. And to keep them in chronological order on a bookshelf. Even to maintain an ongoing list of vocabulary, or plant and bird encounters. How do you organize or work with your notebooks to help with memory and recognition?

JK: What a splendid idea to index each notebook. A simple chronological order is all I have achieved so far, with notebooks tucked into ziplock bags with attendant ephemeral postcards, clippings, and notes. They provide a kind of rangy history of self, and encounters with, at least, the weather.

Bird sightings have their own book, where the dates of returning flocks are noted—for example two years ago the large mixed species flock of sparrows which used to show up like magic on April 23 and leave on September 21 have stopped arriving, after almost forty years of hosting them locally near my house. At least there is a record. And the yearly nesting of the quail flock, which lives here, is noted, along with the offspring that have survived cats and hawks.

AS: Any idea how many notebooks you have? And is there any particular type of notebook you like to work with?

JK: I have over 200 notebooks. I like to use a spiral binding, as I can lay the book flat to write on. Art stores usually carry the 5.5" x 8.5" sketch books with a medium weight paper that takes ink well, and I use those. I also keep little spiral bound books that can be carried in the pocket for short observations, and the ever-continuing list of things to do.

AS: John Whalen-Bridge, the scholar who specializes in Buddhist influence on North American writers, did an interview with you a couple of years ago. I could not quite get from it whether you have had any formal Buddhist training. In "Basho Says Plant Stones Utensils," you write—

> I'm still   waiting
>   for the 'Buddhist'
>   poem to arrive
>
>   Darn it takes so long
>   for the Dharma

Did you learn to sit meditation in Japan?

JK: I learned to sit on my own, from books of course. In 1959 I joined Shunryu Suzuki after he had arrived in San Francisco as abbot of Japan Town's Sokoji Temple on Bush Street. He started early morning sitting at the temple, a new innovation. I was living a few blocks away at the East West House, so it was not a heavy task to get there. Getting up early for six a.m. sitting was more difficult. Suzuki's English was almost nonexistent at the time, but it went well with Soto Zen's "just sitting" practice of meditation.

During the four years I lived in Japan (1960–1964) I sat at Ryosen-an, the First Zen Institute's Zendo in Kyoto, and then later at Daitoku-ji's main temple where, at one point, they made a place for a few foreigners to sit. I never had a formal teacher for *sanzen* (going to a Zen teacher for individual instruction) as there was a mutual language difficulty—my Japanese never became that skilled, and there were no teachers that were speaking English.

There were almost no books in English on Zen, or translations of sutras. The feeling was, one just sat and "discovered" on one's own their "Buddha nature."

AS: With so many appearances of non-human animals in your poetry, I'd think some of the Zen folklore would excite you. A number of famous koans, like Pai-chang and the fox, have central figures that are non-human. What Buddhist literature has drawn you the most? Zen collections? Tibetan biographies? *Jataka Tales* (former lives of the Buddha, often in animal form)?

JK: Don't you think that Buddhist literature in English is a fairly new phenomenon? I met up with the *Jataka Tales*, in English in the early '60s in India, and was delighted by many aspects of non-human Buddha-hood. Even before the birth of the Buddha.

All of Evans-Wentz's translations seemed important in the '60s to me—especially the life of Milarepa. Lama Govinda's books were full of Tibetan Buddhism but also magic and adventures in the Himalayas. And someone as simple and dogged as Alexandra David-Neel was very attractive to read. All those early Buddhist travelers who actually had to endure hard and difficult conditions in order to find their sources in Tibet were amazing.

Monkey as translated by Arthur Waley is a delightful folk mixture of monkey, pig and monk on the road to the west to find a sacred Buddhist text—the *Tripitika*.²

I can't think of koans as literature in the usual sense—but the wild fox in Japan is a mysterious and often dangerous other worldly creature, and not above cause and effect by any means. Better watch out for fox women in Japan! They aren't of this world.

AS: Do the fox women remind us that cause and effect still operate in poetry?

JK: I don't think poetry is free from cause and effect; in fact it rattles around with it. And Fox Spirit Woman, being both animal and human, with the ability to create illusion-like realities, is not free from causa-tion even though she is "supernatural." She can bear children with a human form, is a devoted wife, and probably operates in an inspiring manner within the realm of poetry.

AS: One of the poetic gifts Japan has provided the world is haiku. I saw one critic call it Japan's greatest "post-war export." It has become an international form, with all sorts of little innovations attached—and if you go into a bookstore you are likely to find lots of anthologies and

how-to books for writing it. It was your generation that really brought
North America's attention to haiku, with that sensitivity to the seasons,
to the little moments of nature and human nature, and gave us a way
of writing poetry that I find refreshingly free. Free, that is, from pro-
phetic, oracular, metaphysical or epic noise. Small as it is, haiku is still
profoundly spiritual in intent, and gets closely identified with Zen
insight. You've got an American-style haiku that is postmodern in its
self-reflection—

> I have to go water
> the lettuce
> then I have to go listen to Zen tonight

Do you feel that a Zen sensibility, or a blinking open of spiritual insight
through language, is one of the goals or attitudes of your own poetry?

JK: As for haiku, and writing in general, yes one hopes to give flashes
of spirit and insight which could be called "Zen," but could survive
without that label. But I don't know if it's a "goal" as such—that would
be a bit self conscious. It's the ordinary, after all, that mostly provides
"spiritual insight." Traditional haiku's formality is not really useful to
my writing. I always loved how Jack Collom described haiku—"They
are short poems, but they must be very, very short."

Some of the grand masters of the haiku/senryu[3] tradition right now,
like John Brandi and Steve Sanfield are really razor sharp. Besides
writing their own books, they exchange lines in a haiku correspondence
which bring one, often, to that "aha!" place. Which is why I love to read
them. Some of the "prettier" and more self-conscious attempts at haiku
translated into three-line English poems make one think, why bother
with all those rules. Just be as concise and aware as possible.

AS: I know you and Donald are about to leave for Oaxaca. You spend
a lot of time in Mexico, with many poems in recent years originating
there. Dated December, 2004, you have this:

> Here in Oaxaca it's the Night of the Radishes
> Now I wave from the green
> balcony above the gardenia

in my shoes without socks the sun
is frankly generous
today when everyone needs
room at the inn   Time to put
the Buddha back in place
He doesn't mind being 'catholic'
in Mexico

What does life south of the border provide for your poetry? Animism? Vegetable nights like in the above poem? Catholicism? Or just ordinary experience that is harder and harder to find in the States?

JK: Life in Mexico provides lots and lots of "spirit" and "soul." It's fascinating to observe very old civilizations in their archeological sites, and realize that the many "indigenous" tribes of people there today are part of that history—here on this North American continent. The Catholicism practiced in Mexico today is often a cover story for the old religious practices and festivals. And yes, the everyday on a much simpler and direct level is absorbing to participate in—like the daily market.

Notes

1. See Robert Aitken, *The Gateless Barrier: The Wu-Men Kwan (Mumonkan)* (North Point Press, 1991).

2. W.Y. Evans-Wentz was a friend of W. B. Yeats. His early work was on Celtic fairy lore. He eventually discovered Tibetan Buddhism and published influential early volumes of translation, including famously *The Tibetan Book of the Dead* and *Tibet's Great Yogi Milarepa*. Lama Govinda and Alexandra David-Neel's accounts of Tibetan travel were widely available at one time—some of the only books on Buddhism readily found in North America during the 1960s. In Arthur Wayley's translation, *Monkey*, the folklore characters travel from China to India in search of the *Tripitika*, or three "baskets": the three divisions of the Buddhist canonical texts.

3. Senryu: Written in the same form as haiku (i.e., seventeen syllables) in Japan. It focuses on the "human realm" however, so it typically lacks the seasonal words that are a hallmark of traditional haiku. Senryu employs a level of street humor and irony also absent in haiku. Much so-called North American haiku is, from the traditional standpoint, actually senryu.

The Exact Temperature of a Hand
Melissa Kwasny and the Mystical Imagination
Rusty Morrison

Henry Corbin, whose writings have illuminated the Sufi tradition for the western mind, states that the symbolic image "announces a plane of consciousness distinct from rational evidence; it is the 'cipher' of a mystery."[1] A number of women writing poems today are able to manifest that "cipher," that zero, that code which allows us to access mystery, without attempting to de-cipher it, or bring it back to materialistic logic. Melissa Kwasny's poetry is an excellent example of how a writer can use image to extend her awareness—to move outward, using image as cipher, beyond the parameters of the known.

Corbin claims that when we access the imaginal, we can experience an "articulation between the intellect and sense,"[2] a mediation between the abstract and the world of appearances, between the mystical and the material. Tom Cheetham—another scholar of the imaginal—expresses this as the domain "between the purely physical and the purely spiritual."[3] Cheetham asserts that "the function of *poesis*, whether musical, poetic, religious, or scientific, is the creation and revelation of spaces: qualitative, complex and complexified, personified spaces."[4] And he discusses "*poesis*" as encouraging "the passionate imagination of connections between ourselves and those 'real presences' that lie beyond the merely human world."[5]

In her book *The Nine Senses*, Melissa Kwasny is particularly adept at exercising a reader's ability to use the senses to seek more than what is most commonly available to us. In accord with Cheetham's speculation, Kwasny uses image to open, within the poem, a fertile space between the knowable material of our existence and what is unknown and perhaps unknowable. One might call it an intuition of spirit or a sense of presence beyond our understanding, which arrives, however fleetingly or illogically, through access to the imaginal as perceived with the senses. *How many* senses remains an open question.

Most significantly, it is in responding to the natural world—where animal, vegetable, and or mineral existence still enliven this planet—that Kwasny finds this interface most viable, most essential, and most fraught. And it is to the natural world that she returns again and again.

In the poem "Clairvoyance (Your Word)," she writes:

> The ocean, with its huge shoulders, moves its furniture across the floor. Our mouths are not wide enough to make that sound. We unfold our small words, one by one, against the rock walls. Only pool echoes.[6]

Even as Kwasny keeps her descriptions closely attuned to actual experience, her images put pressure on the personal and cultural beliefs that normally guide and limit our understanding. For example, in the poem "Red Moon," she considers one of our common euphemisms for the catastrophic impact of technologies on our planet's atmosphere: "global warming." She suggests

> We choose the word *warming*, in itself a safe word, so that we don't have to use the word *threat*. Which is incandescent this evening, yellow as a sulphur's wing. The flicker of a living creek through foliage.[7]

Kwasny juxtaposes how we can be numb to our denial *and* to the beauty surrounding us in our crisis-filled present, and thus shows us that there is always more available to us in our experiences. As Gilles Deleuze suggests, we can experience "a sum but not a whole. . . . Nature is not attributive but rather conjunctive: it expresses itself through 'and.'"[8] "Nature"—which the dictionary defines as *all* the phenomena of the physical world—offers us the essence of a radical continuity, an "andness," which is constantly offering us insights outside of the lockstep of our normative logic.[9]

In seeking to embrace this "andness," Kwasny nonetheless remains keenly aware of the fallibility of our subjective experience, how the limits of our culturally-inscribed perceptual interpretations lock us out of experiencing nature's otherness. As she tells us in her poem "Talk to the Milkweed Pod":

> The ditch is filled with milkweed, Wind is tugging hard. The rain is warm, a plant-warmth, an ideal. Can I join them? Can I open the trapdoor, a patch made of grass slats, with a rope—which is the wind— to hoist it? No time to be sacred.[10]

Here is Kwasny's poignant paradox: On the one hand, she holds in mind "an ideal," "the plant warmth," a sense of kinship to the natural world, and it is from such ideals that we create a sense of the "sacred." But she senses, too, that ideas from our past experience of "the ideal" and the "sacred" actually can come between us and what is happening in the moment. We lose the moment's otherness; we fall away from our actual experience, if we think too hard. Yet, on the other hand, we do need our mental constructs to call back previous experiences, in the hopes of building a kinship with that sense of otherness, of sacredness.

Of course, a mental construct can only be an approximation—a representation held in mind—which is, by the nature of mind, separate from, divided from actual experience. This division, created by our yearning to know and to be in union with the natural world, cannot be escaped. All the intellect can do is create a more skillful, more subtle, more sensately detailed awareness to mediate between ourselves and what remains *other* to us, separate from us.

Georges Bataille deftly points out how different we are, as thinking beings, from the non-human beings who live in an unmediated state, when he describes animal existence as being "in the world like water in water."[11]

The history of our differentiation as thinking beings from non-human beings is the history of the development of human consciousness. As Cheetham explains "you can analyze the Neolithic transition in terms of a kind of disjunction between humans and nature."[12]

Yet, as Cheetham and Kwasny would agree, it is this very differentiation—this very ability to continually form an internal image of what is outside our consciousness—that allows us to marvel at the natural world's mystery, and to manifest that sense of marvel, that sense of awe, in poems. And it is in using the image, sometimes in unexpected ways, to examine the differentiation between human and nature, self and other, which allows the poet to further extend the shifting boundary of what remains outside our comprehension. In the epigraph to *The Nine Senses*, Henry Corbin proposes that our ability to perceive the "Earth" as more than material, and "encounter" it in "the person of its Angel," is

> . . . much less a matter of answering questions concerning essences ("what is it?") than questions concerning persons ("who is it?" or "to whom does it correspond?") for example, who is the earth? who are the waters, the plants, the mountains? or, to whom do they correspond.[13]

Following this epigraph, Kwasny begins many poems—such as "Talk to the Golden Birches," "Talk to the Water Dipper," "Talk to the Milkweed Pod," "Talk to the Great Suffering"—by invoking what may seem at first a naïve, implausibly direct communication with essences in her external environment, be they human or nonhuman, concrete or abstract. By speaking directly, Kwasny animates a longing for intimacy with otherness that so many of us feel, but shy away from. By acting upon all such longings, despite their seeming implausibility, she causes possibilities to emerge. As she tells us in her poem "The Book of Spells,"

> I read, in the book of spells, there are four steps to dispersing fear: to name it, to place it, to breathe into that place. The next step is where to go from there. Mouth of water chewing the world to soft, spitting the hard pebbles of shale and slate and shadow.[14]

Though she calls these the steps to disperse fear, I will say that they are also the steps to examine and unsettle the limited names we use to understand the earth and our place upon it. She begins with language, and moves into the physical realm of location, and then uses breath to destabilize both: thus her perceptions are heightened. Perhaps this process lets the image of a "mouth of water" (a personalized, familiarized image of non-human otherness) act upon the world she sees, softening it, blurring the distinctions normally limiting her awareness. Here, we move from what we can humanly relate to (a "mouth" "chewing") to a world changed beyond our previous conceptions of it.

Kwasny takes us from the safe perceptions of a world that we hold by name, in language, and lets the image, which is her language of inquiry, "breathe into that place." Kwasny does not expect "The Golden Birches" or "The Great Suffering" to speak back to her in the language of logic. Rather, the "next step" is to continue asking "where to go from there." In Kwasny's poetry, the next image will allow us to hear a possibility offered directly from her own intuitive experience, implausible as it might first appear. Yet, that next sentence's improbability is a lesson in opening ourselves to the audacious, disquieting, reconstituting possibility of the imaginal in our own experience. Cheetham, using Corbin's terminology, calls this the "*mundus imaginalis* (the imaginal *world*), to underscore the fact that it is not imaginary, not unreal."[15]

Kwasny begins *The Nine Senses* with a poem that enacts this awareness of the imaginal as a shifting boundary, which is also a conduit, to what can be sensed outside our materialist logic. In it, she begins by offering an example of the kind of fixed ideas that we use to label and organize our world. Such ideas have their uses, but can too easily limit our intuition of what we might find if we heighten our attention to actual experience. The poem's title, "The Language of Flowers," alludes to a Persian system popular in the 1900s in Europe for assigning attributes to each type of flower. Of course, our human desire to create fixed referents with attributable meanings or allegoric labels is understandable. We name and use the name's concomitant associations to navigate the otherwise incomprehensible experiences of our lives. Kwasny respects our longing to qualify what we know, and who we know, even as she lets us see that these meanings we hold are as ephemeral as the budding and seeding and decline of the flowers themselves. Yet, in any moment, these meanings seem as resonantly real to us as a beloved. Kwasny speaks to the flowers of this poem as one might to a lover, with directness and desire:

> I wish you were here on my arm. I wish I could crawl beneath your sheets. My Poppy. My Tulip Tree. My Sweet Basil.[16]

Is this her lover, named as flower, or is she responding to the flower as a lover? Whichever way we read it, Kwasny calls attention to the customary and yet limiting method of naming what we love with a label from our past experience. The poem continues:

> You are what I used to dream of as a child, what my mother did, not so much a dress as its fabric, pink dotted swiss, a white voile shirt with French cuffs. Tell me your name, what you seek, and to what you aspire. I will mount a campaign for your world. Magnolia, cloudy and thick, each petal the exact temperature of a hand.[17]

Here, the flower is not perceived as a dress from her childhood, whole and complete, but as what she dreamed of that dress—its textural elements and design. These would be most alive to a child: the fabric, its colors and qualities, the aspects most closely observed by the senses, rather than their usefulness as a dress, a covering, societally correct. As intimate as this connection seems, we sense that it is devoid of the flower's actual presence, its otherness. And it is at this moment that the speaker, with all of her memories and preconceptions exposed, suddenly asks the flower, "Tell me your name." She senses that she does not know it; the word "poppy" isn't *its* name, but merely the accepted name that her language has given it. How childlike is the notion that the speaker can "mount a campaign" for the flower, for its needs and aspirations. I am reminded of all the well-intentioned attempts in books and films to bring more understanding of the natural world into our culture. We can hear in her tone, and in the word "campaign," that she is chiding herself, even as she is suggesting, desiring this course of action. Thus, the desire stands: To offer to the flower what we would want if we were in its place, what we think it would want. What else can we do in order to welcome a guest, to make a friend of a stranger? Yet there's more in this: the speaker wants to "campaign for your [the flower's] world": not simply welcome the otherness into her human world, but somehow make room in our human world for its world to enter. She asks questions of the flower, and it makes us laugh, yet we have to laugh with recognition. The speaker queries the flower with the only language she has. Which, we implicitly understand, is inde-cipherable to the flower. Or is it? The magnolia's petals are the "exact temperature of a hand." Are we tempted to believe a relation, a kind of understanding that passes between the flower and the hand? through touch? is that "exact[ness]" of temperature a shared language?

When a poetic image invokes such questions, the *mundus imaginalis* mediates between what one might call a physical and metaphysical accounting of our perceptions—if one wants to use such polarizing labels. But rather than focusing on the differences that such labels connote, in Kwasny's poems we attend to a surprising continuum within experience between what Cheetham calls "the purely physical and purely spiritual."[18] For Kwasny, as for other poets who engage the mystical imagination, the image is constantly reforming a meaning of vision, a measure of the field of perception. We are offered a clairvoyance that glimpses what Deleuze calls the "Harlequin's cloak" of nature, made of "solid patches and empty spaces," "plentitude and void, beings and nonbeings, with each one of the two posing as unlimited while limiting the other," an "addition of indivisibles."[19]

In the image, all sensations—call their arrival physical or metaphysical—are intensified, even those which common logic proscribes. Testing the proscriptions in our preconceived notions is, of course, one of the primary aims of much innovative writing. But in each poet's work, we ask ourselves, to what end? Kwasny seeks to enact what Cheetham proposes: in the imaginal space we "reclaim a sense of the substantial presence and concrete significance of human life,"[20] finding more in the materiality of our world than our logic had previously allowed. When our attention is attuned by the imaginal, then "the dichotomy between substance and spirit collapses." Thus we "avoid . . . the realist leveling of the cosmos proposed by literal science and literal religion."[21] Perhaps one of the most significant opportunities we gain from Kwasny's images is to learn to ask more probing, more courageous questions of our own perceptions—to increase the space of possibility that our intellect inhabits.

Cheetham goes on to clarify that "[a]ll our imaginings are necessary. But none of them should be grasped too tightly, none of them taken too literally."[22] For Cheetham, no methodology, no hierarchy of understanding, no scientific truth, no poem's revelation, should be held as sacrosanct, no matter how inspired it may seem at its inception. In Kwasny's work, we experience not only how a poet uses image to open intuitions outside her normal ken, but also how a poet demonstrates the freedom, the spaciousness, to question the turns of awareness that the images have suggested to her. I recall the writings of I. Rice Pereira, an American artist known for her work as an abstract expressionist. She tells us "life is the unknown essence concealed in the space which supports it."[23] Kwasny does not suggest that she can make that essence knowable; rather she offers a sense of space in which mystery comes sensually alive to us.

Notes

1. Corbin, *Creative Imagination in the Sufism of Ibn Arabi*, 12.
2. Corbin, *Spiritual Body and Celestial Earth*, xviii.
3. Cheetham, *Green Man, Earth Angel*, 100.
4. Cheetham. *Green Man, Earth Angel*, 26.
5. Cheetham, 26.
6. Kwasny, *The Nine Senses*, 56.
7. Kwasny. *The Nine Senses*, 57.
8. Deleuze, *The Logic of Sense*, 267.
9. Deleuze, *The Logic of Sense*, 267.
10. Kwasny, 89.
11. Bataille, *Theory of Religion*, 23.
12. Cheetham, 2.
13. Kwasny, 3.
14. Kwasny, 53.
15. Cheetham, 3.
16. Kwasny, 5.
17. Kwasny, 5.
18. Cheetham, 39.
19. Deleuze, 267.
20. Cheetham, 26.
21. Cheetham, 26.
22. Cheetham, 26–27.
23. Pereira, *The Nature of Space: A Metaphysical and Aesthetic Inquiry*, 3.

Bibliography

Bataille, Georges. *Theory of Religion*. Translated by Robert Hurley. New York: Zone Books, 1992.

Cheetham, Tom. *Green Man, Earth Angel: The Prophetic Tradition and the Battle for the Soul of the World*. Albany: State University of New York Press, 2005.

Corbin, Henry. *Creative Imagination in the Sufism of Ibn Arabi*. Translated by Ralph Manheim. Princeton: Princeton University Press, 1969.

Corbin, Henry. *Spiritual Body and Celestial Earth*. Translated by Nancy Pearson. Princeton: Princeton University Press, 1989.

Deleuze, Gilles. *The Logic of Sense*. Edited by Constantin V. Boundas. Translated by Mark Lester with Charles Stivale. New York: Columbia University Press, 1990.

Kwasny, Melissa. *The Nine Senses*. Minneapolis: Milkweed Editions, 2011.

Pereira, I. Rice. *The Nature of Space: A Metaphysical and Aesthetic Inquiry*. New York: Privately Published, 1956.

leap with nature)
poem by Colleen Lookingbill

leaves netted with broken margins
streams of watertight atmosphere

dialogue saying "let me decide
which fruit is carried on the wind"

as sunflower's turning stem
draws gentle dart restored sight
away like grains of sand

silvery contrast describes
inconspicuous names of day
a cause, a result, an old rampart

rain soaked orange blossoms
languidly undermine mnemonic trick

window pane against the dusk
blooming waters reach home

seasons keep us waiting long enough
while counting out our rhymes

Third Eye Who Sees

On the Source of Spiritual Search in Sappho's Gymnasium
by T Begley and Olga Broumas
Kazim Ali

No matter how much religion is organized, the very wild act of an individual human soul married to a physical body attempting to whisper its breath into the universal mouth of endlessness would be impossible to buckle down to one form, impossible to write into little books with approved versions. Instead such utterance must escape free like the screams of Antigone or Electra in the ancient Greek plays; between the human and divine there is a place where language breaks. Such a place too might be called god.

Olga Broumas and T Begley created *Sappho's Gymnasium* in a collaborative act. They describe their process in an essay jointly uttered:

> But who speaks? A voice of pluracination, heard partially, as always, gracing one of us with particulars, the other with the hallucinated breath of verbally unintelligible but musically incontrovertible dictions... the field it requires us to serve—eros: gracious, philoxenous, augmenting, lubricant, remorseless faith.[1]

Every space between two bodies, I once thought, was a place of danger. But if there is a danger, it is the danger or losing one's own self, risking transforming into the other. We want to hold ourselves close. But in between the bodies of the two women, or—according to Broumas (email conversation)—words originating in the mouth of one (Begley) and through the breath and mouth of the other into syntax and structure (Broumas), a third voice, not "disembodied" but actually "re-embodied," issues forth.

They open the series of lyrics with a quote from Sappho, the spirit-muse who rules the roost here, for more reasons than one: "Tears unbecome the house of poets." The transformation here—a rejection of grief or stasis, an embrace therefore of *ex stasis* or "ecstasy"—poetry, really—is by negation an active "unbecoming." Unbecoming means to stay in a newborn state or to travel backwards even earlier, to whatever that formless state might be. To be "ecstatic" is to be outside of one's own "self"—however that self be constructed.

What house would a poet live in? The gymnasium where one is "nude, trained, exposed" is a school here of language, of joy and poetry. The body utters and the intellect, the part that wants to organize these prayers into sense, is left behind or at least suspends itself for a moment.

"Any utterance runs the risk of being ideological," Roland Barthes wrote, as invoked later in the "proem" that opens the book.[2] Here the poets, always plural, want to reject the "thought police" and "recorded grammar" and move out on their own, see what can be discovered while—here two make one—lost in the woods of language. The "proem" ends with a series of quotes from W. S. Merwin, ending with this meditation on unity between two bodies making a single work: "Each of us is one / side of the rain / we have only one shadow."[3]

The book is comprised of ten long sequences, each made of small fragments and fractures of poetry that assemble themselves loosely around themes or images. The boundaries between the sections quiver a little bit—when *Sappho's Gymnasium* (excluding the first and longest sequence, "Prayerfields,") was republished in Broumas's collected poems *Rave*, the most significant and obvious difference was the compression of page space that republication can require. Gone were the wide-open spaces of the page in which single lines or stanzas would float—the poems instead ran straight in a series after the title. But the more significant difference was that often poems at the end of a sequence would be removed and appear instead as the beginning poems of the following sequence. Some pieces were inverted and some few were excluded. More on this presence of two differing versions of the text later.

"Prayerfields," the longest and opening sequence of the book, is a seemingly autobiographical series of short poems that travel from a position of "invocation" to the lip of "ecstasy." "Invocation" means you are calling on a force outside yourself—a "prayer," not always "for" something, but often that is indeed the case. The "field" of the title also means you are not whole and complete unto yourself, but need to depend on some particular external "location" to create that spiritual matrix in which a communion or communication with the divine or god-like can occur. When you move to the "lip" of ecstasy—the state in which you can travel outside your fleshly confine or perhaps realize the borderless condition of the spirit—it means you are beginning to understand *you* are actually *inside* something, in this case your physical frame and body, inextricably a part of it but also, in fact, Some Other Thing at once.

The form of language cannot contain the impossibility of god. It is one thing to believe in a *via negativa*—that God is fundamentally unknowable—but when you do have to live inside your body and in the actual material world it is not much help. *Via negativa* means you still believe god can be defined, but in this case defined by what it is *not*. *Sappho's Gymnasium* does not accept this dichotomy and chooses a third way.

Here is a piece early in "Prayerfields"[4]:

best friend and half-wild protector named
comfort for the body I can always
pray keep me in god coherent form
of light like memory also distributed
where it is not dimension only

Each phrase can leak into the other—god as best friend and half-wild protector? Did he (always lowercase in this book) comfort the body? And what is the prayer: to be kept in coherent form or to be kept "in god" and what is coherent—the body or the form of light; these two perhaps can be the same thing—at any rate, body, god and light all wish to be beyond the fact of mere "dimension" or physical shape.

The tender body, the one that is mortal, the one that dies, needs a tender god as well. The human, understanding this, walks "out onto the ice finite and helpless in return his soft / parts ventral know to die."[5] It seems a bitter lesson to learn—that after this glorious awareness, after learning to love one must (we all *must)* learn how to die.

Is that it? We live to love and die? You are on your own but it will have to be enough the poets seem to say in this short pair:[6]

> this helpless desire your own suffering the
> work of grace makes us visible
> flocking on small
> islands of inland waters the near
> shore of unsayable
>
> each
> had vivid memories of portions of
> their Good Friday experience the only
> one who can initiate you
> is your soul

The usual religious practice of seeking "grace" does nothing more than make humans "visible" on their little islands that hover near what cannot be expressed. It is the drama of "Prayerfields" to seek to understand not where one body ends and another begins—it was this dilemma that caused Atalanta to lose her wrestling match (and with it her sovereignty) to Meleager—but rather where the human and mortal part ends and the endless spirit matter begins. Is this the border between life and death? Not "life" nor "death" the way we think of it anyhow: solely in terms of the physical body that we can touch and smell and taste and hear and see.

Christ, rather than being the bodily incarnation of God-in-flesh, the key that can open the lock to everlasting life, is instead in this book a "jailer" (22). The "father" to whom one might ordinarily pray or depend on for support is asked to "burn the river down" since once the river, giver of sustenance, disappears one might in the "lighted flexion receive god unspasmed."[7]

The father reappears later:[8]

> father whose voice had not been completely
> destroyed is it okay now
> to love the actual
> watchful
> young adult genital oral

This is the actual world then that one lives in. The body, even with its spiritual leanings, wants the world genitally, orally, lustfully. Though in a poem that depicts childbirth the poets do say "borderlines they need," between a mother and a child being then created out of the material of her body and through the "movement of her own / body she wishes to be small / again."[9]

"The tablet is broken" could mean here those received laws of the father; though of course those tablets were broken because they were flung by their authority (Moses) at people who were disbelievers.[10] It is as if Creation itself were that rupture, that cells broke apart and multiplied the way those tablets broke.

The body becomes visible through the sunlight of this creation, this rupture. Though Anne Carson has written compellingly about the "erotic" space being the gap between two bodies, here in the gap between two poets the moment of touch is the transformative moment, not the climax of eros but only the beginning—(or in the space between two women's bodies, lesbian bodies, an argument against the notion of climax?):[11]

> if this one holds me so
> pleasurable does so long
> enough I came visibly to
> love

In the closing poems of "Prayerfields" there is a growing awareness of the qualities of the individual body and recognition that to be able to communicate with "god" or That Name, one does have to use the tools and tricks one has: one's voice, one's bones, the strings in the throat, and the so-called box of wonder. Small wonder ancient Indian sages identified the seven places of communion inside the human body, the chakra wheels around which we turn.

> only the analyst of souls knows how
> to exhume them to the breathing it is necessary
> for the caller to anoint
> the newborn[12]

We come to language through existence then, or said more directly, through actual breathing. It's the selfsoul here that takes you through,

and still one has to be handled, "anointed," or baptized—validated by
some external office. Later on in the book the emphasis will move even
farther out to the intangible, but only once the body is fully understood
and "prayer," such as it is, becomes possible at all.

All the speakers want seems summed up in the prefatory one-line
"invocation" that opens "Prayerfields":[13]

faithful the present I see you

By the end of the sequence, one doesn't require the locality of the
"field," rather, one understands, "the impossible world is / all around
us indistinguishably / one is this act the cause can be / anywhere."[14]

We attended a birth to understand the necessary way a body separates
from another and in this were able to see a microcosm of all creation—
cells breaking forth from cells, the entropy of the universe that splits to
join, ceases in order to continue. And so later we attend such ceasing:[15]

> . . . I sit by the death bed she is
> so beautiful a transparence one speaks
> is the beginning of
> memory of sensation let me make
> it good light being unborn

When Sappho suggests that tears "unbecome" a poet, she enjoins a
return to initial or original states at the beginning, now one (by
"dying") engages not in a ceasing but in a continuance of transforma-
tion into new matter and energy: being "unborn." It's not mere euphe-
mism here; it has something real at stake—the poets go on to say "I
committed all the necessary murders within myself / to acquire faith."
It brings my mind back to Arjuna's argument with Krishna at the
beginning of the *Bagavad Gita*: what is it within yourself you are willing
to part with in order to transcend the limitations of mind and body
both. And what, after all, *is* the "soul"?

Can we at all follow one of the final wishes in the field:[16]

> alone daily peace
> to honor without coveting
> the possibility of life
> without meeting boundaries or ever turning back

At the close of this sequence, with this wish to really *know* the body, the boundary between it and the spirit both within and beyond, we are left at another moment of birth: "when this was done an eggshell forms / us light hammering a spasm of sound."[17]

That eggshell may call to mind for the mythologically minded reader Helen herself, born immortal from a swan's egg, pure beauty and brilliant besides (for more on Helen's brilliant mind, see her appearance early in *The Odyssey*!): who better to take us on the next stage of this journey—the drama of the body knowing its own spiritual capabilities, seeing itself not as a limited vessel that prevents spiritual enlightenment but actual vehicle of absolute potential to travel those air-light roads.

From the broad open space of the field to a more concentrated arboreal venue, the opening section of "Helen Groves" sets the stage for the drama to come:[18]

what if there were no sea
to take up the table of our hearts
breath which is everywhere curved
hand from infinity broken (57)

The poets question what the individual will do without the infinity outside and beyond. Now turned inward how could one *not* feel lonely? One does float after all in the saline sea. The "floating" is not merely superficial (one floats by talking enough air into the lungs to remain buoyant—one only sinks, and thus drowns, by taking water into the lungs) but deeper even that that: the result of millions of years of evolution since our emergence from the ocean, the salt content of blood and seawater remains precisely identical. The "heart" then of the sea and the body is the same, a table on which one floats.

What if our anxiety—the anxiety of death, of what will happen to us "after"—is the same as the anxiety of the soul *before* birth: will we be received? What happens on the other side of this existence? Like the question of who we are in a dream this one remains unanswerable. Breath turns in the lungs the way space bends in the universe. A human body is fashioned out of another human body and *somehow* in the womb cells transition from tissue into incarnate being. No one can say when and no one can say really how. Human bodies—flesh—"broken" perhaps from the beginningless store of universal energy that is still to this day being categorized and understood—seen for what it really is: none of it has either appeared or disappeared, it seems, since the very so-called beginning of time. It has always Been.

So the bodies that broke off, the humans, have a role to play:[19]

Went walking and walking
far off to get water
two people with your birds
mirrors for multiplying light
we serve

Peaceful limbs
had been a little breathless
branches of new humans
the gods are open mouthed

One delight of the queer line breaks and eschewing of any punctuation at all is that sometimes clauses lead both backward and forward. Who are the mirrors meant to multiply light, the birds or the humans? And who is being served?

Humans, at any rate, by dint of the vulnerability of our forms, are tasked with the coarser chores of life. The two humans in this case, peaceful, having walked a long way for water, are breathless. It is unclear whether it is during their breathlessness the gods open their mouths, or whether *they* themselves are the gods in question. Either way one is left to consider the conditions under which one is "open mouthed": exertion, intimacy, communication, desire...

"The idea of a book held me as icons hold others," the poets quote Odysseas Elytis in the "Proem" to this book.[20] "I had but to fill it as you fill a row of empty glasses and, immediately, what power, what freedom, what disdain toward bombs and death it gave me." So the book or icon is something to be entered, to be interacted with in some way. Here in "Helen Groves" the poets say, "by long kiss the icon is / worn a lighter color / than the rest of the face / bathing the living."[21]

It is these physical interactions—birth, a kiss, bathing, caressing, sexual intimacy—that bodies come to know each other. The sun-soaked mythology of Broumas and Begley traffics in Greek idiom, landscape and sensibility but runs counter to the myths of alienation so prevalent in the ancient stories: Psyche who should not look, Eros who would not be seen; Orpheus who should not look, Eurydice who could not be seen; Echo who could not speak, Narcissus who would not hear, Atalanta who did not know where bodies ended, Medusa who could not be looked upon, Cassandra who could not be understood, the Sirens who could not be listened to. And so on.

The speaker here, like Homer's Telemachus, is unworried by the question of actual "origin." When Athena disguised as Mentor asks Telemachus whether he is Odysseus's son the young man says with the blithe unconcern of youth, "My mother says I am his son; I know not surely. Who has known his own engendering?"[22] The poets here clarify, "I don't know virgin / when I was made I was made," meaning there's no "blank" state or "pure" state, the answer to that old Zen question of "who were you before your parents were born" seems suddenly to be a somewhat stark though simple "No one." Is it too philosophical for the actual and ongoing world? The body with the mind in it, unaware of the infinity or eternity of the spiritual energy inside, is left with few ways of understanding it:[23]

It's not the herbs on my lips
we have freedom to be
infinite or not at all
infinite or not yet

It's a wonderful little musing, turning away from sensory experiences as a route to spiritual awakening and declaring the right of the human to ignore all this philosophy, to ignore the infinite inside, to be what one chooses to be, though the second choice implies that the awareness is inevitable, one is only left with deciding "infinite" or not yet infinite . . .

Though these poets of course dare to actualize. They confess in the very next poem, "I am optimistic I am scared a little"—how lovely to read both emotions in the same line, unmediated by connective language or comma. "My friend it is possible," they go on to say, "to drink the ecstatic one's ecstasy / over the source of energy I drink it."[24]

"I come single," the poets declare in their twin voice, "alone / under my clothes."[25] "Alone here" has echoes of what we really *are* under our clothes—naked. In this original state, "alone," profoundly alone, we arrive prepared for the journey. As one reads an echo of "naked" under "alone," one too hears the sexual *double-entendre* in the spare declaration "I come."

The supplicant, washed in the eros of knowledge, ready to light the lamp and stare then at its sleeping body, is given a little motivational speech at the end of the section:[26]

> You'll like the worshippers
> the sky with its seacoasts of Greece
> what kind leaves home for home
> send me

Here the seemingly infinite and intangible sky possesses inside itself the physical seacoasts of the former homeland. But there's no nostalgia in it because the poets dream of leaving "home for home," ask then—who is it they are asking?—to be sent. The body then, though explored as an instrument of liberation, is asking here to be acted upon. How can it be? Can you believe in both things at once—that infinity is inside but that the self is still separated from it, that you still must beseech that separate thing, pray *to* it? It seems a contradiction, a return to a more dualistic way of thinking, here in two small words, the first *actual* "prayer" since the initial line of "Prayerfields."

Prayers in every religious tradition always depend on their being uttered in the "proper" language for complete efficacy, whether—for example—Sanskrit, Arabic, Hindi, or Latin. The *intention* of the supplicant is secondary to the breath flowing through and animating the consonants of need.

The word "vowel" from the section "Vowel Imprint" opens with a "vow" of course, and opens its mouth to modulate and end on the liquid "l" (a yogic changer is reminded of pronouncing "Aummmmmm"). And the word "imprint" itself "im" "prints" when the close-lipped breath of its first "m" (said by linguists to be a human body's first consonantal pronunciation—in infancy, the mouth surrounding a nipple) meets the "p" (our second sound, the sound the mouth makes upon releasing said nipple).

The imprint of a vowel must be that depression made—on earth, sand or skin—by the breath of another. One also remembers the Islamic version of the story of the Virgin Mary, giving birth under a date palm, alone and ostracized. To give her sustenance the date palms drops fruit into her lap; taking one, she expels a breath in pain and the humble date is thus forever imprinted with her breath and made the holiest of fruits.

"Vowel Imprint" contains mostly short utterances, or expulsions, some of them only a single line long, as if in effort to pack greater impact into as brief a possible vessel of poetry. Indeed the first line of "Vowel Imprint" is one that has captivated me for years, one which has written itself in breath and in other kinds of ink all along the measures of my skin:[27]

Transitive body this fresco amen I mouth

The vowels of this opening line begin hemmed in by multiple hard consonants of the first word "transitive." They open wider in the word "body," but it isn't until "fresco" with its multiple liquid consonants "f," "r" and "s" that they really open free. The hard "c" of "fresco" causes a little expulsion of the vowel sound. It is notable that the turn from hemming consonants to releasing consonants happens on the neutral word "this." "This" holds a lot of power here—referring to the "fresco," which is of course also the body. The open vowels of "amen," "I" and "mouth" open the poem out as breath, though the final word "mouth" of course imitates the body—a vessel container of the boundless open inside—the "ou" in "mouth" is the same as the "Au" in "Aum."

The body is both transitive here, a passage, a bridge of flesh for breath between states of before and after, but also a fresco, made of pieces from all eras of time and all places throughout the universe. If the body is a fresco could it be the eternal matter that is painted onto the flesh of the body? But in a fresco that paint itself has bonded, become part of the wall; they are no longer separable.

The appearance of the speaking "I" (relatively late in such a brief poem) is the bridge between internal acknowledgement of infinity—"amen"—and the act of the individual actualizing herself into the external world, the exhalation of breath in "I mouth."

Of course what makes the line *truly* interesting is that it moves beyond standard syntax of prose declaration and into the queer strange language of ecstasy reminiscent of the odd choral ejaculations in ancient Greek drama. It's never fully clear what the subject, main verb, and object of this line are. Is the fresco being mouthed or the body or is the mouth an open space at the end of the line, mere descriptor for the "I"?

In the short poems of "Vowel Imprint" there is always a challenge or danger in lingering in the half-real zone between the actual physical world and spiritual awareness. At one point the poets worry, "Will these floors burst in oxygen / my life spent swimming."[28] Later they warn, "You feel the bruising mid-flight as one born / to dazzle god with your heat."[29] The encounters between the individual human and her spiritual sound are fraught with the essential difference between asceticism and human needs, the "hot burning off of self which exhausts it."

How is one, as a faulty human, a hungry one, supposed to continue in the face of such dangers? The poets muse:[30]

Honey of clarity and strength laboring light
the yes of song and its relentless ear
the actual words

There's no complicated solution ultimately. The desire toward song, toward affirmation comes accompanied by its "relentless ear." The "actual words" at the end may be song or they may be ordinary human utterance. Or it may be—best of all—that ordinary human utterance *is* song if only we could learn to hear it as such.

Thus reassured the poets realize:[31]

I am not alone
facing the sun
lover of all

Out of all the fragments and lines and scraps of Sappho there is a single poem to bear witness that Sappho was not mere ancient post-modern poetess marrying broken phrase with profound insight like Myung Mi Kim or Susan Howe. Her single poem shows a musical poet working wonderfully within the musical and metrical conventions of the time, a poet like Dickinson perhaps. So among the shreds and shards of *Sappho's Gymnasium*, around halfway through the book significantly, we come upon the first page of "Flower Parry," a poem written in a more standard performance mode but with all the metaphysical worries and flurries of the poems that came before and that follow.

This opening poem uses repeated lines almost like a blues musician repeats lyrics. It's an apt comparison since throughout *Sappho's Gymnasium* the poets riff on themes, words and phrases:[32]

> Clear blue temple I'm taken in
> clear blue temple I'm taken in
> god would talk if I did
> god would talk if I did
>
> got a mouth wants to know
>
> I was seeing someone burst open
> I was seeing someone burst open
> the door she was being
> the door she was being fucked
>
> hurt as a virtue
>
> hurt as a virtue makes me
> vertigo piss-scared
> seeing someone burst open
> god would talk if I did

Is it true then that god demands the submission of the individual ego, so equating spiritual enlightenment with a violence? In which case the idea of being thus "hurt"—that is to say "enlightened"—is not necessarily appealing to the individual person. *Why* should we give up our own individual perceptions, our own distinctive uniqueness? If even under the worst of circumstances we are afraid of change then small wonder we are chary of "realizing" infinity or immortality.

The line that rings in my ear is, of course, "got a mouth wants to know." Who is it that has a mouth? The human "I"? And what is it I want to know? The poem gives no chance to find out. Is it true that god will only talk if we see someone "burst open"? The thought gives scant comfort. Barring actual god-talk or prophecy the poets are left only with their own powers of ecstasy and utterance. As they say in their essay on the collaboration, "I need a wafer, equal in body and propulsion, that develops an entirely immaculate congregation of the tongue so that we might address you in words your love shapes."[33]

"Flower Parry" goes on to challenge the easy notions of obtaining wisdom by exploring some of the real dangers and difficulties that lie in wait for the individual human, the one who has a body and mind vulnerable to attack. "Let go your hammering," one poem begins, saying "I can miss with effort . . . no matter how painful . . . if it came from my heart."[34] In one place the effort of spiritual struggle is not conscious. In talking about a failing garden the speaker observes:[35]

> I should rest and not water the
> shoots but wait until dark to
> uncover them

"God with restraints I'm not," the poets say, as if to re-emphasize that one is caught in a swing between an understanding of "God" in strictly human terms and a refusal to categorize god at all.[36] There seems sometimes in the swinging to be no in-between space. In the closing poem the moment of creation and destruction is explored:[37]

> I don't know why I serve or want to dance wake up be born
> . . .
> I do myself o solitude
> at the birthing of sea level
> my undesired you ask undestroyed

It's the unmentionable things there, the reversed things that exist in the present moment always, actually "unasked" for. In a quest to reach spiritual enlightenment the individual human suffers precisely because the body has its sensory limitations, is trapped in a sensory existence. The lustful supplicant is rife with unquenchable desires so how is it possible to move forward at all? The image of the Fool, the first card of the tarot's major arcane, seems suddenly to be the position of knowledge, the simple saint, the sacred idiot, the only one able to achieve wisdom.

The lyrics of "Your Sacred Idiot With Me" splinter into brief and compressed two-and three-line epigrams, almost as if devolving into child speech or baby talk:[38]

After the roots have spoken
your night cries

Look after me true
true wherever

In these brief moments we are able to grasp or explore insights without
some of the verbal and rhythmic fireworks that characterized early
sections of the book. The syntax stripped down here, the line breaks
less unconventional; yet the extreme compression itself offers a kind
of shivering sometimes:[39]

A soul I did insist upon
I live superimposed

One thinks of the earlier "fresco" here. If we are superimposed though,
superimposed on *what*? What is the nature of the connection itself
between the material world and the spirit world? Because if there is a
duality between them, then spiritual search in the material world must
be limited to the realm of "preparation;" there will be no achieving in
the mortal frame of a life. It might be the job of poetry like this to
expose the cracks or rents in our perception of the world and the actual
physical world to show the places and possibilities where there is actual
transit between the material and spiritual. In other words, "in the
visible / time poets shine."[40]

In a hymn or choral ode the language transforms from the plain-
spoken of the rest of the section into the more ecstatic musically infused
rhythms of the earlier sections of the book:[41]

your translated trance I am performing it
asylum through my clearest my solid birthright singing
full time mercy break god

In the first line there is a trance that is given by one person, "translated"
from somewhere—from the spiritual realm of formless energy in the
matter, meaning *words*?—and passed along to the other who is then able
to "mouth it" or perform it. Here then is the story of the writing/
speaking of this book, two poets who pass the words and lines across
the space between them.

The words in this case become an "asylum" or "birthright" both of which imply transitional states—"asylum," meaning a freedom from past oppression or sanctuary with other like-minded individuals otherwise unable to function within mainstream society, and "birthright," which means a reclaiming in some way of something intrinsic which has gone unrecognized or has been lost.

When the poets sing "full time mercy break god," god breaks free in the poem. "He" has been previously mentioned by name very rarely but here god breaks at the end of a line, a chain of associations which evinces not worry or apprehension but rhythmic and spiritual release into open expression.

Wood can be joined to itself by pegs which means held together but by its own material, fastened but not splintered, not pierced. In "Joinery" body and soul, matter and energy or human and human thus weld together and become "structure."

"Long my heart has been / home," one lover may say to another, "home you feel the most / my arms will tell."[42] The limbs of the body narrate the story of lust and love here, as in the Quranic story of the body which speaks of the deeds of the person on the Day of Judgment. If the body can speak out (to divine force in this case, one presumes) then maybe the body can speak inward to the self and not in after-time but now immediately in this-time:[43]

> Art is climax over conduct
> zen of no color by sunrise I do

Perhaps "intention" or motion of the mind into the physical world is what is meant by "art" here, an art which trumps actual conduct. The second line of the couplet uses the language of the vow. Broumas, a Zen Buddhist, has written elsewhere of her work in massage and its counterpoint in meditation practice. She greets this practice of the body without "color," without intention, each and every day. In her essay "Moon," she says, "I have neither hope nor the absence of hope. I have the sweeping."[44]

It seems passive but in the next poem of "Joinery" the poets praise not willingness to sing but the gift of being "willing to be sung."[45] The body itself, the human life becomes expression of something else ineffable, something with agency. Imagine it: that you are not singer but thing *being sung*.

Other metaphors besides joining, music and meditation throughout this section include photography, gardening and sonar location. The actual spiritual symbols aren't all Buddhist though. In one poem the poets consider "reincarnation" with Christian symbols, meant for all supplicants though, not limited here to god (in the form of the Son):[46]

Cure for water is water
one very blue throughout the trees
divine indulgence yesterday
the cross dove from the wall
naked cross get into lifeboat
reincarnation of not

It's the "not" at the end of the poem, the doubt that quickly questions everything that came before that really drives the point home: No matter what is believed or disbelieved, no matter what poetry works to reveal, the fundamental unknowability of spiritual conditions is a wall not to be breached. In other words, "My belief and aggression took so long / sowing ground in her prophetic tropic."[47] "I'm done reading your book and admiring you / grape-sized obedience," the poets say tartly in the very next poem. What point is there indulging in this so-called minderror mirror, they wonder.[48]

"There is no way of rainbow for looking in broke / child behind unknown tongue," they say. It is some reassurance to know it is impossible to have any such revelation.[49] After all the looking, eye is "broke." Unlike the knowledge that seemed possible at the beginning when the body first broke from infinity, here it seems the eye *can't* see, won't be able to after all. One puts faith then not in the tongue that can speak in the actual world but the other tongue, the unknown tongue.

The path of the artist—and only that one—can lead the human not to revelations that will fill in the blank of received or expected outlines but of the actual confusing world with all of its contradictions, countermandings and, yes, countertexts. "On faith from some artist's image / a sheet of paper saying you are possible," reassure the poets, "values I stand on I invent / and in the very middle of that gap / the givers."[50]

Once more we are left in the space between the seeker and what could be known. Neither can be achieved. Only the material actual physical world can be sensed and perceived by the human incarnate body. What wisdom there can be can only be achieved in quotidian and ordinary things. The body must know its own processes then—birth, love, breath, age and death—to have any hope of deeper connection. Is it possible? That remains to be seen.

"I AM TASTING MYSELF / IN THE MOUTH OF THE SUN," June Jordan says in a poem, dreaming herself born of that (seemingly) eternal source of (seemingly) endless energy.[51] What's digested by the sun must then be transformed. Birth images open this section. To contrast the earlier "hand from infinity broken," here we find "spit sharpened so her tongue / finds the newly torn."[52] The difference between "broken" and "torn" is that the "torn" does imply an external force acting upon a previously whole matter, whereas "broken" may be a present condition which has its own agency, i.e. a small part "broken off" of a whole but also in itself whole. While it may be a Christian idea that liberation is dependent on the external factor, whether "grace" or an actual actor, the Son of God or whoever, there might also be something to the thought that other humans are required for the liberation of the individual.

"Give me your hand candidate of light," one seeker says to another, reassuring "the light won't wake you."[53] There is an in-and-out movement like the tide or breath that enables one to harmlessly engage with oneself and the community at large:[54]

Language you surge
language you try me
I set a place for you
who would have guessed there were so many
similars to you with your light
plotted across my window
we are walking toward it arm around
shoulder what else

Once again the poem fragments and splinters off at the end reminding the reader there is more to go, that the journey is endless process. Besides an ode to language, of course, it is also an ode to touch, ending with the human connection of one's arm resting around the shoulder of the other. Language and the body meet as one here and in many erotic lyrics that thread and rethread their way through the sequences of the book.

What the poets call the "sunny addiction" and "barely possible thirst" feels many times like it could equally apply to spiritual or sexual thirst. "I lie all night with her / I live where she is many," the breathless poets intone, "I look forward to it / I get on my knees."[55] As Atalanta thrashes in the moment of being unable to tell whether her body and Meleager's body are actually different, the searcher feels an erotic moment wondering where boundaries of skin truly lie:[56]

Her hours alone allure
mind makes mind need to cure
our work before us shape to be
receiving skin amid unceasing

If what's "digestible" is something that passes through the Sun, or the energetic power of the universe, the "insomniac" must be someone unable to interface in any meaningful way with the restorative and intangible energies of the universe. Sleep thus denied, the conscious mind moves into a different and skewed relationship with the reality around one. "The light upon me a kind of body," the insomniac realizes suddenly in her sleep-deprived clarity. Talking about the woods, she thinks, "The twigs snow soft / fetch knots of spring then eager morning."

It's almost as if, because of its inability to engage, the separated body can detect a greater subtlety in the absences of perception. In this case she is attuned to both the physical manifestation of time ("knots") and the *feeling* of time ("eager") in the motion of spring.

Throughout the sections "Digestibles of the Sun" and "Insomniac of a Zen-Garden Fruit," the shortest in the book, the images of childhood, natural landscapes and marriage presented all along in earlier sections recur and recur as if in waves. One is reminded of the genderedness of certain experiences: in a book written by and in the interchange and exchange between two female bodies, climaxes may be multiple ones.

The penultimate sequence, "Photovoltaic," does indeed "turn" in "light"; it turns from a pure climactic moment of lingual ecstasy to an earnest injunction to "Write poems / starve off death."[57] It continues to alternate between an address to an outside "Lord" and later "you," and an internal observational voice. The "you" shifts and changes throughout the sequence, and unlike—for example—in Louise Glück's *The Wild Iris* (another work which deals with the traffic between human and divine in which the speaker of the poems alternate among flowers, gardener and god), here it is harder to say (or perhaps better to say the question is irrelevant) who the "you" in any given poem is: a human addressee, the "Lord" or divine element or the speakers herself (herselves!).

It's appropriate to have that level of confusion for a poem that in its first line seems to use the phrase "wild cherry" as a *verb:*[58]

> Lord let me all I can wild cherry
> I'm dazed all my ways of arriving bear tracks
> failure of being torn to pieces is me
> mumbling anxiety and I love my heart

"Dazed" indeed, the supplicant finds in this poem her path is intersected not only with "bear tracks" (animal beings) but also "dew stars," and the earth in repeated iterations. The ecstatic uncoupled language she actually refers to as "vernacular"—not the heightened and ritualistic language of prayer with its human hierarchy of entry (priesthood, scholarship, etc.) and its imagined divine hierarchy of reception (who is worthy or washed clean enough for prayer, whose prayers will actually be answered, etc.)—but rather the plain speech of those "uneducated," the perhaps always "unwashed!"

The vernacular is confused, stumbles along (note the inverted subject in line 3), and moves against the linearity of address expected in a prayer designed for communal worship. No "mass" here but individual address, moreover not even between supplicant and "God" but between two human women who declare:

> I do each day lightly suffering desire
> for kindness vividly today
> idiot red unselfish green blue threadbare of cloud
> outside the labyrinth imagining my life

The "idiot" or wise person again makes an appearance here suffering, though lightly, desire. The scintillation of colors seems to belie this suffering; though threadbare or not she is still engaged in the highest form of praise, "imagining." The labyrinth, place of confusion and even danger, is abandoned here, and threads—*sutras* or sacred texts, threads the devoted tie around their wrists, threads made to weave tapestries or laws, threads that prisoners can use to escape said labyrinths—all flutter away in the stuttering music and assonance of the praising phrases.

Of course what priesthood, scholarship, or institutions offer is precisely this: the *organization* of knowledge, and the "inside"-*insight* of achieved wisdom. When we say "received" knowledge we mean someone has collected it, passed it down, given it *to* us. But *who* has given it to us? The books of the bible were voted on and included based on decisions of a council. A caliph ordered the writing down and binding of the oral document that was the Quran, and then of course he ordered it "ordered." All variant versions were collected and burned.

An ecstatic document, a document passed between two people from one mouth to another, would have to be comfortable with its variants, its impermanence. Of course, as I mentioned before, the two published versions of *Sappho's Gymnasium* do differ textually in more than one way. I myself catalogued more than forty differences between the two texts, some small, some large. There were eighteen examples of stanzas and lines that were transposed and appear in different places in their section or in different sections, there were around fourteen new stanzas in the work that appeared in *Rave*, and about as many that were removed, not including the entire first section "Prayerfields," which is not reprinted. Such differences do not seem to be of concern to the text itself—permanence doesn't have much to add to the seeking of a body for sensual or spiritual knowledge: "Insistent love I won't outlive the words I lamb into your mouth."[59]

At any rate, any text that uses both "wild cherry" and "lamb" as verbs is a scripture I'll sign up for. And the text of the section of "Photovoltaic," alone out of all the other sections in the book, is unchanged in both of its appearances in print.

Whether or not permanence is at stake, it *is* a seeking: "Empty of shit the race is on," the poets urge:[60]

> empty of eyes made of wood with indifference
> don't you straighten it
> don't pretend your mouth is not on fire
> that stupidity bursts the needle

And then they urge:

> race for the oar light sleeps to dream
> travel through shining the ration before you
> for every hurt be my large palm
> Poetry

"Poetry," at the end is the rescuer then, from the hurt, from the mouth on fire, from the indifference, even from the animal panic of bowel expulsion in times of grave danger. And what is the danger here? Death of the body? Loss of knowledge? The poets who traffic in oral ecstasy are channeling Sappho, of course, but doesn't that precisely outline the problem: the woman who sang, tenth of the muses, whose work was strafed to scraps by sand and war and history. The ancient epic of blood and death and the fall of the city were lovingly tendered from hand to hand, but the songs in a woman's voice, the songs of love and the body and Aphrodite, they drift away . . .

So how then are we supposed to continue on our path? Not by learning the chapter and verse, but by bringing into our *own* body the process itself for searching. And for that you need a school of certain sort.

If one can actually learn to "write" or pronounce out the words oneself, to lamb them into the mouth of another, then perhaps one can "read" *anything* as a sacred text. "Bird is drunk inside me," the poets observe later.

The final and titular section "Sappho's Gymnasium" opens, like any good school, with a series of dicta. But these dicta are meant not to contain but to open wide possibilities for "misbehavior" for its rowdy rabble of students:[61]

> Outside memory worship never dies
> . . .
> Torn mists the doves I will love
> . . .
> Light struts cannot be broken
>
> Make praise populations will last

When the poets say "outside memory," they may mean "besides memory," but they may also mean that "memory worship," or a writing in and through the body, is the thing that never dies, the thing that connects the finite body (not really finite at all because made of the infinite undying matter of the universe which neither begins nor ends and only transforms) to the infinite condition of energy (not really infinite at all because subject to the conditions of all matter and antimatter—if space bends perhaps time does as well? And if time does then what *about* energy . . . ?).

Thus laced one to another in a spiral that does and undoes itself endlessly we have not necessarily "read" or "recite" but rather "remember" and "sing." Here follows then an epigraph of the curriculum itself, fittingly, as delineated in the notes of Sappho's Gymnasium, a fragment from the Headmistress herself:[62]

I have a young girl good as blossoming gold

her ephemeral face I have formed a of a key

dearer than skylark homelands

The love for the girl is a portal into emotion more dear than even a "homeland." Of this power metaphor the poets outline what's really at stake: that human love, connection with another, is deeper than nation, than "home," a surer form of worship than any other. This fragment, by Sappho, enters into the stream of the poem, mixed with the words of Begley and Broumas seamlessly.

In this moment even the eros of the breakdown of linguistic structures starts to disappear. "Dutyfree dove seapitched Eleni," the poets sing to Helen, muse of ultimate beauty, "nectar your carafe seafounder."

Sappho and Eleni—Helen's Greek name—weave themselves into the fabric of Broumas and Begley's own words and in this way there seems a generosity of intent in the text. There is in the poems that follow a real commitment to connection, to actual communication, not solely utterance tossed out into the winds of the world. "Tongue I owe you," the poets say, and they mean both that the tongue is a recipient of a debt but also that the tongue itself *is* the debt that must be gifted to another. Spiritual and sexy at once indeed and in deed.

This form of rapt bodily attention has been arrived at by a long and careful exploration of the body and its possibilities. What happens when one rolls back knowledge of the intellect and seeks instead knowledge of the body and its senses:

Preumbilical eros preclassical brain

Preumbilical eros would be the one body literally inside the other even *before* the stage of separateness. This is eros not of separate bodies meeting each other skin on skin but swimming *inside* one another's sensory awareness. The preclassical brain is one unhindered by discipline or disciplines, that separation of knowledge that seeks also to problematize and alienate the human mind from the body's most significant physical processes: birth, sexual awakening, grief, ecstasy, beautiful age, death.

And what if life in its limb-loosening sweetbitter hem of experience is the illuminated part, then death even after death is diffuse, unknowable and unknown? What if "we" (all part of the same source?) transfuse "ourself" *into* flesh from the unknowing state precisely to do what the body can do: learn and know and with each death carry back a little bit more of that understanding?

"Pansappho unscalp unfleece unscalpel unskin of flowers our kin," the poets sing next.[63] This line sings musically even somewhat more when one remembers that in the Greek, Sappho's name has a hard "p" sound which precedes the "f" in the middle of her name and would properly be pronounced "Sapfo." When the poets wrote in their essay on the collaboration, "My skin is the volunteer cipher of your emotion," they are not speaking to an abstract other but to me actually. To you. Actually. They equals you equals me equals who.

And so how could I be surprised then when on the next page I found a short letter, written actually to me—six years before I met Broumas in New York City, when I still lived in Washington, DC, was working in social justice organizing and having panic attacks at my constricted and constricting life, before I had started on the path of poetry at all, she pronounced this verse out loud. And then how could I be surprised when six years later I read this book for the first time and missed it?

Not until late 2010, ten years after I read this book for the first time, longing for mentors who kept leaving me by geography or by death, did I suddenly come across the note, cast directly at me—*me*—from across time:[64]

> Justice missed hyperventilates poet
> Buddha vowel in Mohammed child dared cross
> far from mother olivegroves father almonds
> lyric sap of maple far from Lesvos

I am far from my sources—parental, spiritual, and otherwise. I dream my way home. My consonants—the religion I was born with, the rules I learned, the body I inhabit—may be that of a "Mohammad Kazim," but my vowels—the breath that moves through them—are from Buddha, Krishna, and from innumerable other places. There was a time in my life when I knew that far from my sources in every way—far from "God" and far from poetry—I would have to make everything up myself, in a language quite before unheard.

This is a book both individual and expansive, both immediately local and quite endless, as open as the wide southern Mediterranean. And why say anything at the end of the essay at all except pronounce more words from traveling; it seems the end of the known universe:[65]

> In the dark before the candle
> where the archetype takes our unconscious to build
> this work is forever

Notes

1. Olga Broumas, *Rave*, 361.
2. Barthes, qtd in Olga Broumas and T Begley, *Sappho's Gymnasium*, ix.
3. Merwin, qtd in Broumas, *Sappho's Gymnasium*, xi.
4. Broumas, *Sappho's Gymnasium*, 13.
5. Broumas, *Sappho's Gymnasium*, 14.
6. Broumas, *Sappho's Gymnasium*, 20–21.
7. Broumas, *Sappho's Gymnasium*, 28.
8. Broumas, *Sappho's Gymnasium*, 37.
9. Broumas, *Sappho's Gymnasium*, 38.

10. Broumas, *Sappho's Gymnasium*, 40.
11. Broumas, *Sappho's Gymnasium*, 43.
12. Broumas, *Sappho's Gymnasium*, 46.
13. Broumas, *Sappho's Gymnasium*, 5.
14. Broumas, *Sappho's Gymnasium*, 47.
15. Broumas, *Sappho's Gymnasium*, 50.
16. Broumas, *Sappho's Gymnasium*, 52.
17. Broumas, *Sappho's Gymnasium*, 53.
18. Broumas, *Sappho's Gymnasium*, 57.
19. Broumas, *Sappho's Gymnasium*, 58–59.
20. Elytis, qtd in Broumas, *Sappho's Gymnasium*, viii.
21. Broumas, *Sappho's Gymnasium*, 62.
22. Homer, *The Odyssey*, 8.
23. Broumas, *Sappho's Gymnasium*, 65.
24. Broumas, *Sappho's Gymnasium*, 66.
25. Broumas, *Sappho's Gymnasium*, 70.
26. Broumas, *Sappho's Gymnasium*, 73.
27. Broumas, *Sappho's Gymnasium*, 77.
28. Broumas, *Sappho's Gymnasium*, 80.
29. Broumas, *Sappho's Gymnasium*, 81.
30. Broumas, *Sappho's Gymnasium*, 89.
31. Broumas, *Sappho's Gymnasium*, 90.
32. Broumas, *Sappho's Gymnasium*, 93.
33. Broumas, *Rave*, 362.
34. Broumas, *Sappho's Gymnasium*, 94.
35. Broumas, *Sappho's Gymnasium*, 96.
36. Broumas, *Sappho's Gymnasium*, 98.
37. Broumas, *Sappho's Gymnasium*, 105.
38. Broumas, *Sappho's Gymnasium*, 110.
39. Broumas, *Sappho's Gymnasium*, 111.
40. Broumas, *Sappho's Gymnasium*, 112.
41. Broumas, *Sappho's Gymnasium*, 113.
42. Broumas, *Sappho's Gymnasium*, 117.
43. Broumas, *Sappho's Gymnasium*, 118.
44. Broumas, *Rave*, 207.
45. Broumas, *Sappho's Gymnasium*, 119.
46. Broumas, *Sappho's Gymnasium*, 124.
47. Broumas, *Sappho's Gymnasium*, 126.
48. Broumas, *Sappho's Gymnasium*, 127.
49. Broumas, *Sappho's Gymnasium*, 129.
50. Broumas, *Sappho's Gymnasium*, 133.
51. Jordan, *Directed by Desire*, 564.
52. Broumas, *Sappho's Gymnasium*, 137.
53. Broumas, *Sappho's Gymnasium*, 138.
54. Broumas, *Sappho's Gymnasium*, 139.
55. Broumas, *Sappho's Gymnasium*, 146.
56. Broumas, *Sappho's Gymnasium*, 149.
57. Broumas, *Sappho's Gymnasium*, 162.

58. Broumas, *Sappho's Gymnasium*, 161.
59. Broumas, *Sappho's Gymnasium*, 167.
60. Broumas, *Sappho's Gymnasium*, 168.
61. Broumas, *Sappho's Gymnasium*, 171.
62. Broumas, *Sappho's Gymnasium*, 172. Alternate translations of this stanza of Sappho can be found on p. 89 of the Barnstone translation, p. 269 of the Carson translation and is number 17 of Mary Bernard's fragments.
63. Broumas, *Sappho's Gymnasium*, 177.
64. Broumas, *Sappho's Gymnasium*, 181.
65. Broumas, *Sappho's Gymnasium*, 183.

Bibliography

Barnstone, Willis, trans. *The Complete Poems of Sappho*. Boston: Shambhala Publications, 2006.

Bernard, Mary. *Sappho*. Berkeley: University of California Press, 1986.

Broumas, Olga. *Rave: Poems 1975–1999*, Port Townsend, WA: Copper Canyon Press, 2000.

Broumas, Olga and T Begley, *Sappho's Gymnasium*, Port Townsend, WA: Copper Canyon Press. 1993.

Carson, Anne, trans. *If Not, Winter: Fragments of Sappho*. New York: Vintage Books, 2002.

Jordan, June. *Directed by Desire: Collected Poems*. Port Townsend, WA: Copper Canyon Press, 2007.

Can I Do this Spiritual Drag

on kari edwards

Michelle Auerbach

"[C]an I do this spiritual drag, collective agony wishful thinking, fearful peek-a-boo actuality about to be read in unapologetic disinterested participation against fantasy without benefit familiarity..."
—kari edwards[1]

"uggghhhhh, i am only halfway through this interview between akilah oliver and kari edwards on queer subjectivity in poetry (queer as in: how to actually make language supple enough address the material realities of LGBTQ people) and i am a little bit high and i hate that they are dead and i hate that passing for me is pretending that chris kraus's *i love dick* has anything to do with my life and i hate that we are always talking about the abject straight girl's abject love for straight men and i don't think we can talk enough about akilah oliver and kari edwards and why isn't everyone talking about them and where are my queer poet mentors and how many fucking academics get paid for a lecture on halberstam and fucking gagafeminism and how many shits do i give about your boyfriend and how much of my life have i spent trying to identify with gay men and how much of my life have i spent trying to identify with straight women and how much of my life have i spent hating my dykey-ness and how much do i need kari and akilah tonight and why am i thinking about lorca addressing whitman and ginsberg addressing lorca and whitman and where are the other chronologies where is my imagined space of address where can we speak to the other dead queers where are we where are we where they where are they"
—Jane Cope[2]

"There was no one I knew with a deeper commitment to looking for something real in the heart of the façade. Maybe she would learn to face the truth, and like the truth she faced? (She was 45 when I first met her, and would be 55 today if she had lived.)"
—Kevin Killian[3]

"[R]elating to or affecting the human spirit or soul as opposed to material or physical things..."[4]

The Lord Shiva in the Hindu tradition can appear as both male and female, either/or both/and all of the above. There are statues of Shiva with one side of his body dressed and adorned as female with an identifiable female anatomy and the other side in male garments with male anatomy. The statues are dynamic, moving, dancing, never still, always in flux and in transition. In the Shaivite tradition, the play of the masculine and the feminine manifests both strong gendered roles and fluid sexuality, but always winks at the illusory, cardinal identification with the physical form as essential and dangerous. In the diverse and eclectic history of Hinduism there are myriad ways to approach the problematic physical body in a spiritual world. There are strategies of going in deeper, getting out faster, cooling, heating, moving, stilling, and flagellating. There are moves to engage in dangerous and transformative magic and ways to leave behind individuality in favor of divine connectivity. The body is crucial to the undertaking of spiritual evolution. It is a transitory vehicle for incarnation and engagement or disengagement with the illusory world of the sensate.

kari edwards's philosophical poetics and spiritual philosophy show us the differences (none) between spirituality and poetics. edwards's poetry and philosophy wants to find a way to break us out of the illusion and give us a glimpse of the divine. This was a sentiment edwards elaborated on in conversation with Akilah Oliver and in an online interview, "poetry attempts to get to a deeper truth by trying to describe the indescribable."[5] All the poetic tricks and turns and jumps, for edwards, boiled down to conveying a slanted, altered, other view of reality that moves us deeper into our bodies—negating our existence and exploding and exploring and staking out the no space of the subject who will not stay still. In *Bharat jiva*, edwards writes, "when we mention the people, we do not mean the confessional body of the people, we mean the particularly itinerant bodies in mechanic flux..."[6]

The perplexing tension in edwards's work is that the body is there to be transcended at the same time as it is the tool, the vehicle, the necessary and perfect structure with which to be taking "a joy ride though the absurd."[7] The body, according to edwards, is "what allows me to feel others and the universe. if I want to speak of the possible I have to be in touch with the present present in the body that is my body."[8] The bodily experience is both singular and plural. It is made of distinct singularities that never quite adhere to the rules of the dominant culture, yet provide little interstices that both separate and bind. The body, that other to spirit, is necessary to accrue the details of worldliness in order to see how the individual differences manifest as the overarching idea of difference and exclusion—"if beyond the self, is the self beyond essential multiworld universal non-escapable caring."[9]

The epigram at the beginning of *Bharat jiva* is from Patti Smith, "oh to be not anyone, gone / this maze of being skin."[10] Escape from the body and the illusion of this reality as separate and individual appealed to edwards. In fact, edwards followed this branch of Hindu metaphysics all the way to Sri Aurobindo's ashram in India. Central to Aurobindo's teachings is the idea that we are transitional beings in transitional bodies on our way to an involution and evolution of consciousness. We can see this reflected in *Bharat jiva* when edwards writes, "despite the body / there is a universe / despite the universe / both waves of existence..."[11] Aurobindo's dialectic of salvation was based on a very poetic undertaking of moving to the depths, finding revelation, and having a complete transformation of experience—bodily, emotive, and intellectual. There is no doubt that this view on the body is also tied to Patti Smith's and intrigued edwards in the quest for no gender.

Yet, the deeply embodied pursuit of the luminous details of the quotidian is at odds: "remembering through bodies / and thoughts of thoughts..."[12] The entirety of edwards's poetry is taken up with details of incarnation that bring the reader back into a sexual experience of the body without sex characteristics where fuck stands in for connection and reality is defined as what connects us: "in reality this is it, the end, or maybe a deep understanding that two good fucks is worth one hundred thousand, one hundred thousand dollars and change."[13]

It is possible to read the classic narrative of the spiritual searcher in edwards's work: dissatisfied with this plane and with bodily existence, the seeker looks to break the barriers between self and the cosmos and find a sense of belonging to mitigate the yearning and sorrow this realm has to offer to anyone who navigates it in human form. The escape from the body and the escape from illusion are both tropes in the retelling of spiritual awakening. However, instead of this tired but sturdy story, edwards pursues a path of tension of opposites between the body and spirit that holds the both/and instead of the neither/nor. While edwards describes the experience of being in a body in "Having Been Blue for Charity" as "I crouch in a body episode,"[14] there is also the feel of a "sense of polish and satin"[15] when skin meets skin or mind meets mind that burnishes edwards's jarring, difficult work.

In other words, the body and the experience of being in a body are complex. The more complex, the better for edwards as the language of the poetry reflects:

> falling in and out of the service of "truth," to another, for another, in love with "truth." Repeating you have to believe, you must believe, listen to the mother and the father read books and repeat after me, I can not represent myself, we must represent the not representable whole impossible to represent...[16]

This complexity, a fractal iterative form of subjective possibility is the spiritual core of edwards's work. As Judith Butler writes and edwards uses as an epigram in *obedience*, "Possibility is not a luxury; it is as crucial as bread."[17] Juxtaposed with grammatical terms and flashes of suburbia and India in edwards's work are definitions of modern life—bank accounts and burger joints and 800 numbers, "call 1-800-complete resignation"—with lurid light and a trip through "a field of time, where / there is a choke hold on language."[18] These are such glorious descriptions and beloved touches that edwards's deep love and confusion around a body's purpose and necessity is evident. These moments, along with the always more and eternally fecund world of the poetic and spiritual unconscious illuminate spaces "where the lakes, rivers and oceans are no longer lakes, rivers and oceans but mud covered hunger living in bodies."[19]

Another aim of certain Hindu metaphysical technologies is to quell hunger, desire, and other physical needs and demands of embodiment. While edwards mocks conventional religion in America, chalking it up to "cheap prayer to a god subdivision,"[20] there is the yearning to use yogic traditions to escape the inevitable suffering of being spirit in a body. Lines in *Bharat jiva* such as "neither delight or aversion / no difference between a thing"[21] echo the Bhagavad Gita. Even so, edwards is not a classical yogi looking to still desire and evade this world in search of transcendence. Rather, in the way Hindu philosophical traditions are always in conversation with each other—questioning, arguing, reflecting, engaging, demanding—edwards turns over experience and looks at it from different angles. In an essay edwards writes: "shifting and causing interference, not knowing where the 'I' is going, creates the possible out of the impossible."[22] The polyphony of voices and images in edwards's work is a both/and/all strategy to take in human consciousness. The divine is present in the universal spaces around self that form very personal connections in the search for where the world, language, our bodies, consciousness, and experience meet and mingle, captivate, and repulse. Though edwards uses the first person singular, the uncomfortable, unreliable "I," it is in the service of a "you" and an "us." As Robin Blaser puts it, this pronoun is "neither first, nor a person, nor singular."[23] In "having been blue for charity" edwards writes "just words. You are my consciousness. I am you, sitting there reading of listening, content and embellished."[24] The receptivity and reflectivity of consciousness throughout edwards's work values Aurobindo's tradition, where "the most indispensable thing in every case is receptivity."[25]

In Hindu temporal concerns, receptivity, openness, confusion, and calamity are all parts of the experience of the body. They are universals that, even in dissolving gender and questioning the body as solid or real, draw us together and define the encounter with form and incarnation. However, edwards warns against using "the 'I' as the ultimate achievement, where the endgame is the epiphany of late capitalism," lest we become "a consuming self-controlling anorexic life form on automatic."[26]

These words invite us to experience the "I" without trying to control or define it. And to taste and enjoy the "I" without trying to morph it when it becomes uncomfortable. The tribulations of moving through this escapade of incarnation are, in Sri Aurobindo's yogic teachings, what creates enough discomfort to open the well-defended shell of ignorance and break the ties with illusion. In other words, to crack a person open and make space for something new: "The task remains as always about reducing suffering."[27]

Emmanuel Levinas writes, "The biological, with the notion of inevitability it implies, becomes more than an object of spiritual life. It becomes its heart."[28] So, too, with edwards, where as difficult as the body may be, the body sits itself at the center of experience and then starts causing important trouble. Yet, without a body, there is no heart to crack open and no fragile, precious human existence in which to work towards enlightenment, and edwards knows "it is time to detonate the heart."[29] To have the experience of an "I" who does not fit into the either/or gender constructs and to question the version of reality regurgitated in American culture is to feel essential brokenness or failure as sweet, divine, tender and most importantly universal. "[O]ur blood is your blood / our house is your house, listening / for another other's cry for love . . ."[30] As the offering of our transitory, temporary, excruciatingly beautiful time here, edwards's work gives the reader an elemental connection of feeling self to feeling self. Subjectivity, like grammar and gender, is part of how a consciousness placed in a body articulates finiteness. Without something at stake, be it self or death, gender or transcendence, or entanglement of feeling, there is no wedge with which to open to each other and to describe what the "I" knows.

The deep "now" and "I" and "us" and "this"-ness of edwards's work is the boon that has carried on, brought people into intimacy and conversation, and fed the need for history and placement of a reflection of self that is skittish, needy, human, and real. If we are to move with edwards's spiritual gesture, it would be towards building a community of vulnerability and lack of stable self that opens us to the possibility of a state in between this and that, now and then, here and there, I and thou, in and out, and singular and plural. This is the gift edwards brings to an awkward, frenetic, unstable search for reality and freedom. The good tidings of incarnation—we are here, this is it, this is reality as I experience it at this fraught moment—can appear to be problems to solve or damage to be avoided. The pain and the trashy ugliness of our culture and of this illusion of time and space might be enough to drive someone to search out something better, cleaner, bigger, and more comforting. This kind of retreat may wall off the individual into a spiritual materialistic grab for abatement of suffering. Not so with kari edwards, who bravely and gorgeously uses poetic gesticulation to describe and embrace the volatile spaces between illusion and reality. This negative capability, this ability to hold both the arduousness of existence and the possibilities is at last the deepest move of the spiritual: "Today I watch the cement crumble. Juxtapose love with everything."[31]

Notes

1. edwards, *Bharat jiva*.
2. Cope, "akilah and kari."
3. Killian, "Long Ago Tomorrow."
4. *Oxford English Dictionary*, 2nd ed. (2 vols.), s.v. "spiritual."
5. Oliver, "Shifting the Subject."
6. edwards, *Bharat jiva*, 3.
7. edwards, *Instructions on the Impossible*.
8. edwards, interviewed by Lance Phillips, in "Here Comes Everybody." Note: Phillips's blog is no longer available online, but this quote can also be found on Ron Silliman's blog, "Tuesday, January 13, 2009," *Silliman's Blog*, http://ronsilliman.blogspot .com/2009/01/lance-phillips-in-1953-when-paris.html.
9. edwards, *Bharat jiva*, 76.
10. edwards, *Bharat jiva*, 76.
11. edwards, *Bharat jiva*, 104.
12. edwards, *Bharat jiva*, 106.
13. edwards, *having been blue for charity*, 14.
14. edwards, *having been blue for charity*, 9.
15. edwards, *having been blue for charity*, 9.
16. edwards, *TRANSSUBMUTATION*.
17. edwards, *obedience*.
18. edwards, *Bharat jiva*, 67.
19. edwards, *Bharat jiva*, 74.
20. edwards, *Bharat jiva*, 71.
21. edwards, *Bharat jiva*, 19.
22. edwards, "a narrative of resistance," 267.
23. Blaser, qtd in *kari edwards: No Gender*, 179.
24. edwards, *having been blue for charity*, 12.
25. Alfassa, *Collected Works of the Mother, Volume 7*, 257.
26. edwards, "a narrative of resistance," 266.

27. edwards, "a narrative of resistance," 267.
28. Levinas, *Some Reflections on the Philosophy of Hitlerism*, 18-19.
29. edwards, *Bharat jiva*, 3.
30. edwards, *Bharat jiva*, 75.
31. edwards, *Bharat jiva*, 99.

Bibliography

Alfassa, Mirra. *Collected Works of the Mother, Volume 7: Questions and Answers 1955.* Pondicherry, India: Sri Aurobindo Ashram, 1979.

Brolaski, Julian T., Erica Kaufman, and E. Tracy Grinnell, eds. *kari edwards: No Gender: Reflections on the Life & Work of kari Edwards.* Brooklyn, NY: Belladonna Books/Litmus Press, 2009.

Cope, Jane. "akilah and kari." *Travelcoat Tumblr* (blog). Accessed June 11, 2012. https://www.travelcoat.tumblr.com.

edwards, kari. "a narrative of resistance." In *Biting the Error*. Edited by Mary Burger, Robert Glück, Camille Roy, and Gail Scott. Toronto: Coach House Books, 2004.

edwards, kari. *Bharat jiva*. Brooklyn, NY: Belladonna Books/Litmus Press, 2009.

edwards, kari. *having been blue for charity*. Buffalo, NY: BlazeVox Books, 2003.

edwards, kari. "Here Comes Everybody: Interview with Lance Phillips" (blog). December 4, 2006.

edwards, kari. "let us say goodbye." *Tarpaulin Sky 4*. no. 1 (Spring/Summer 2006). https://tarpaulinsky.com/Summer06/edwards.html.

edwards, kari. *obedience*. Ithaca, NY: Factory School, 2005.

edwards, kari with Cole Swenson, Robin Blaser, Samuel R. Delaney, Michael du Plessis, Akilah Oliver, Eileen Myles, Roberto Tejada. "Panel: Politics of Identity." In *Civil Disobediences*. Edited by Anne Waldman and Lisa Birman. Minneapolis: Coffeehouse Press, 2004.

edwards, kari. *TRANSSUBMUTATION* (blog). http://transdada3.blogspot.com/.

Killian, Kevin. "Long Ago Tomorrow." *Keep the Lights On* (blog). August 17, 2011. http://keepthelightsonfilm.com/archives/art-and-autobiography/long-ago-tomorrow.

Kraus, Chris. *I Love Dick*. Los Angeles: Semiotext(e), 2006.

Levinas, Emmanuel. *Some Reflections on the Philosophy of Hitlerism*. Paris: Payot-Rivages, 1997.

Oliver, Akilah. "Shifting the Subject: an interview with kari edwards." *Rain Taxi Online* (Spring 2003). http://www.raintaxi.com/shifting-the-subject-an-interview-with-kari-edwards/.

A [Prayerful] Ingenuity that is Erratic
Patricia Dienstfrey's Theopoetics
Elizabeth Savage

When Kelsey Street Press published Patricia Dienstfrey's *The Woman Without Experiences* in 1995, important experimental writers, including Kathleen Fraser and Carole Maso, reviewed the book immediately. Soon after, excerpts from *The Woman Without Experiences* appeared in the 1997 keystone anthology *Moving Borders: Three Decades of Innovative Writing by Women*, edited by Mary Margaret Sloan; and Dienstfrey edited with Brenda Hillman the 2003 collection *The Grand Permission: New Writings on Poetics and Motherhood*. In 1974, Dienstfrey co-founded Berkeley's Kelsey Street Press, a small operation established "to address the marginalization of women writers from small press and mainstream publishers."[1] Recognizable innovators of feminist poetics who have published books with Kelsey Street—Mei-Mei Berssenbrugge, Barbara Guest, and Erica Hunt among them—have gradually secured critical attention. Given Dienstfrey's important contributions to feminist poetics, the position of *The Woman Without Experiences* on the periphery of critical awareness seems mysterious and outrageous.

Though they admire and respect *The Woman Without Experiences*, feminist scholars have perhaps avoided writing about this book because of its unusual confrontations with religion and sexuality. In Fraser's interview with Dienstfrey[2] and in reviews, these issues do not come up, despite their obvious centrality to the book, importance declared in sub-headings like "Architectures of Explosion: The Cross" and "Incest and Myth /

Between Two Holes: Trussed, Softly Bound." Certainly, a fear of getting it wrong, of violating by misunderstanding the book's considerations of sex and God, body and spirit, has delayed my own writing about this astonishing work. No topic is more private than religion; sex is a distant second, although transgressive sexuality closes the gap considerably. Carole Maso hints at these matters when she concludes her review, "Indeed, the book asks us to question our assumptions. [. . .] It gently presses me to question the desire to take stances: it asks in thinking and articulating positions, one leave room, as the text itself does, for doubt, for forgiveness . . . for being less quick to judge in the old ways."[3] Hoping to answer the book's call for courage, I leave the quiet room of my long-term relationship with its pages by opening the door to conversation.

The Woman Without Experiences begins and ends with an address that imitates prayer and represents words' ability to access invisible dimensions through which personal longings can be pursued. These passages literalize the embodiment of world in words:

> *I come back to the room to look for you. I come back to the room to look, to bring my eyes up to the words "to look for you," to look, as through a pair of glasses. I press the double o of room.*
> *I say, "Oh, room. Mm. Mm fleur, flower."*
> And a door opens.[4]

The unidentified speaker is the book's central figure and sometimes narrator, Nina Mansfield-Schorr, also Dienstfrey's alter ego.[5] The "you" addressed is possibly God, the reader, Nina's mother, the book's many cited writers and literary characters, or Nina herself. She "comes back to the room," introducing the book's theme of revision, rereading, and return and its vision of spiritual quest as movement through everyday domestic routines like misplacing and recovering things, thoughts, and people. Revising the opening sentence in the second so that "to look for you" becomes "to look," the passage uses words as literal instruments for uncovering what's concealed: the speaker takes up the articulated words first as lenses and then presses the "double o of room," which operates like buttons on a secret panel. Words and letters are visual, touchable objects linked to spiritual desires and fulfillment. Pressing and speaking in surprise, recollection, recognition, or pleasure *("Oh")*, the speaker savors the terminal consonant of "room" in an expression of contemplation, hunger, and satiation. The repetition of *"Mm. Mm"* links the sensual and spiritual to the linguistic: the hum between the speaker's lips, both expression and origin of the flowering/ opening that follows, delivers the password first in French, then English, which calls attention to the implicit chain of etymological association among choices and impulses of the body.

In these framing moments, *The Woman Without Experiences* demonstrates in miniature the theopoetics of its entirety, one in which divinity is revealed as the persistent opening of reality through changes in vision, which require the difficult work of learning to look, to see, and to read differently. Prayer presses on reality by using words to change and open the self and surroundings to different understanding. In cooperation with divinity, prayer brings consciousness to bear on intention; praying redistributes attention in order to gather and redirect forces of self and bring into understanding the meaning of one's presence in the world. Dienstfrey's Nina seeks contact with divinity that will refit the structures of her selfhood so she may enter her present life, in which she feels those physically and emotionally nearest to her are remote and her sense of absence criminal, painful, and furtively carried out:

> What is missing surrounds Nina as a moat. She looks up and her children are at the table rolling Play-Doh around on plates. She can't see to the other side of the moat. Her children are in the watery move-ments which the walls confine, her little ones bearing the roundness of the inner, the shapes that multiply suspended between heaven and earth in cells in the dark.[6]

In narratives of western culture, particularly those supported by gender scripts of Judeo-Christian traditions, Nina's alienation from her chil-dren is a sure sign of madness or monstrosity. Her belief that her life is empty and uneventful, likewise, makes no sense in these contexts because she has achieved the female part of the heteronormative dream:

> "I am thirty-three. I am married to a man I love. We have three chil-dren, each of whom I think I love more than I love myself. I have traveled. I have loved cities, countrysides, mountains. And nothing has happened."[7]

Nina searches for a form through which to enter her life and pull her experiences close, but she isn't looking for acceptance, a way to trim her life to conform to existing scripts of presence and happiness. This book illustrates the sought substance of divinity very differently, "A mother-father in one body. Sacred and secular love, one and inseparable."[8] God, the "mother-father," is the continual opening—noun and verb—of psychic spaces in the secular and sublunary realms. Looking itself impels Nina's return to familiar places and texts where she discovers new rooms and meanings that reciprocally revise the terms, especially the paradigms of interiority and externality, through which self is understood in relationship to experience.

In theorizing the ethical and spiritual powers of experimental writing, Joan Retallack explains the belief motivating "interrogative" work like Dienstfrey's that radically departs from "'nature' narratives" of self and language: "What we long for is implanted in our grammatical structures as much as it is in our vocabularies."[9] Dienstfrey's theopoetics proceeds from Nina's crisis of experience and emerges as a collage of findings, fragments, readings, and memories unsuited to the unifying (and universalizing) imperatives of genre categories and the reading practices they dictate that are at the bottom of Nina's isolation. Nina's creation of ways to be present in her experiences begins in the study of spoken and written words, the shapes of letters, books she's read, images of memory, and childhood fantasy to recover in their deep structures what she has wanted. *The Woman Without Experiences* develops "a purposeful ingenuity that is erratic,"[10] a hybrid prayer capable of revealing and reshaping longing, looking, and seeing from an assembly of literary tools and appetites. And what is seen there is another shape of experience, one freed from the "unifying aspect of experience" reinforced by most texts, measures of memory and notions of truth that, as Joan W. Scott points out, also "exclud[e] whole realms of human activity by simply not counting them as experience, at least not with any consequences...."[11]

Rethinking experience is closely bound up with formal innovation and with encountering divinity in writing. L.B.C. Keefe-Perry usefully describes theopoetics as "the study and practice of making God known through text" and "a means of making God, of shaping experience of the divine, and the ways people come to know the Spirit."[12] Keefe-Perry's collapse of revelation, "making God known," and creation, "making God," resembles the paradoxical operations of Dienstfrey's book and of experimental poetics. In "The Experimental Feminine," Retallack speaks of literary experimentation as a moral pursuit, the fabric of creation itself, arguing, "the form that the experiment takes is not preliminary to the answer, not preliminary to the creation of the art object. It *is* the answer. It *is* the art."[13] Remake the discursive grounds of self and remake the world.

The Woman Without Experiences dissolves paradigms of interiority and exteriority, form and content troubling Nina's experience of self and creation. In "Sort, Sortie I," a subchapter, Nina's beloved husband Jake insists (in what is a likely a perennial disagreement) that Nina must "live in the world as it is" and, the conversation implies, accept physical laws that preclude metaphysical uncertainty.[14] They agree that "to sort is important," but the tasks each assigns to the infinitive "to sort" differ in both denotation and philosophy:

> They agree that to sort is important. Jake: "Sort means you keep it or you don't. It's on the table or it's off."
> Nina: "Sorting is finding an order, this then that. Everything stays on the table."[15]

Jake's definition upholds dualisms, the either/or logic of gender and genre, self and other, creativity and form that entail exclusion (on or off) to protect an order established on categories. A self-described "Jewish mother,"[16] suggesting comfort with gender slippage, his sorting practice maintains conventional taxonomies that order experience according to externally verifiable events: "living in the world as it is."[17] Based on a very different premise, Nina's sorting is a way of looking and rearranging without eliminating possibility, "Everything stays on the table." Her world exceeds judgments, although she has since early childhood suffered from what she describes as "envy . . . a legless feeling" tied to seeing herself as excluded from "a world she hasn't made,"[18] one accepted by Jake and most people who appear to inhabit it.

Nina's world, created in the process of *The Woman Without Experiences*, becomes known through intuition, traces, glimpses, sensual imaginings.

At times, the book positions the world of her experiences as a world "within" Jake's empirical world, but at other times, Jake's is a world Nina pushes off from to swing or fly beyond. Nina "rocks" between and within worlds that revolve around the expansive realm of conflicting sensations, belief, and faith. The generation of Nina's logic—the departure signaled by the pairing of the French "sortie" with sort—takes on more profound connections to God and experience in the chapter "Womb, Table" that begins with a substantial statement by Elaine Scarry, which I quote only in part:

> The relation between the three shapes of womb, well and altar should for a moment here be placed side by side. . . . [I]n each it is not the outside surface but the inside surface that functions to 'contain,' that holds what is precious. [. . .] That the altar's surface is the reversed lining of the body is made more imagistically immediate in all those places where blood is poured across the altar.[19]

Scarry's claim articulates Nina's own revision of conventional givens, including that language is separate from but accurately records "the world as it is." Scarry's complication of insides and outsides inverts also the relations among worship, sacrifice, the basic component of human life (water), and the female body. By releasing the literal and symbolic from dualisms, this inversion spills out meanings eclipsed by the model of self-dictating individuation. The humanist idea of the mind separate from and ruling over the body echoes in the contradictory voice of God Nina hears in childhood, first approving her self-comfort, "Stay in bed [Little One], read, amuse yourself," then turning on her to berate, "You are becoming yourself the wrong way, from the outside in."[20] To comply with this command to "become [herself] from the inside out" would be to settle for the alienation she often feels because so much of her self is rooted in belief, not fact, formed in the images of her body in childhood, the germination of her inner life through reading and touch.

The opening and closing passages in which Nina reads and touches words she's spoken applies Scarry's revised relations to solve the metaphysical problems posed by God's reprimands and modern civilization that diagnose her as "wrong." Near its conclusion, the book cites Scarry again to support Nina's methods as a faith practice, *"Belief... is the act of turning one's own body inside out—imagining, creating."*[21] The resonances of this statement for Nina appear immediately after the first-person address ("I come back to the room"), when the narrative shifts to a third-person, present-tense voice of an unidentified woman who has not cleared the breakfast table. The narrative then names her and tells the origin of her name, Nina; the "I" then returns in the section immediately following, "Nina Reading Our Lady of the Flowers / Berkeley, Spring 197_." Here, the "I" combines Nina reading and Genet's narrator before shifting back to a third-person description of the author writing the book, "Thus I lived in the midst of an infinity of holes in the forms of men."[22] Voices continue to multiply so that Nina and Genet seem to travel through "an infinity of holes" that are both voids and doors. Genet's metaphor "holes in the forms of men" functions like the "double o of room," sound-signs through which Nina passes "in parts, phonemes, traces."[23]

The passage headed "A Mother in a Field of Writing" describes Nina's mixture of "horror? excitement?" as she recognizes herself as both "a mother at home with her children" and "a woman who knows she has been replaced" while she enters and is entered by Genet's book: For instance, just now reading Genet, she imagined a man writing, curled up under covers—and she became a man/child creating in a cell, her face his over the page. She sat in her kitchen, the father/creator of her children. The woman, he in a bathrobe, rocking on a kitchen stool. A hole in an infinity of holes . . .[24]

This passage turns "inside out" many expectations about reading, namely that the reader acts on a book, giving it meaning through critical reflection. Here and throughout *The Woman Without Experiences*, however, books interpret Nina, and she becomes part of them. She joins Genet writing his book as she earlier collaborated with Jo March scribbling away at her manuscripts and, with Alcott, Jo's creator; but these characters also call Nina into being from the white light of pages she claims as her own. Dienstfrey's book insists that reading (especially, in Nina's case, childhood reading) is experience, not an escape from reality, as much a part of one's history as mealtimes, houses, and neighbors. *The Woman Without Experiences* dissolves past and present into the well of memory, the womb and altar of the adult self. Retallack comments provocatively that "[h]istory is nothing other than the infinitely intricate present that surrounds us—the panoply of residues and effects, accidental and chosen—that adorn and litter the landscapes of our desires."[25] In this temporal configuration, history remains on the table; the present does not replace the past, but is the sorting (or reading) of "the panoply of residues and effects" steadily reinterpreting each other. Nina's infinitely intricate present is bound by a day she spends with her children, one that is punctured and punctuated with readings and remembrances, invocations and intrusions. This day is haunted by two particular concerns the book moves between: motherhood and childhood. In these culturally fraught, interconnected arenas, *The Woman Without Experiences* accomplishes its most daunting task. The book's ingenuities, pursued through acts of reading and writing, recognize children's erotic experiences of divinity without defaulting to nostalgia for innocence. Scholar of postmodern theology Romana Huk explains theopoetics as way of writing in "phenomenological mode, bracketing perception against preconceptions about the matter at hand."[26] In the chapter "DIVIDING CREATION, a portion titled "Incest and Myth / Between Two Holes: Trussed, Softly Bound," brackets preconceptions that children are nonsexual and must be protected from the damage sex would cause them. Speaking of child Nina in the present tense, the passage discretely unfolds its title's significance in a vignette from Nina's childhood summers at the family lake house:

> Between lunch and the afternoon swim, Nina rocks herself to sleep under the patched summer sheets. She turns in the world. Holes open—her intensely viewed and now pronounceable "mouth"; her nameless, dark vagina. She turns the world out of the pole of her body that links them. Her hole-pole: it empties and fills and the sun rises and sets over the horizon. This is a certainty.
>
> While Rob's penis is an object of doubt, as to whether it is the inside of a hole turned out, or a pole that is missing one way to enter and leave.
>
> They share it. Rob slips it into her mouth, and she remembers it on her tongue. He tells her about its life—*Sshh! sshh!*—the story of the hunter-prince in flower-dotted meadows.
>
> He looks out for her and she looks in for him.[27]

Like the book itself, Nina's early awareness of her body eludes expectations. As Nina ages into girlhood, her self-mothering and self-pleasuring ("Nina rocks herself") become intolerable to her tyrannically Christian father, Chester, who punishes her "with dinners with no dessert, bedtimes / without kisses."[28] At this very young age (she has just begun to pronounce "mouth"), however, she experiences her body as a sign and source of information about the world and as a world itself. The center, axis, and creator, Nina's body fills with imaginative illumination that unsettles (and does so quite directly and comically) the Freudian rubric of childhood sexuality measuring Nina's "nameless, dark vagina" as a deficiency. Her revelations counter contemporary Romantic views that childhood is "innocent" and therefore sensual experiences like Nina's are meaningless—either "harmless" or "deviant." Nina's rocking activates her imagination of a/the world; she "turns the world" with what her uncivilized mind envisions as a route and connection rather than as a lack.

This experience of embodied power and belief sadly contrasts with the adult Nina's sense of displacement, her sense of failure to be present in the world much less to turn it. On "patched summer sheets," Nina's playful exchanges with her brother ("the story of the hunter-prince"), as we are told, have helped articulate her body's connection with the world. Paced between blank spaces, the ensuing paragraphs reveal that Rob's penis is not merely something Nina has seen and speculated about but that she and Rob "share it." At this, the reader of Dienstfrey's book faces the choice to refute Nina's fulfilling interpretations of her body or to accept Nina's account as truth. Nina's reflections, without pathology or pity, state her adult relationship to her early childhood eroticism with unusual levity. Gayle Rubin has argued persuasively that "our culture denies and punishes erotic interest and activity by anyone under the local age of consent" and that the assumption that "sex per se is harmful to the young has been chiseled into extensive social and legal structures designed to insulate minors from sexual knowledge and experience."[29] And so it is also chiseled into our psychological structures. The challenge to resist the draw of conditioning mounts when, in the next three paragraphs, we witness Rob abused physically by his father, who is feared by all who enter the Mansfields's house "muttering prayers to carry them safely into the hall," and then we are told Rob brings a group of boys home to receive oral sex from Nina at his instruction.[30] In the section immediately following, we're told Rob goes away to school at thirteen, when Nina is four, an age gap that raises difficult questions about who counts as a child.

The most accessible and culturally supportable interpretation is that the intimacy, pleasure, and empowerment Nina associates with her specifically female body is an innocent misunderstanding of trauma and transgression or an elaborate psychological defense against it. We can understand Rob's sexual exploitation of a toddler as carrying on a cycle of abuse initiated by his father. It is far more difficult to consider that both Nina and Rob have experiences that lie outside these meanings but could exist alongside them.

Offering helpful contexts in which to consider these difficult ideas, the book references the influence of Romanticism in the intricate present of the late twentieth century. Waking from a nap at age two to watch neighbor children laughing in the snow through a window against which she breathes the word "Romance," Nina's intuitive identification of the boy and girl's rough play as "Romance" ties the tales and situations of Rob's "hunter-prince" to the founding tropes of modern childhood: "Everything is in it. It is the word before the word she can pronounce or spell."[31] While we have inherited with little skepticism the Romantic idealization of the child (at once godly and innocent), cultural efforts to preserve this ideal, as Gayle Rubin suggests, strangely ignore many children's experiences of the expanded vision lost to adults through socialization. In Blake's *Songs of Innocence and Experience*, for example, innocent children see comfort and love in a world obviously miserable to the experienced, but the beliefs of the innocent, however discordant with adult culpability, are not supposed to be overturned by the experienced. One version of the world is not truer than the other. Blake's anti-dualist cosmology, his theopoetics, requires both to stay on the table.

Keeping both on the table, for Nina and for Dienstfrey, is a matter of experimental tools made for retrieval through "the laws of negotiation and forgiveness."[32] An earlier version of Nina's and Rob's incest appears in Dienstfrey's 1987 poetry collection *Small Salvations*. In the poem "The House Behind the Field," the adult speaker tries to figure out when the incest started, glancing briefly at her brother's motivation:

> on his way toward the dream of innocence
> I was closest to—
>   The youngest
>
> "Stoopie" my brother took
> as his own, some time
> in that sleep that's childhood
> before memory.
> [. . .]
> This has been spoken of publicly
> in the radiant civilization
> of my mind, in traffic
> no one sees.[33]

The poem speaks of childhood trauma in familiar terms and implies that what happened created a weighty and terrible family secret. Only in the paradoxical description of having told the secret "publicly / in the radiant civilization / of my mind" does the poem gesture toward the speaker's awareness that her experiences in "the sleep" before memory and language may hold something invisible in the colonizing light of civilization. The characterization of children's sexuality as only subjection and damage correlates with the stable genre of the poem.

The book's irregular form corresponds with its recovery of meanings lost in "traffic / no one sees," a goal stated explicitly. In "Writing Presence," a section within "Album of the Girlhoods of Nina Mansfield-Schorr and Simone Weil," Nina enters the narrative in the first person ("I enter here")[34] and announces intentions to make intelligible experiences suppressed through western individuation. The book states a main tenet of its theopoetics, that finding is creating:

> I am making an alphabet for the next step. To find the first letter is
> to create it. For this, I devise an act. I draw a circle, divide it in half
> and write it on the page facing two ways:
>
>   (
>   )
>
>   A body comes to the parting and surrounds it. Mouths open,vows
> are spoken and bonds cut.[35]

This first "letter" resembles both an "o" cut open, as if to keep ajar the door activated in the book's first passage, and a disabled parenthesis, redesigned to release enclosed meaning. The line "vows are spoken and bonds cut" explains the letter/act is capable of holding the paradoxical metaphors at the heart of the book's theopoetical vision that looking is finding and finding is creating. Dienstfrey's note explains another level of paradox in the word "cut," one that illustrates more precisely the power of Nina's alphabetic invention that can cut open "any other thing."[36] Instead of division and renunciation (disloyalty, divorce, estrangement), cutting bonds and binds: "In Biblical Hebrew, covenants were not 'made,' but 'cut' or 'passed through,' 'come into,' 'stood in.'"[37] Nina's ingenuities effect her conversion into a world of meanings more radiant than civilization's.

With this ability to open and to bind (to sort without losing) experience, Nina returns to preoccupations rooted in childhood that haunt her adult life. (My wording suggests causality the book's flowering form actually ignores.) Nina's relationship with her sons seems freighted with the loss of her own mother, Beatrice, who has died recently but was lost to Nina in moments throughout her childhood. Jealous and manipulative as the Old Testament God he quotes, Dr. Chester Mansfield rules over Nina and Beatrice with the force of his anger; he seems to have made his disobedient son, Rob, disappear at thirteen, sending him off to school and ordering his bedroom door closed for good. The tensions of growing up a sensual, "egregious" girl with a severe father caused Nina to develop an exclusive attachment to her mother that became an obligation to save her from Chester. Like Dante's Beatrice, Nina's mother is divine, the muse of Nina's childhood romance: "For Nina, at four years old, there is no goodness in the world unless it is Beatrice. . . . No one feeds Nina and nothing comforts her, unless her mother appears."[38] At ten, Nina sees herself as Beatrice's knight in shining armor who vows "[s]he will protect this lady" from her suffering, but "fails to save her, the one she / loves and who loves her—they share a common heart."[39]

Nina's sense of failure pervades her own mothering. Beatrice's goodness could be tasted in the bread she baked for her children, but Nina's children "taste her absence in the stew [she makes]: carrots and nothing, / onions and aporias."[40] In Nina's memory, Beatrice appears glowing and pure, like paintings of saints. To Nina, Beatrice and Christ are nearly the same, both folding her in the "Infinite Love"[41] of their sacrifices. Nina does not feel and cannot imitate this sort of love, maternal and divine, self-annihilating yet fully present. Defiant and led by her appetites, Nina only sometimes glimpses the woman she thought she was going to become[42] in the traces of Beatrice's memory.

When Nina enters *The Woman Without Experiences* in "Album of the Girlhoods of Nina Mansfield-Schorr and Simone Weil," she does so "as a girl who is looking" and as a woman asking, "How do I appear?" and "How do I care?"[43] Here, Nina threads her childhood through writings by and about Weil that combine in an obverse narrative of individuation and devotion. Nina grieves the theologian's self-effacement, especially the attenuation of her body through starvation and physical labor, in pursuit of God and in her flight from God. While Weil's family tried to spoil Simone, Nina's family was driven by fear of displeasing God with indulgence. Weil fed her belief through abstinence and self-denial, while Nina was pulled to abundance, always craving more. In the subsection titled "For the Beginning of an Album of Unmothered Pages / (A Variation on a Bouquet, Cut and Contained)," Nina usurps Weil's abject life governance:

> I work my scissors around the outline of your head. The circle fits the center of the absence we have created, the woman you would not become and the one I cannot follow. I affix your image to her surfaceless surface, an act of addition and invasion. It opens a doorway into a past and future that we share . . .[44]

In this moment, Nina, emerging as the God of her world and Weil's, cuts a picture of Weil's face from the cover of *Formative Writings: 1929–1941* and seizes the woman Weil refused to be, one Nina might have emulated. Seeing Weil as God sees, with all the possibilities of becoming in view, Nina creates an album in which her own girlhood is reassembled. Desecrating Weil's book in order to preserve Weil's discarded image among the folds of her own life, Nina brings onto the altar of maternity and selfhood the complexities of memory, character, parenting, and love excluded by the dualism father/tyrant and mother/sacrifice. The section's title references the flowers Chester raised and railed over when they did not grow as he wished. The only scene in which Chester is not threatening, "Father and Daughter in Reflected Light: Filled, Framed, Held," features a joyful young Nina sitting in her father's lap after dinner looking at the flowers he'd permitted her to pick arranged on the table, "a sign of our possible liberation."[45] In cutting Weil for her own bouquet (a trope for the book), Nina arrives at a new covenant of compassion through which she understands Chester's drive to overpower as a form of love.

Perhaps most importantly, Nina's achievement of presence that brings lost experience back to the table also deidealizes Beatrice. On the penultimate page, a strikingly different memory returns to Nina, the only one in which Beatrice does not appear beatific:

> She remembers coming home when she was twelve. She has been riding, and it is dark when she sets out across the field, her boots slipping on the frost. Ahead, the kitchen windows float above the fence, and her mother is pacing back and forth in a fury. "Why aren't they home? Why aren't they *in*? *Why aren't they all here by now?*" She stops and gives the pot a few vicious stirs.[46]

Through *The Woman Without Experiences*'s theopoetical album, Nina sees Beatrice perhaps as God sees, both inside and outside the house, as waiting mother and returning child, and this view restores her human dimensions. Citing David Miller, Keefe-Perry comments on the change of vision attending theopoetics: this perspective "means, especially, reading everything in life and work poetically. It does not mean stepping out of the depths through to anything else [but] walking through everything more deeply, seeing through life deeply."[47] Dienstfrey's theopoetics reminds us that reading the world poetically does not promise just to release more beauty in the world, although surely it does, but to bring a necessary confusion to our certainties, chinks in our ideals, and discomfiting realizations about a variety of human appetites, emotions, and practices. Nina's deidealization of Beatrice reminds us that unlocking the "infinite intricacies" of the world around us, however difficult, is a critical form of love.[48] As readers and writers of poetry, we take as our moral obligation the grinding of lenses, the opening of doors.

Notes

1. "About Kelsey Street." *Kelsey Street Press.*
2. Fraser, "Ideas as Architectures," 1–3.
3. Maso, "Escape Artist," 1.
4. Dienstfrey, *The Woman Without*, 3, 121.
5. Dienstfrey candidly discusses the book as inspired by her own experience in the 1970s as a mother with three young children, but the book is not an autobiography or memoir.
6. Dienstfrey, *Woman Without*, 7.
7. Dienstfrey, *Woman Without*, 107.
8. Dienstfrey, *Woman Without*, 6.
9. Retallack, "What is Experimental Poetry," para 36, 12,
10. Dienstfrey, *Woman Without*, 69.
11. Scott, "The Evidence of Experience," 404.
12. Keefe-Perry, "Theopoetics: Process and Perspective," 579–580.
13. Joan Retallack, "The Experimental Feminine," 98.
14. Dienstfrey, *Woman Without*, 6.
15. Dienstfrey, *Woman Without*, 8.
16. Dienstfrey, *Woman Without*, 8.
17. Dienstfrey, *Woman Without*, 8.
18. Dienstfrey, *Woman Without*, 5.
19. Dienstfrey, *Woman Without*, 84.
20. Dienstfrey, *Woman Without*, 48.
21. Dienstfrey, *Woman Without*, 101, Dienstfrey's ellipsis.
22. Dienstfrey, *Woman Without*, 4.
23. Dienstfrey, *Woman Without*, 7.
24. Dienstfrey, *Woman Without* 7, Dienstfrey's emphasis.
25. Retallack, "Feminine," 96.
26. Romana Huk, "A single liturgy": Fanny Howe's *The Wedding Dress*," *Christianity and Literature* 58, no. 4 (2009): 658. Huk is characterizing Fanny Howe's "a/theological poetics" in this statement, but the conversion of human sight and judgment to see as God sees or to find new values and meanings themselves a revelation of divine presence applies to Dienstfrey's work and echoes through discussions of other theopoetical projects.
27. Dienstfrey, *Woman Without*, 28.
28. Dienstfrey, *Woman Without*, 14.
29. Gayle Rubin, "Thinking Sex," 20, 24.
30. Dienstfrey, *Woman Without*, 29.
31. Dienstfrey, *Woman Without*, 9. "Romance" suggests, of course, the Latinate family of languages, too, but the context of playing children and Nina's almost supernatural understanding of the word makes the religious, political, and literary force more relevant in this instant.
32. Dienstfrey, *Woman Without*, 40.
33. Dienstfrey, *Small Salvations*, n.p.
34. Dienstfrey, *Woman Without*, 55.
35. Dienstfrey, *Woman Without*, 69.
36. Dienstfrey, *Woman Without*, 69.
37. Dienstfrey, *Woman Without*, n 124.
38. Dienstfrey, *Woman Without*, 23.

39. Dienstfrey, *Woman Without*, 31.
40. Dienstfrey, *Woman Without*, 98.
41. Dienstfrey, *Woman Without*, 63.
42. Dienstfrey, *Woman Without*, 71.
43. Dienstfrey, *Woman Without*, 55.
44. Dienstfrey, *Woman Without*, 71.
45. Dienstfrey, *Woman Without*, 59. The resurrection of Chester as not a despot but as a loving parent also happens when Nina conducts a drag show in which she dresses up in her father's clothes and gold watch as Dr. Nina Mansfield-Schorr and goes on rounds, inspecting her sons approvingly. Dienstfrey, *Woman Without*, 32.
46. Dienstfrey, *Woman Without*, 120.
47. Keefe-Perry, 586.
48. Love, "Truth and Consequences," 249. I am grateful to Heather Love for this welcome insight, which comes from an essay in which Love calls for a more complex reading of mentor Eve Kosofsky Sedgwick's writing: "Recognizing that it is not only reparation but damage at work in Sedgwick's late essays will let us begin the hard work of deidealization. And that's love too."

Bibliography

"About Kelsey Street." *Kelsey Street Press*. Accessed July 21 2011. http://www .kelseyst.com/about.htm.

Dienstfrey, Patricia. *Small Salvations*. Berkeley: Kelsey Street Press, 1987.

Dienstfrey, Patricia. *The Woman Without Experiences*. Berkeley: Kelsey Street Press, 1995.

Fraser, Kathleen. "Ideas as Architectures: A Talk with Patricia Dienstfrey." *Poetry Flash* 268, 1996, 1–3.

Huk, Romana. "A single liturgy": Fanny Howe's *The Wedding Dress*." *Christianity and Literature* 58, no. 4 (2009): 657–693.

Keefe-Perry, L.B.C, "Theopoetics: Process and Perspective." *Christianity and Literature* 58, no. 4 (2009): 579–601.

Kinnahan, Linda A. *Lyric Interventions: Feminism, Experimental Poetry, and Contemporary Discourse*. Iowa City: Iowa University Press, 2004.

Love, Heather. "Truth and Consequences: On Paranoid and Reparative Reading." *Criticism*, 52, no. 2 (2010): 235–249.

Maso, Carole. "Escape Artist," *The Woman Without Experiences* by Patricia Dienstfrey," *Women's Review of Books* 13, no. 10–11 (1996).

Retallack, Joan. *The Poethical Wager*. Berkeley: University of California Press, 2003.

Retallack, Joan. "What is Experimental Poetry & Why Do We Need It?" *Jacket Magazine* 32 (2007). Accessed February 2, 2011. http://jacketmagazine .com/32/p-retallack.shtml.

Rubin, Gayle S. "Thinking Sex." In *The Lesbian and Gay Studies Reader*, edited by Henry Abelove, Michele Aina Barale, and David M. Halperin, 3–44. New York: Routledge, 1993.

Scott, Joan W. "The Evidence of Experience." In *The Lesbian and Gay Studies Reader*, edited by Henry Abelove, Michele Aina Barale, & David M. Halpern, 397–415. New York: Routledge, 1993.

"The Woman Without Experiences." *Publishers Weekly* (review). January 2, 1995. http://www.publishersweekly.com/978-0-932716-37-8.

Porous and Continuous with the World

Mei-Mei Berssenbrugge's Four Year Old Girl

Sasha Steensen

> "I think a lot about fate and if and how it can be changed. I've had so much experience with illness that I came to see it as a crisis of being. And I began thinking of how not to pass on illness to my (then) four-year-old daughter Martha. My poem ("The Four Year Old Girl") is the result of being desperately sick and trying to figure out a way spiritually to overcome illness."
> —Mei-Mei Berssenbrugge[1]

> "The charge of the parent and poet is to live on the unraveled edges of death and stitch them together as regeneration."
> —Elizabeth Robinson[2]

Mei-Mei Berssenbrugge's poem, "The Four Year Old Girl," and by extension, the larger book in which it appears, are concerned with mothering, illness, fate, and spirituality.[3] The book begins with a paradox central, but not exclusive, to motherhood. It is the paradox of the transient being thinking, experiencing, perceiving, existences that exceed her without "annulling their transcendence."[4] What is a mother if not someone who recognizes the transitory nature of herself and her child, but struggles to assure the child's longevity? In *Four Year Old Girl*, Berssenbrugge, while recognizing the inevitable death of both mother and child, explores ways of prolonging life, of "spiritually... overcom[ing] illness," and in doing so, she glimpses an afterlife. While the mother knows that "Each girl is transitory," she desires to "see the world as implicit promise, something human that leaves the body at death and goes off on its own."[5] This paradox, this possibility that something *of* us *exceeds* us, is felt keenly during pregnancy, birthing, and nurturing a child. Mothering, both because of its biological and quotidian circumstances, is a state in which selfhood is experienced as permeable and interdependent at one moment, and painfully discrete the next. But this is not unlike the paradox facing the poet. Words miss and meet their mark, fail and exceed their intentions. The mother-child relationship serves as a useful metaphor for Berssenbrugge as she works through the dynamic interplay of signification. Megan Simpson, commenting on several passages from the book's poem "Daughters," observes: "These passages taken together seem to suggest that mother-child relations function as a meaning-making process or problem, even partaking of the gap which always exists between signifier and signified."[6]

The work of the poet and the work of the parent are the same work, a work of regeneration in the face of certain obliteration. Because, according to Berssenbrugge, "discourse on death contains a rhetoric of borders," she turns her attention to these "unraveled edges."[7] It is crucial that these borders are "unraveled," that they are not clearly delineated. The poet recognizes the borders and edges as not merely actual, but as a function of language, as "rhetoric[al]." Just as mother and child work in symbiotic extension of one another, in Berssenbrugge's considerations, so do life and death, immanence and transcendence. Berssenbrugge is searching for a way to account for the subtlety of these relations, and when she glimpses the many "misty, lighted edge[s]" that populate *Four Year Old Girl*, she hesitates before she names. She writes, "It makes me hesitate, as between poles of an alternative, like a peacock, the way nonduality looks in the face of her longing, to a mother inconsolable before a blessing."[8] This sentence is characteristic of what Berssenbrugge describes as a line that asks the reader to "keep letting go and surrender themselves to the language or the dynamics of the poem."[9] While Berssenbrugge employs long sentence-lines because "you can't grasp the whole line in your mind," these lines are also restless, displaying a chain of comparison that both relishes in analogy and doubts its accuracy.[10] Hesitation *and* restlessness.

For the reader, many questions arise: *who* or *what* is between two poles; *who* or *what* is being compared to a peacock; *what* looks like non-duality in the face of *whose* longing; and is the mother inconsolable *prior to* a blessing or *in the face of* a blessing? These are not questions that find answers; these are questions that restlessly proliferate, reverberate. What Berssenbrugge offers in the space of this hesitation is an alternative to oppositional thinking, one that need not choose between transcendence and immanence, but instead relies on relational interplay and seeks an "interaction between an ethereal object and an organism."[11] As Charles Alitieri notes, Berssenbrugge proposes that "spirit becomes manifest as the folding and unfolding of surfaces that we produce as we engage in various relationships."[12]

For Berssenbrugge, any consideration of "spirit" must start with a consideration of the body and the "folding and unfolding of surfaces" that contact the body. This imperative leads Berssenbrugge to consider the ways in which scientific language might help her explore the permeability of subjectivity. In a dialogue with Charles Bernstein, she notes:

> I first used scientific concepts, because it seemed interesting to try and feminize scientific language by altering its context and tone. This was in the late '70s. Later, I appropriated texts from philosophy, Buddhism and contemporary art as well. A self encompassing or embodying what it interacts with was more articulate than trying to speak for myself. This is the literal situation of our bodies which are porous and continuous with the world. Tom White told me, after a few days in the Sierras, one's internal flora has more in common with the surrounding pine trees than with people back in Berkeley.[13]

Though a detailed investigation of Berssenbrugge's use of scientific texts is outside of the scope of this essay, it is important to note that when she herself addresses this topic, she does so in terms that help us further understand the nature of her interest in nondualistic thinking. While she began using scientific language so as to "feminize" a traditionally masculine discourse, by the late '70s, the use of scientific language helped her to "create a continuum between the abstract and the concrete, a continuum between the material and the immaterial—to make a world like that."[14] Again, for Berssenbrugge, the figure of the mother—someone who is both intimately tied to, and undeniably separate from her child—illustrates the nature of the continuous, relational world Berssenbrugge hopes to re-present in her poems. In her "Eighty-Five Notes," a selection of passages on maternity and motherhood, she writes, "The mother is anonymous and social as language, but simultaneously concrete, filled with specific content, with many locations and identity of forces."[15] The expansive nature of the mother allows for a continuum in which binaries—abstract and concrete, individual and collective, transcendent and immanent, among others—might be reconfigured as continuous and interactive. In such a reconfiguration, "energy is continually dispersed along the web of the inter-relation."[16] In *Four Year Old Girl*, the material and the spiritual worlds are so interwoven that any attempt to distinguish one from the other is not only misguided, it is futile. Instead, our attention is turned to the dynamics of inter-relation.

Many images in *Four Year Old Girl* are characterized by this interplay, but none more so than the flower. Flowers spring up on nearly every page of the book. While flowers have long been associated with female sexuality and reproduction, more important for Berssenbrugge is the flower's symbiotic relationship to its environment. She writes, "When I look at a blossom, I'm surprised how it reverberates between something going from it to its context and something coming from this context."[17] The flower, an organism that relies on pollinators for reproduction, presents us with a model of inter-relation that beautifully illustrates the interactive and continuous world Berssenbrugge experiences and aims to articulate. The flower's "reverberat[ion]" of exchange promises the continuation of life. But what is this "context" that both feeds and is fed by the blossom? Beyond our understanding of "context" as the conditions or environment in which something exists or occurs, the word's etymology is rooted in the Latin contextus, "connection," and contextere, "to weave together." The reciprocal connection between flower and environment constructs a continuous texture in which one thread cradles, and is cradled by, the other. In the section "Pollen," Berssenbrugge writes, "An orange cliff holds the light, concave and convex from wind, as between alive and not alive, the boundary of a person touching you, as if the person were moisture leaving air, skin's respiration. You hold her, like pollen in the air, gold and durable, more like a dry spring that continues holding sky."[18] Just as the flower, like all plants, breathes, breaking down the barrier between itself and its environment, the boundary between self and other is permeable. Berssenbrugge looks at the relation between cliff and light, pollen and air, wind and land, life and death, self and other, and sees that these relations, reverberating with simultaneity and similarity ("as between;" "like a dry spring"), are not two-fold, but manifold.

How, then, can one "hold" the entirety of any one person, or any one thing? Just as dry air can hold pollen only until it begins to rain, holding the other is temporary. In the first section of "Daughter," subtitled "The Dream," Berssenbrugge writes, "holding her face in my hands is holding a bowl from where I was born."[19] Though Berssenbrugge has commented that the four-year-old girl of this book is actually herself as a four year old, it is obvious that mothering, and in particular, "thinking of how not to pass on illness to my (then) four-year-old daughter Martha" is at the heart of this book.[20] Additionally, Berssenbrugge adds, "finding a way to spiritually overcome [her own] illness" was just as crucial.[21] The interchangeability of mother and child suggests that the child's survival depends, in part, upon the mother's survival. But it isn't only that Berssenbrugge wants to physically overcome illness by becoming healthy; she wants to spiritually overcome illness. If, to recall Altieri's quote, Berssenbrugge proposes that "spirit becomes manifest as the folding and unfolding of surfaces that we produce as we engage in various relationships," then treating illness spiritually requires an attunement to the dynamics of relation.[22] The surfaces we produce are not simply those that have actual weight in the material world, but they are the weighty presences of "empathy," "love," and "compassion," to use words that appear again and again in Berssenbrugge's work. Toward the end of her meditation on motherhood, Berssenbrugge writes, "she and I together form the other for matter."[23] The mother-child relationship, while clearly transitory, also produces something—"the other for matter—" which endures. The "bowl" in which the speaker holds the girl's "face in her hands" emerges again a few lines later, still in the context of the dream: "The bowl represents his feeling for the immanent structure of what appears delicate and vulnerable, but almost inorganic, like feathers."[24]

Again, this restless sentence complicates our tendencies toward dualistic thinking and forces us as readers to question the interplay between the material and the immaterial, the transcendent and the immanent, the self and the other. The bowl here is not necessarily an actual bowl made of matter; as a function of the dreaming mind, it represents feeling, it holds. And yet, it does not represent the speaker's feeling, but rather it represents his feeling "for the immanent structure" of something that "appears delicate and vulnerable." This unnamed "something" is "almost inorganic," and it is "like feathers." Immanence, or divine presence, if locatable at all, seems to be "continually dispersed along the web of the inter-relation."[25] And unlike our conventional depiction of divinity as eternal, this immanence is associated, at least in appearance, with vulnerability. While the mother-child relationship is characterized by interdependence, vulnerability lurks at the heart of this symbiotic affair. In fact, relationships of all kinds are dynamic, synergistic, and subject to destruction. Berssenbrugge uses the mother-child relationship as a model because it has important implications for all relationships. As Megan Simpson notes, "what makes Berssenbrugge's treatment of motherhood in these poems especially compelling is that the poetry represents an act of thinking about mothering at the same time that it is a thinking through, from the perspective of, mothering . . . Berssenbrugge has succeeded in producing a poetic maternal discourse of radical relationality."[26] And it is only through this "radical relationality," through this "folding and unfolding of surfaces that we produce as we engage in various relationships" that the spirit might become manifest.[27]

And what role does language play in this manifestation of spirit? Does language ornament, communicate, distort, initiate, or belittle this manifestation? According to Berssenbrugge, "No one can describe the relation between an experience that needs to be communicated and the form of that communication."[28] By no means a description of this relation, Berssenbrugge does suggest that representation of an experience and its beautification are part and parcel of one another—a dream, a feeling, a thought is "beautiful because of my attempt to contain it."[29] It is, then, the impossibility of representation that makes these attempts beautiful, and so Berssenbrugge relishes in language that draws attention to the restlessness of reference. She writes, "The angel's ribbon fell across her eyes while she was looking at something, like light over a wide part in the river, and like the pink wall of a house through buds of the trees. It was like these two things, the way yellow fruit is like a feeling, though this color changes."[30] In such a passage riddled with similes, the vehicle and the tenor shift places, reach outward, then inward, then expand, mimicking the web of inter-relation at the heart of this book. And when she looks at the material world, the angel's ribbon does not so much obstruct her view as offer access to something normally out of view. The ribbon, like light on the river, allows her to see all the more clearly. These are not similes that transfer once; they transfer and transfer again. The simile, for Berssenbrugge, is a linguistic structure that mirrors the process whereby an individual comes in contact with her world. The simile has the potential to serve as messenger, carrying from speaker to reader, the ineffable experience of interrelation that is a crucial component of Berssenbrugge's spirituality.

In Greek mythology, Iris, messenger goddess of golden wings and swift feet, is the embodiment of inter-relation. Just as the flower reverberates with connectivity to its environment, Iris assiduously carries messages in all directions, from gods to mortals, from mortals to gods, and from gods to gods. Though her name means "the speaker or messenger," according to the classical scholar Sir William Smith, "it is not impossible that it may be connected with eirô, 'I join,' whence eirênê; so that Iris, the goddess of the rainbow, would be the joiner or conciliator, or the messenger of heaven, who restores peace in nature."[31] Evoking both goddess and flower, Berssenbrugge begins *Four Year Old Girl* with a poem entitled "Irises," in which she writes, "The more wispy the mind, as at the edge of greenness of a dogwood blossom, the more fit to catch sight of such an invisible entity as 'parallel,' its distinct substance capable of having all mountains thought away and still being around."[32] As messenger, Iris resides both in the human and the divine worlds, cultivating a mind that sees the substance of an invisible entity.

This ability is hers because she appears and disappears in the space of a moment, not unlike the rainbow with which she is associated. In Iris's charge, language joins the material and the immaterial worlds so that they are no longer distinct, creating a "continuum between the abstract and the concrete, a continuum between the material and the immaterial."[33] Similarly, Iris's mobility between the human and divine worlds suggests that the material and the spiritual, rather than existing at some distance from one another, are in fact intimately connected. If the divine—neither immanent nor transcendent—brings much to be bear on the physical world, then perhaps Berssenbrugge might realize her desire to "spiritually overcome illness."

But this is not the same as escaping death. In fact, just as the mother's body becomes vulnerable to make room for the child, as the book proceeds, Berssenbrugge's speaker commits herself to inevitable death. While the book begins with Iris, messenger goddess, it ends with Kali, a Hindu goddess of death. Associated with destruction, darkness, and power, Kali's appearance at the end of *Four Year Old Girl* might seem surprising. But Kali offers her devotees an opportunity to confront death, and to overcome, not its reality, but its terror. The question, for Berssenbrugge, is not so much what Kali represents as what she brings forth, and this is true for *Four Year Old Girl* as well. "The poem," Berssenbrugge writes, "presents a situation with various kinds of darkness, but it only generates a love."[34] According to David Kinsley, author of *The Sword and the Flute: Dark Visions of the Terrible and the Sublime in Hindu Mythology*, the same could be said of Kali. He writes:

> The boon granted to him who confronts Kali, as already suggested, is that of things as they really are and the consequent tendency or ability to see beyond the finite destiny of an ego-centered life.... From this point of view, Kali's overall presence may be understood as benign. Her raised and bloodied sword suggests the death of ignorance, her disheveled hair suggests the freedom of release, and her girdle of severed arms may suggest the end of grasping.[35]

Or, as Berssenbrugge notes, "Black means she's unknown by people full of ignorance, since it stands for their ignorance."[36] To confront Kali is to worship her and receive her protection, the reward of which is a release from ignorance and fear. These incredible gifts—the gifts of courage, protection, knowledge—are the gifts the mother gives the child, and thus Kali is also figured as a mother goddess capable of nurturing and sustaining life. In one myth, Kali, celebrating success on the battlefield, hears baby Shiva's cry and spots him lying beside her slain victims. Instantly calmed, Kali embraces the baby and nurses him, moving, in the space of a moment, from taking life to saving it. Like the parent and the poet, Kali "live[s] on the unraveled edges of death . . . stitch[ing] them together as regeneration."[37] In this final section, Berssenbrugge writes, "Experience of her shifts like a pronoun or originary transcendence and is specified through some other thing, surface of emergence (motherhood, environment)."[38] It is not clear whether this "she" is Kali, the four-year-old girl, or the mother, but what is clear is that the speaker's experience of the "she" is one that undergoes transformation and is specified only via comparison. It is a relation that she cannot articulate without seeing it in terms of "some other thing," equally hard to name. The shifting pronoun here, and elsewhere in the book, is a function of Berssenbrugge's recognition of interrelation, in which our bodies are "porous and continuous with the world."[39]

This recognition comes with much difficulty; it is not uncommon for us to imagine ourselves as separate and distinct from those around us. But Berssenbrugge's illness, her maternity, and not least of all, her work as a poet, demonstrate that this sense of our existence is inaccurate. As Robert Duncan writes, "the 'our,' 'my,' 'us,' 'we,' 'I,' 'me' of the poet's work, and the other 'you,' 'your,' 'they,' 'them,' are pronouns of play, members or persons of a world drama in division. These are no more at liberty, no more seek liberty than they pursue happiness."[40] Like Berssenbrugge's "she" whose identity constantly shifts, Duncan's pronouns are part of a "chorus," not because he seeks harmony, but because this world—neither spiritual nor material, but both at once—is characterized by, even built upon, this "web of the inter-relation." In this way, the child and mother extend into each other; the choruses of birthing and burying sing similar songs.

Notes

1. Tabios, "Interview with Mei-Mei Berssenbrugge," 134.
2. Elizabeth Robinson, "Gaps, Overflow, Linkage," 259.
3. Tabios, *Black Lightning*, 134. Berssenbrugge often uses fate and spirituality interchangeably, as in the following quote, also referencing *The Four Year Old Girl*, "I was really trying to mix up the spiritual—considerations of fate—and the hard rock of genetics."
4. Berssenbrugge, 11.
5. Berssenbrugge, *Four Year Old Girl*, 12.
6. Simpson, "Mei-Mei Berssenbrugge's *The Four Year Old Girl* and the Phenomenology of Mothering," 9
7. Berssenbrugge, *Four Year Old Girl*, 59.
8. Berssenbrugge, *Four Year Old Girl*, 66.
9. Tabios, *Black Lightning*, 144.
10. Tabios, *Black Lightning*, 144.
11. Berssenbrugge, *Four Year Old Girl*, 23.
12. Altieri, "Intimacy and Experiment in Mei-Mei Berssenbrugge's *Empathy*," 1
13. Bernstein and Berssenbrugge, "A Dialogue."
14. Tabios, *Black Lightning*, 137.
15. Mei-Mei Berssenbrugge, "Eighty-Five Notes," 214.
16. Berssenbrugge, "Eighty-Five Notes," 216.
17. Berssenbrugge, *Four Year Old Girl*, 67.
18. Berssenbrugge, *Four Year Old Girl*, 67.
19. Berssenbrugge, *Four Year Old Girl*, 21.
20. Tabios, *Black Lightning*, 134.
21. As Megan Simpson writes of "Four Year Old Girl": "while the poem is not unproblematically or transparently 'about' the poet's experience mothering her four year old, it is nonetheless steeped in concerns that originate in that relationship." And, as I will argue later, the ambiguity of the pronoun "she" in many sections of this book serves to remind us of the "porous and continuous" nature of the mother-child relationship.
22. Altieri, "Intimacy and Experiment in Mei-Mei Berssenbrugge's *Empathy*."
23. Berssenbrugge, "Eighty-Five Notes," 216.
24. Berssenbrugge, *Four Year Old Girl*, 21.
25. Berssenbrugge, "Eighty-Five Notes," 216.
26. Simpson, "Mei-Mei Berssenbrugge's *Four Year Old Girl*."
27. Altieri, "Intimacy and Experiment in Mei-Mei Berssenbrugge's *Empathy*."
28. Berssenbrugge, *Four Year Old Girl*, 15.
29. Berssenbrugge, *Four Year Old Girl*, 11.
30. Berssenbrugge, *Four Year Old Girl*, 22.
31. William Smith, ed., *Dictionary of Greek and Roman Biography and Mythology*, 621.
32. Berssenbrugge, *Four Year Old Girl*, 12.
33. Tabios, *Black Lightning*, 137.
34. Tabios, *Black Lightning*, 140.
35. Kinsley, *Sword and the Flute*, 143.
36. Berssenbrugge, *Four Year Old Girl*, 71.
37. Robinson, "Gaps, Overflow, Linkage."
38. Berssenbrugge, *Four Year Old Girl,* 73.
39. Bernstein and Berssenbrugge, "A Dialogue."
40. Duncan, *The H.D. Book*, 560.

Bibliography

Altieri, Charles. "Intimacy and Experiment in Mei-Mei Berssenbrugge's *Empathy.*" *Electronic Poetry Center*. State University of New York. http://epc .buffalo.edu/authors/berssenbrugge/altieri.html

Bernstein, Charles and Mei-Mei Berssenbrugge, "A Dialogue." *Electronic Poetry Center*. State University of New York. http://epc.buffalo.edu/authors /berssenbrugge/bernstein.html

Berssenbrugge, Mei-Mei. *Four Year Old Girl*. Berkeley: Kelsey Street Press, 1998.

Berssenbrugge, Mei-Mei. "Eighty-Five Notes." In *Grand Permission: New Writings on Poetics and Motherhood*, edited by Patricia Dientsfrey and Brenda Hillman, 211–216. Middletown: Wesleyan University Press, 2003.

Duncan, Robert. *The H.D. Book*. Berkeley: University of California Press, 2011.

Kinsley, David. *The Sword and the Flute: Dark Visions of the Terrible and the Sublime in Hindu Mythology*. Berkeley: University of California Press, 2000.

Robinson, Elizabeth. "Gaps, Overflow, Linkage: A Synesthesiac Look at Motherhood and Writing." In *Grand Permission: New Writings on Poetics and Motherhood*, edited by Patricia Dientsfrey and Brenda Hillman, 255–262. Middletown: Wesleyan University Press, 2003.

Simpson, Megan. "Mei-Mei Berssenbrugge's *Four Year Old Girl* and the Phenomenology of Mothering." *Women's Studies* 32, no. 4, (2003) http://www .tandfonline.com/doi/abs/10.1080/00497870310089.

Simpson, Megan. *Poetic Epistemologies: Gender and Knowing in Women's Language-Oriented Writing*. Albany: State University of New York Press, 2000.

Smith, William, ed. A Dictionary of Greek and Roman Biography and Mythology. Vol. 2. New York: AMS Press, 1967.

Tabios, Eileen, ed. *Black Lightning: Poetry-in-Progress*. New York: Asian American Writers Workshop, 1998.

part iv.

all things leave themselves behind

Beginning with a Dark House
poetic statement by Beverly Dahlen

> As always, in memory of my grandmother
> Mary Magdalene Swanson Dahlen
>
> and with gratitude for the work of Dr. Sigmund Freud,
> Dr. Elaine Pagels, and the poet H.D.
>
> Beverly Dahlen, September 8–28, 2012

In the photographic replica of a dark house a light suddenly goes on and my friend says, "That's spiritual!" I think, but don't say, it's probably just someone going to the bathroom. But of course it's nothing one can know. It's a sort of movie or video in the museum. And we walk on. But I have been thinking about it all this time (it happened years ago) and now here it is again. The memory of a light going on in a dark house: someone going to the bathroom.

Do we always think of the spiritual in visual terms as a light, or even a great light, a sudden revelation?

What about the darkness, then, the visions of the other side of light, the negative, the dark, which is the sign of evil. Martin Luther was struck with a vision while sitting on a toilet. He saw that the Pope was the Devil. He linked evil with shit. Dirt. And that vision was also a spiritual vision, one that ultimately propelled the Protestant revolution.

*

We walk upright and too far from the ground to know the smell of shit, to sniff a message as dogs do instinctively. We have a sense of the blue sky, clouds, stars, even angels, invisible beings. *The Heads of the Town Up to the Aether.*

A lost Gnostic work.

By their works ye shall know them. It turns and turns. So who would you count a spiritual adviser or mentor or teacher? That "you" in the first place, which signifies "I" and there, is a clue. The "I" that is another, the ego that Freud deconstructed and showed us was a fragmentary entity, not exactly an illusion, but something not quite real either. Real? What is the Real. And here I am reminded of the first words of my work called *A Reading*: "before that and before that. everything in a line. where it was broken into, the house. not a body but still I could not see that it didn't have a roof." In the Freudian tradition of free association, this image arose, and it was the image of the playhouse my father built for my sister and me when we were children. When the playhouse was half-finished I took my dolls inside and left them overnight. And because it rained in the night, my dolls were ruined. There were "lines" for the roof, that is, beams in place, but no roof. The lines represented a roof to me, as they would have in a drawing, but the house was open to the elements.

Piaget's theory of the development of cognitive ability includes a period when children have not yet grasped logic fully. He calls it a time when we perceive "semi-logically."

It seems to me that this event, this trauma, really, arose from my inability then to see fully and logically. *When I was a child I thought as a child.*

*

Coming back to the quotation: "not a body . . ." Not a body broken into, but a house broken into by rain. Is the body a house? Do we, did I, think of the house as a body?

This is my body. As children, we had a sense of the integrity of our bodies. I had that sense. And if the body is narcissistically also the house, then there was "something to cry about" and the babies, my dolls, were ruined by the rain. The rain which came in the night and broke into the house.

"before that and before that . . ." A regression into the past, "a regression in the service of the ego" (Freud). Because the ego for all its illusoriness is *something*, a social construct, who we are in the world.

The ego learns to speak, and to read, and to write. It learns family and friends and all sorts of complicated social relationships as it grows. But the body is silent and that silence is a mystery among many mysteries. Where it came from, why it's here. Why does it disappear? Where does it go? A child may lie awake at night and wonder about these things. They are, though the child may not know it at the time, philosophical questions, even the most fundamental questions. Heidegger asks, "Why are there *essents* rather than nothing?"

Why? The forbidden question.

When I was in my teens, I joined a Baptist church. I was very active in my church. I sang in the choir, I went to service on Sundays and met with my youth group every week. I read Scripture, I listened closely to the sermons. And then one day, on my way home from school, it all fell apart for me. I stood stock still on the sidewalk and thought *God is not just.* I may even have said it aloud, I was so struck by the thought that Jesus would say "no man cometh to the Father except by me." What about everyone else? Would all Muslims, Buddhists, Hindus, etc. etc., be condemned to Hell?

Why? There is no justice in Heaven.

And that was pretty much the end of my life in an organized church. But there had been an opening to poetry and that had happened several years before. It had come to me quite suddenly as I was walking down the street a block or so from home. The poem had come as a "dictation," perhaps not in Jack Spicer's sense, but still it was not *my* poem; I was simply a medium for the poem. I did not hear a voice but I knew what the poem was and I went home and wrote it. It was a real poem. (Creeley: "Is that a real poem or did you just make it up?") And then there were no more poems, at least not poems that were given to me. That gift, or grace, does not often occur. I went back to writing "made-up" poems, romantic fantasies. I had been reading E. A. Poe, and the influence was clear, though not to me at the time. After I showed these verses to a teacher, she said, "This is all very well, but why don't you write about something you know?" Every young poet has to be told that at some point. Poetry must also be grounded in reality. So I wrote, in great detail, about the bus ride home from school.

It was not until I began college that I met a professor, a teacher who would influence my writing, probably for most of my life afterward. He was Reginald White and he was a Freudian. He introduced me to the idea of writing in a freely-associative way, to begin in silence, *this is my body*, and to write, without editing, almost without thinking, the words which come to mind, one after another. Of course, Freud had always credited the poets with having discovered "the unconscious." So the poet turns, and the process of writing becomes part of the project of the "return of the repressed." That unspeakable, even unthinkable task.

One, that "I" seeks for revelation, the spiritual (to call it that) which is some part of the truth as it occurs to "I."

*

To end it. Whose body? My body, but also the body of Christ, in whose memory we commune with one another, but also in memory of the broken bodies of the gods Dionysus, Osiris, with the dead in Hades, unnamable. The end. "Surely I come quickly. Amen. Even so, come, Lord Jesus."

"And now it may be expected that the other of the two 'heavenly forces,' eternal Eros, will put forth his strength so as to maintain himself alongside of his equally immortal adversary."

Sigmund Freud: *Civilization and its Discontents*.

The last words.

Empty Sleeve
poem by Kimberly Lyons

If your silence wraps the chilly hour

of 7 am and tints it violet

and gray and silver

then, the sound of breathing as I walk

intrudes. Silence, plus thought,

pink cherry blossoms plus cigarette smoke

blue cement under brown shoe.

I still feel hope

which is a concentrated aquamarine

the variegated water the fish

is placed within a mosaic on a wall.

Still, yet representing motion.

Or maybe the glittering segments lock the creature in.

Is it Christos? I don't know

Why you don't write or call.

Same as him who says: I am here, I am with you.

But where? Always ahead and behind

just seen by guys up the road

who told the story last night in the bar.

It's the fragment held by a few threads

to the larger body

of the Gnostic cloth

that I remember this morning

as though the essential message, what you

meant for me to know,

is the empty sleeve

the color of reddish early dirt

someone's small garden in the shadow

as I pass by.

Mysticpoetics
Writing the Alchemical Self in Brenda Hillman's Poetry
Jennifer Phelps

Brenda Hillman's poetry circumnavigates around the overarching interest of spirit, matter, and everything in between. Even though Hillman's work is often uncategorizable, she works within a vein that combines traditional lyric as well as more experimental forms. In addition, she incorporates various theologies and esoteric philosophies in her writing. Hillman has said of herself, "I think of myself as a mystic in a practical way."[1] Hillman blends cultural references, nature, and the spiritual with an open lyric form that leaves room for mystical experiences to occur on the page. Hillman's poetry can be read as enacting an alchemical process where spirit is turned into matter and matter into spirit.

Hillman is often deemed "a school of one" because "her poems can maddeningly lurch from the sacred to the profane, from the most quotidian and anecdotal writing to passages of darkly brooding gravity."[2] Yet despite her use of innovative form, she still identifies herself as a lyric poet: "I've never left the lyric behind. I've not only been influenced by lyric, I am a lyric poet."[3] Playing with lyric and innovation, Hillman sets aside all assumption of how poetry has been written previously to do something new. Through experiments with form, Hillman disrupts assumptions of what poetry is. She creates a sense of bafflement by juxtaposing ordinary events in her poems with the imaginative and mysterious. Fanny Howe calls this a poetics of "bewilderment," where one composes in a state of wonder, awe, and disorientation.[4] A poetics of bewilderment can also be understood within the terms of what psychologist Carl G. Jung (1875–1961) describes as a way of uncovering true uniqueness: "If I want to understand an individual human being, I must lay aside all scientific knowledge of the average man and discard all theories in order to adopt a completely new and unprejudiced attitude."[5] Hillman has a similar theory of composition: "The place where we make poetry is outside any familiar state. Poetry sort of makes us stranger so we can wake up in a place where everything hangs off the edges, creating itself."[6]

Carl Jung and Brenda Hillman

Jung developed a model of the psyche with an organizing center known as the self: "The self is not only the centre, but also the whole circumference which embraces both conscious and unconscious; it is the centre of this totality, just as the ego is the centre of consciousness."[7] His concept of the self was revolutionary because Jung claimed that humans carry an element of the divine within their psyches and that the goal of one's life should be the search for selfhood, which is known as the process of individuation:

> Individuation means becoming an "in-dividual," and, in so far as "individuality" embraces our innermost, last, and incomparable uniqueness, it also implies becoming one's own self. We could therefore translate individuation as "coming to selfhood" or "self-realization."[8]

Jung's conception of self-knowledge, however, is not to be understood in a rational sense, but rather in a divine sense—discovering and integrating the spiritual into one's life. This union can bring about a more fulfilling communion with the larger world. His model includes various stages in which a person gains specific knowledge about one's soul; at the center of this inner work is the ongoing formulation of a unique self and creating a relationship with that self, and this lifelong process may never be entirely realized. Jeff Raff, a contemporary Jungian analyst, reminds us that "the formation of the self is never fully complete, for there always remains material not yet integrated into (or harmonized by) the center."[9]

Jung provided a map for the psyche by categorizing it into parts, with the ego as the center of consciousness and the self as the center of personality which includes both conscious (the ego) and unconscious impulses. Jung's unconscious consists of both a personal level or "contents that . . . lost their intensity and were forgotten"[10] and a collective level or "the ancestral heritage of possibilities of representation . . . common to all men, and perhaps even to all animals, [that] is the true basis of the individual psyche." The collective unconscious includes archetypes—images or figures—that "give form to countless typical experiences of our ancestors. They are, so to speak, the psychic residua of innumerable experiences of the same type."[11] Jung used symbols and images to interpret dreams, yet he hypothesized that there was more to the unconscious than the personal. He was often deemed a mystic by his contemporaries because his archetypal theory held elements that could never be empirically explained, and he relied upon various disciplines such as mythology, religion, and alchemy to exemplify his theories:

> I noticed to my amazement that European and American men and
> women coming to me for psychological advice were producing in their
> dreams and fantasies symbols similar to, and often identical with,
> the symbols found in the mystery religions of antiquity, in mythology,
> folklore, fairytales, and the apparently meaningless formulations of
> such esoteric cults as alchemy . . .[12]

Just as Jung "found parallels to his psychic perspective in the lineage of alchemy and Gnosticism" and "consistently referred to and quoted from older religious traditions to shed light on the workings of the unconscious,"[13] Brenda Hillman uses Gnostic and alchemical language in her writing.

As Hillman has clearly identified herself as a lyric poet, let's examine this term more in depth. A lyric implies a rhythmically interesting line in a poem that could be sung; this is often where the emotive function plays a larger role. In addition, the lyric frequently refers to a category of poetic literature representational of music in its sound patterns which are characterized by subjectivity and sensuality of expression—usually in a highly enthusiastic and exuberant way. As indicated in Jung's model of the psyche, if the ego is the center of consciousness, then in order to create a self, it must be in relationship with both the personal and the collective unconscious. This is how I see the Jungian model working in a poetic model of a self: the words on the page represent the ego or consciousness, the personal anecdotes represent the personal unconscious, and the lyric form represents the collective unconscious. Hillman uses a lyric form when she conjures mysterious experiences, and I will present specific examples of this form through a close reading of her poetry.

Hillman's poetry has been described as conveying "the necessity of otherness, to write, to be the amanuensis of the visible world, joined with the necessity of inclusiveness, of participation."[14] Hillman uses the lyric to bring out ecstatic insight from human experience. In the necessary disorientation one feels when creating a poem, Fanny Howe expands the definition of the lyric as "searching for something that can't be found. It is an air that blows and buoys and settles. It says, 'Not this, not this,' instead of, 'I have it.' "[15] This searching is continual in Hillman's poetry. The lyric recurs, but Hillman simultaneously redefines selfhood by introducing new forms into her poems as she explains: "The idea of knowledge in process does have to do with the experiments and explorations of writing, I think, and not just arriving at a spiritual center."[16] Jung might call this a search for self-knowledge. By wavering between two elements or approaches, "not this, not this"[17] separations can dissolve, activating a process of individuation, the aim of which is "nothing less than to divest the self of the false wrappings of the persona on the one hand, and of the suggestive power of primordial images on the other."[18]

Through the arc of Hillman's poetry collections, one can see that she "has in recent years written poems that question the continuity and cohesiveness of what we think of as the self."[19] Hillman's sense of the "I" constantly shifts and expands, making her work an exciting place to trace the self's alchemical development.

The alchemical self

In the most literal terms, alchemy is known as the medieval philosophy concerned with the chemical transformation of metal into gold. However, often the "gold" was of a more spiritual nature. In alchemy, various sequences are associated with different stages of transformation. First, the alchemists must find a substance they believe contains the *prima materia*[20] that after losing its form can go back to its primal state. This stage is known as *mortificatio* or the *nigredo*, in which the material undergoes an alarmingly dramatic breakdown. Since this matter loses its original form, it is often reduced to liquid (*solutio*) or formlessness. The alchemist then introduces the chaotic liquid substance to sulfur which creates a new form. Thus, a continual process of separation (*separatio*) and joining (*coniunctio*) of various states of matter and substances takes place, sometimes with violent reactions and sometimes with a balanced reaction that produces a solid and organized matter. This organized matter is referred to the philosopher's stone.[21]

Fire or *Calcinatio* is another key symbol in alchemy, which reduces a substance to ash in a type of purification process. Fire also resulted in separation, "splitting the ash or body of the material from the spirit, which rose to the top of the alchemical vessel as vapor."[22] In alchemy, the separation and reunification process continues until the ultimate goal of gold (either spiritual or physical) is produced. As the alchemists experienced, this process of turning metal into gold often ended in failure, but the attempts to transform matter did result in self-knowledge. We can also see how this process represents a spiritual or psychological transformation as Jung pointed out with his alchemical model.

Jung did much research on alchemy and was profoundly interested in the work of sixteenth-century alchemist Gerald Dorn. Jung interpreted the three stages of what Dorn called "The Great Work" of alchemy as three stages in the constitution of the self. Jung's alchemical model included a first, second, and third *coniunctio*, or three levels at which opposites unite and "since the self is the union of opposites, each stage corresponds to a different level of self-formation."[23] However, one should realize that the process of alchemy is not linear: "although there is sequence, there is also simultaneity, regression, and chaos."[24] The alchemical process, and often the various *coniunctios*, are repeated many times before the self moves into the next stage of development. It is important to keep this in mind in relation to Hillman's body of work.

Fortress and mortificatio

The alchemical process in Hillman's work begins with *Fortress*.[25] This volume presents the reader with the beginning of a separation process in which opposites emerge in binaries of sorrow/joy, beauty/pain, love/ loss, dark/light, and newness/death, which lead to a breakdown of material (Hillman's life as she knows it) into the *mortificatio* stage of alchemy. Separation seeps through the book's elegiac tone: "In the beautiful void / over the lighted wing, / those ice children seem alive, moving / with no purpose but to be separate" (8); "I see the silk threads / snails put upon the porch / and think how simply / all things leave themselves behind" (43). The *mortificatio* or *nigredo* stage of alchemy is often associated with a dark color, and in *Fortress*, the color gray emerges often: "the gray between decision" (3); "the large, cement-gray-suited woman" (5); "leaves that fall / in gray apostrophes" (56). This darkening world indicates decomposition, or a death. In alchemy, there must be a death before the material can go on to the next stage of joining, or *coniunctio*.

Fortress exemplifies strength in its title, yet its content addresses the experience of disintegration. Mention of dreams, nature, and the other are woven throughout the poems to create a mysterious presence which often questions the origins of things: "Does a poem pre-exist / as dawn pre-exists" (69), and "Sometimes you are known completely / by seeing, known as if by a secret companion: / eyes pressed from the base of an incline / into the depths of your perilous being" (58).

In Jung's alchemical model, the first *coniunctio* takes place in the unconscious: "the first union begins when the ego discovers the reality of the unconscious and makes an effort to pay attention to it . . ."[26] The ego begins to recognize and develop a relationship with an "other," or the unconscious. Hillman juxtaposes her experience of divorce with strong, declarative lines throughout the book: "What we want is simply past our reach" (22); "You could reach inside and make it work" (46); and "The music is the music of failed expectation" (65). The authority in these succinct sentences balances against her personal experience of loss and creates recognition of the "other." *Fortress* provides a glimpse into individual experience through a lyricism that may be filled with wonder or sorrow: "They've taken the larynx out of the dog / so he won't disturb the neighborhood. / But he still opens his soundless mouth, loving his own // subjective barking" (35). These lines evoke grief, yet there are moments of amazement found elsewhere: "The great hurt hangs on for a while, / and then reveals the maps . . . / of a true self no less mysterious"

(57). It is in these moments of lyric bewilderment that the conscious ego reaches toward a symbolic death in order to move out of the *mortificatio* stage to a *coniunctio* with the unconscious or mysterious: "I don't care that my body / will die, for it has not known / its proper freedom" (69).

Death Tractates, Bright Existence, and the first coniunctio

Death Tractates[27] progresses into a splitting process as Hillman deals with the veil between worlds and attempts to find meaning in an experience of loss. The idea that the poem holds its own consciousness, "I had only to trace the pen / over the words; / the poem was already written,"[28] is intertwined with a death: "that death did not subtract, it added something, / her death made me whole."[29] *Death Tractates* (1992) was written as an "interruption" to *Bright Existence* (1993), and the two books serve as companions to one another, representing the alchemical splitting processes of separation and integration. The question of formlessness in one collection of poems is answered with concreteness in the other. *Bright Existence* is filled with experiences of the quotidian: paying tolls at a toll booth, a hair caught in her new lover's throat, even pulling lice from her daughter's hair. No detail is too small or irrelevant. Through observation, Hillman records and makes sense of the transformation taking place in her life.

Death is a central theme in *Death Tractates*[30] and Hillman asks the large spiritual question: "What is this so-called / death what is it" (31). In her exploration of loss, she investigates Gnostic philosophies, asking what comprises matter and spirit and what boundaries might constitute the border of a soul. Hillman searches for a trace of her lost mentor in four sections entitled "Calling Her," "Writing Her," "Losing Her," and "Finding Her." Often a Dickinsonian dash signifies the entrance or exit of a disembodied voice who addresses the speaker of the poem and answers questions that have been posed: "—You think about a poem too much" (11); "—Don't you see? / It doesn't matter what order you put them in" (33); "The choice was simply / whether to live in 'memory' and time / or outside—" (42). Lamenting inquiries continue throughout the text: "What if, despite your false calm, / your brokenness, your self-deception— / in fact, when you were most broken, / her heaven was you?" (35). This insistent questioning leads only to a place of paradox: "—You asked for the difference between life and death.../...and at the moment of your question, / you were handed, / like a black rose, the paradox—" (47).

In alchemical psychology, paradox is a place in which one must learn to dwell comfortably. The tension of opposites must be held during any *coniunctio* stage of alchemy and "the ego must be flexible and able to hold a middle position...consciousness must be balanced with its opposite—the unconscious."[31] In *Death Tractates*, the "I" is distinct from the "you" and space serves as a place of paradox in the uniting of the opposites. Fanny Howe explains that space or emptiness: "teaches us to mistrust the location of the 'I' inside us, since it exists at a 'zero point of orientation,' being both at the source of the physical body and on its periphery where it, too, becomes empty."[32]

The reader experiences this space as it surrounds the central poem located exactly in the middle of *Death Tractates*. Set apart by blank pages, "(untitled poem)" explores the idea that a poem has its own consciousness: "—So the poem is the story of the writing of itself" (25). In this line, Hillman enters the alchemical stage where "the ego carries the principle of consciousness into the darkness of the unconscious and this effects transformation."[33] The poem continues as it speaks to the ego's task in the first *coniunctio* or union:

> So, put yourself in the way
> of the poem. It needed your willing
> impediment to be written...
> You had to be willing to let it through the sunshine
> error of your life,
> be willing not to finish it— (25)

As Hillman explains elsewhere, "It seems as if betweenness, ambiguity, or states of uncertainty are the sites for the most possibility."[34]

And, just as the short, lyrical poems in *Death Tractates* strive for consciousness, the first poem in *Bright Existence*[35] echoes the process:

> The world had been created to comprehend itself
>
> as matter: table, the torn
> veils of spiders....Even consciousness—
> missing my love—

was matter, the metal box of a furnace.
As the obligated flame, so burned my life ... (1)

Hillman struggles with the idea of creation through "real" objects such as a table and the metal box of a furnace. She juxtaposes these with symbols of the imagined world like the "obligated flame." The image of the furnace emerges here, so like the alchemical *calcinatio* or burning stage that purifies and also separates matter and spirit.

Bright Existence's poems reflect a Gnostic belief, that the world was created as a site for the spiritual ones to come to know themselves. In "The Spell" Hillman writes: "This world is my twin / but I was not cut from the same cloth, I passed / through the shadow so I could be / amazed at it—" (32). In Jung's alchemical model, during the first *coniunctio* the ego must become aware of the unconscious in order to move forward in self-formulation: "two as a symbol, and especially doubling or twinning, usually refers to a content within the unconscious that is ready to cross over into the conscious sphere."[36] Hillman explores this idea through form and formlessness. Poems that consider the hardness of form: "trapped in somethingness, in those tiny mosaics with no blood" (30) are juxtaposed with poems that consider spirit: "because at the edge / of your becoming, something kept trying / to erase you" (57). Lines in the title poem "Bright Existence" demonstrate this first *coniunctio* clearly:

there should be more witnesses at the edges of the self
where everything is both
[. . .]
the part that wasn't ready
stayed inside a little longer
and the part that was ready to be something
came forth— (96)

Here, the "part that wasn't ready" and "the part that was ready to be something" signifies a reaching toward consciousness, a doubling, "where everything is both" and there must be recognition of the other for this union to occur.

Hillman ends *Bright Existence* with an image of the snake: "I found its skin of stretchy diamonds / and picked it up, so I could keep / one of the two selves ..." (99). In Jungian thought, the snake is the symbol of transformation and often denotes the *ouroboros* or the serpent eating its own tail—a symbol of union.

Loose Sugar and alchemical ash

After these twin volumes, Hillman embarks on a study of alchemy and depression in *Loose Sugar*,[37] in which she attempts to transcend her dark experience. The series "blue codices" explores the mode of fragmentation. In this series, the "ash poems" are essentially fragments that fall to the bottom of the page, symbolic of alchemical ash from the furnace. The volume is structured in five dualistic sections entitled: "space/time," "time/alchemy," etc., mirroring the unresolved nature of the poems themselves. Things heat up: "Once you were immortal in the flame. / You were not the fire / but you were in the fire;—" (3). This image of the burning alchemical furnace is central to the process of alchemy, and just as alchemists hoped for success and often failed in their search for gold, Hillman too, having struggled with depression, uses the idea of alchemy as a way to transform her experience into a different material or as a way to see it as something outside herself. The ash poems become "the ash of depression from which your beauty of spirit will rise, if it doesn't kill you first."[38] So in this alchemical process of separating the ash from spirit, Hillman attempts to allow the spirit to break free from depression. This process is not easy and often contains periods of the *nigredo,* which include darkness and unknowing.

During the second *coniunctio* of Jung's alchemical model, the self takes on a life of its own and begins to function in its own right. The new self is represented by being held between the masculine and feminine. Both energies are needed for the second *coniunctio* to take place. In poetic processes, the writing of a poem can be seen as the act of writing the self, or searching for a relationship between the unknown (the blank page) and the known or perceived known (the word on the page). In Gnostic myth, this is specifically the search for a feminine wisdom: "*Sophia* (or wisdom) fell from the *pleroma* (or pure world), scattering divine sparks. The Archegenetor (or *Demiourgos*)—a secondary god—created humans to enslave these divine sparks in matter."[39] Similarly, in Jungian theory, the unconscious represents the mystery of what is at the depths of uncertainty and is often denoted as a feminine principle.

The poem "The Spark" alludes to this kind of joining in the second *coniunctio*: "You who happened only once: / remember yourself as you are; // when he comes to you" (5–6). The "you" is well established as a feminine presence at this stage in Hillman's writing (in the progression of *Death Tractates* to *Bright Existence* to *Loose Sugar*). Thus, the line "when he comes to you" represents this masculine and feminine union in the formulation of the poetic self and "stands for the psychic totality."[40]

Cascadia and the second coniunctio

Cascadia explores the question of place which "takes us automatically to the problems of reality and the ideal."[41] Unlike her previous books of poetry, carefully organized in separate sections, *Cascadia*[42] is structured like a large striated landscape. Each poem is layered upon the next and the aforementioned feminine principle emerges throughout the book in poems such as "(blank page)" and "(interruption)."

The poem "(blank page)" is precisely that: a page filled with whiteness. It is given a title in the table of contents, but no words are written on the page itself. Symbolically, the blank page can be seen as feminine, a space that is formless and undefined, yet contains multiple possibilities, indicating here that it holds open possibility like that required in the alchemical process of self-formulation. Also, Hillman notes that the blank page can be used as an in-between space: "The alchemists knew that the fallen thing can be retrieved . . . so the marginal voices exist at the side, apart from the lyric, with a lot of white in-between. Seemingly trivial detail offers itself easily to metaphoric space. The *between* is left blank and fertile."[43] We can see this exemplified in the poem "Cascadia":

In the search for the search
During the experiments with wheels
Holiday Inn   After the scripted caverns
When what had been attached
Lompoc   Was no longer attached
After choosing the type of building
hydrangea   In which no one has died
We recalled a land or condition
one of those   Whose shape was formal

> teeth bedspreads   Formality gave pleasure
>   A shadow's shadow dragged it
>   Back to the sea of eyes (55)

Hillman explains that her "poetry and poetics began to evolve unexpect-
edly.... The sense of the single 'voice' in poetry grew to include poly-
phonies, oddly collective dictations."[44] By stretching the "I," Hillman's
work expands from a lyric-narrative tradition to a more innovative mode.
Hillman herself has noted, "The lyric...is also social.... That much
more stretchy sense of 'I' really interests me."[45]

The reader sees this illustrated in *Cascadia*'s "(interruption)" as a
"we" is called forth: "(enter: The 'we' —)" (6). This short fragment is
enclosed in parentheses and is centered directly on the page, sur-
rounded by white space. In Jung's alchemical model, during the second
coniunctio "the self progresses to such a degree that it takes on a life and
reality of its own within the psyche. The self comes alive and begins
to function in its own right."[46] One also sees here the masculine and
feminine union needed to contain the process. As those "above ground"
in consciousness are transformed, the unconscious also undergoes a
transformation, endowing the self with new energy. The parentheses
of Hillman's line signify a generative dewdrop and the "we" represents
the second *coniunctio* in the alchemical process. A "we" of masculine
and feminine unite as a new "we" of the self emerges. Hillman's poetic
self becomes polyphonic and this new "center strives to express itself"[47]
more consciously in *Cascadia* through an inner and outer landscape.

Hillman's "A Geology" plays with the idea that "place is a world and
a word"[48] and crosses boundaries between the internal and external:
"In the expiation of nature, we are required to / experience the dra-
matic narrative of matter... // This was set down in strata so you could
know / what it felt like to have been earth" (14). This poem is grounded
with four words on each corner of the page to anchor it "so it wouldn't
float."[49] The word "fault" is repeated three times on the last page of "A
Geology" (14) suggesting multiple meanings: mistakes, geologic frac-
tures that cause movement in the earth's crust, and/or human weakness.
The fourth word "prevalent" on the bottom right corner of the page
surprises the reader in its difference; it not only helps to anchor the

poem, but also destabilizes it and opens its reader to the experience of the last line: "what it felt like to have been earth."

In an alchemical process of separating and joining matter, substances can react to each other in a violent or balanced manner. When balanced, the substance can emerge as solid matter, or the philosopher's stone. *Cascadia* is about landforms where "shifting internal geographies must be managed in relation to external ones."[50] In alchemical terms, the violent reaction is the poem "written under various kinds of emotional pressure"[51] and the stone emerges as organized matter: "It took quiet / It took stone" (74).

Lines from the poem "Before My Pencil" grapple with the idea of creating a world out of intense feeling. The poem investigates "the mannerism of the curve" of earth or the universe and finishes with the idea that it can "crawl among syllables," creating itself by feeding on dead organic or spiritual matter to produce a "white fact" (74). In alchemy, as the substance continues to change, it reaches "an initial resting-place . . . called the first stone" where it regains form and has "the power to create silver from other metals" and is often "associated with white . . . referred to as the *albedo*."[52] Similarly, this poem touches "the white fact," Hillman reaching a resting place where she creates a solidified poetic self.

Pieces of Air in the Epic: A gesture toward the third coniunctio

In Jung's alchemical model, during the third *coniunctio* the individual self comes into union with the divine world that existed before matter and spirit were separated. The third *coniunctio* is rarely ever achieved except perhaps in death as "the individual self that has been formed comes into union with a level of reality that transcends it, with the divine world . . . the one world before spirit and matter were separated."[53] This is the Gnostic world Hillman explores in much of her poetry, but about which she rarely arrives at a conclusion. The third *coniunctio* denotes the spiritual plane of the elements of air, wings, etc., and is represented by the sun, sky, and clouds. In *Pieces of Air in the Epic*,[54] Hillman explores this elemental world as she "tackles the large metaphysical questions" and "opens up the line and the page's horizon to express the apocalyptic fears of our 'epoch.' "[55]

The poetic self enacts a new way of seeing: "I looked below / the air behind the paintings . . . // I made my eyes pointy to look at air in / corners" (58). The poem "Street Corner" invokes the one world that will ultimately transcend this individual self: "There was an angle / where I went for / centuries not as a / self or feature but / exhaled as a knowing" (3).

Other inquiries on exhalation/breath continue in "Platonic Oxygen" as the poet asks, "What is thought Is it breath / Were you breath" (76). The formlessness of the unknown transforms the solid matter of *Cascadia* into air: "Can we remake elements" (29) Hillman asks in the poem "6 Components from Aristotle." These meditations bring one closer to the elemental world, although "the danger of writing a book on air is that it might disappear at crucial moments."[56] Hillman does not allow this to happen, as the poetic line remains grounded in the everyday: "Some // foolish soul has sold his entire / Liz Phair collection back to Amoeba; // Used jewel cases seem almost tender, / smothered-to-smithereens-type plastic . . ." (66).

Hillman continues to work with polyphony, and in the poem "Air in the Epic" the reader must jump between dense phrases to seemingly disconnected phrases surrounded by space. The lyric which operates in the right-hand margin can be read vertically while the dense poem on the left cannot:

> You look outside the classroom where construction trucks find little Troys. Dust
> rises: part pagan, part looping. Try
> to describe the world, you tell   them—but what is a description? (8)

It is the space between the lyrical phrases that allows the mind to make causal connections that do not exist on the left. Hillman has carefully constructed each line so that it must interact; it must come together and join in an alchemical process while still suggesting gaps. The experimental form of "Air in the Epic" and "String Theory Sutra" produces a tension that reaches toward the transformative third *coniunctio*. The poem remains lyrical, yet continues to question the poetic self:

> There are so many types of
> "personal" in poetry. The "I" is   a needle some find useful, though
> the thread, of course is shadow.
> In writing of experience or beauty,   a cloth emerges as if made
> from a twin existence . . . (80)

In *Pieces of Air*, the poem sees itself existing through the "writing of experience or beauty" as cloth made from a "twin existence" and one can see that Hillman's poetic self has grown and transformed from the "selfhood" of her earlier books. Just as a person might function in life according to what she has consciously experienced, there is also an underlying unconscious myth or archetype at work that creates a life pattern and is expressed in a poem by what Howe calls "the strange Whoever who goes under the name of 'I' . . . where error, errancy, and bewilderment . . . signal a story."[57]

Through the breath, the image, and the lyric, the spiritual elements of the third *coniunctio* are at work in *Pieces of Air*: ". . . there's a patient tap / tap tapping in the text . . . / where stars pass; / stars passed; stars pierced you —" (56). In "Clouds Near San Leandro" the poetic self inquires, "Aren't there visions involving everything?" (67). *Pieces of Air* provides the reader with elated insight and urges one to question spirit and breath: "song outlasts poetry, words / are breath bricks to / support the guardless singing / project. We could have / meant song outlasts poetry" (4). Hillman has indeed found a way to separate matter from spirit and lift the words off the page in rapturous song.

Conclusion

One can clearly see the three *coniunctios* in Jung's alchemical model represented in Hillman's books of poetry, where inner and outer worlds resonate and come together on the page in a redefined notion of self that takes shape in the alchemical imagination of time and space, earth and air. Hillman identifies herself as a poet with Gnostic interests and has carved a niche for herself within an oeuvre of poets who are interested in the mysterious workings of the origins of things, or in Jungian terms, the unconscious. Hillman has even developed a "minifesto" which explains her interests:

= A poem is the rescue of a vanishing body.
= Poems embodying original technique make units smaller than the sentence serve both the sentence and the line. They help rethink the relationship between word, phrase, or sentence every time they make one of those things.[58]

To rescue the vanishing body, the mysticpoet writes words, phrases, or sentences on the page. In doing so, a new body—a poetic self—is developed. Hillman never abandons the lyric, although she often dwells in a place of unknowing with her experimentation of form: "Uncertainty is to be preferred. In those years, many of us found we could reinvent the lyric, however shattered it might be."[59] The process of alchemical separation and joining repeats itself in Hillman's poetry, and after publishing her last element-focused volume of poetry (on fire) in 2013, Hillman's reader might wonder where she will take us next. My guess is that, like alchemy, she will take us through a continued process of refining the self through *gnosis*, just as the image of the burning salamander signals the return to the *prima materia*:

Some animals are warm in paradise;

your little alchemical salamander *taricha tarosa*,
fresh from the being cycles, stumbles

over rocks in its lyric outfit— [60]

And with Brenda Hillman, there will always, always be a "lyric outfit" present.

Notes

1. Lennon, "Episode 025: Brenda Hillman."
2. Wojahn, "Survivalist Selves."
3. Kirkpatrick and August, "An Interview with Brenda Hillman," 2006.
4. Howe, *Wedding Dress*, 15.
5. Jung, *Civilization in Transition*, para. 495.
6. Larimer, "Interview With Poet Brenda Hillman," 8.
7. Jung, *Psychology and Alchemy*, para. 44.
8. Jung, *Two Essays on Analytical Psychology*, para. 266.
9. Raff, *Jung and the Alchemical Imagination*, 12.
10. Jung, *The Portable Jung*, 38.
11. Jung, *Spirit in Man, Art, and Literature*, para. 127.
12. Jung, *Psychology and Alchemy*, v.
13. Raff, *Jung and the Alchemical Imagination*, 4.
14. Mullins, "Introduction," *Readings in Contemporary Poetry*.
15. Howe, *The Wedding Dress*, 21.
16. Kirkpatrick and August, "An Interview with Brenda Hillman."
17. Howe, *The Wedding Dress*, 21.
18. Jung, *The Portable Jung*, 123.
19. Johnston, *Precipitations*, 158.

20. Raff, xxi. "*[P]rima materia* was matter before it was formed, which the alchemists called 'chaos' among other things."

21. Raff, 219–20. "[T]he [philosopher's] stone creates mystical experiences and ecstasy, and offers a door that leads to the celestial world. Their goal in the creation of the stone is direct encounter with divinity."

22. Raff, xxii.

23. Raff, 84.

24. Spiegelman, *Divine WABA*, 159.

25. Hillman, *Fortress*. The following poetic lines in this section are cited from *Fortress* and page numbers are hereafter cited in the body of the essay.

26. Raff, 85.

27. Hillman, *Death Tractates*.

28. Hillman, *Death Tractates*, 32.

29. Hillman, *Death Tractates*, 21.

30. The poetic lines in the following paragraphs are cited from *Death Tractates* and page numbers are hereafter cited in the body of the essay.

31. Raff, 106–107.

32. Howe, 47.

33. Raff, 106.

34. Kirkpatrick and August, "An Interview with Brenda Hillman."

35. Hillman, *Bright Existence*. The poetic lines in the following paragraphs are cited from *Bright Existence* and page numbers are hereafter cited in the body of the essay.

36. Raff, 89.

37. Hillman, *Loose Sugar*. The following poetic lines in this section are cited from *Loose Sugar* and page numbers are hereafter cited in the body of the essay.

38. Lennon, "Episode 025: Brenda Hillman."

39. Johnston, *Precipitations*, 5–6.

40. Jung, *Aion: Researches into the Phenomenology of the Self*, para. 426.

41. Larimer, "An Interview With Poet Brenda Hillman," 3.

42. Hillman, *Cascadia*. The following poetic lines in this section are cited from *Cascadia* and page numbers are hereafter cited in the body of the essay.

43. Hillman, "Split, Spark and Space," 252.

44. Hillman, "Split, Spark and Space," 246.

45. Hillman, "Our Very Greatest Human Thing Is Wild," 28.

46. Raff, 85.

47. Raff, 12.

48. Larimer, "An Interview With Poet Brenda Hillman," 5.

49. Larimer, 7.

50. Larimer, 3.

51. Larimer, 3.

52. Raff, xxiii.

53. Raff, 85.

54. Hillman, *Pieces of Air in the Epic*. The following poetic lines in this section are cited from *Pieces of Air in the Epic* and page numbers are hereafter cited in the body of the essay.

55. McCabe, "Platonic Oxygen," 65–66.

56. McCabe, "Platonic Oxygen," 71.

57. Howe, 6.

58. Hillman, "Split, Spark, and Space," 250.

59. Hillman, "Split, Spark, and Space," 248.
60. Hillman, *Pieces of Air in the Epic*, 67.

Bibliography

Dienstfrey, Patricia and Hillman, Brenda, Eds. *The Grand Permission: New Writings on Poetics and Motherhood*. Middletown: Wesleyan University Press, 2003.

Hillman, Brenda. *Bright Existence*. Hanover, NH: Wesleyan University Press/ University Press of New England, 1993.

Hillman, Brenda. *Cascadia*. Middletown: Wesleyan University Press, 2001.

Hillman, Brenda. *Death Tractates*. Hanover, NH: Wesleyan University Press/ University Press of New England, 1992.

Hillman, Brenda. *Fortress*. Middletown: Wesleyan University Press, 1989.

Hillman, Brenda. *Loose Sugar*. Hanover, NH: Wesleyan University Press/ University Press of New England, 1997.

Hillman, Brenda. *Pieces of Air in the Epic*. Middletown: Wesleyan University Press, 2005.

Howe, Fanny. *The Wedding Dress, Meditations on Word and Life*. Berkeley: University of California Press, 2003.

Johnston, Devin. *Precipitations: Contemporary American Poetry as Occult Practice*. Middletown: Wesleyan Press, 2002.

Jung, C.G. *The Portable Jung*. Translated by R.F.C. Hull. Edited by Joseph Campbell. New York: Penguin Books, 1971.

Jung, C.G. *Two Essays on Analytical Psychology*. Vol. 7 of *The Collected Works of C.G. Jung*. 2nd ed. Edited by Sir Herbert Read, Michael Fordham, Gerhard Adler, and William McGuire. Translated by R.F.C. Hull. Princeton: Princeton University Press, 1966.

Jung, C.G. *Aion: Researches into the Phenomenology of the Self*. Vol. 9ii of *The Collected Works of C.G. Jung*. 2nd ed. Edited by Sir Herbert Read, Michael Fordham, Gerhard Adler, and William McGuire. Translated by R.F.C. Hull. Princeton: Princeton University Press, 1968.

Jung, C.G. *Civilization in Transition*. Vol. 10 of *The Collected Works of C.G. Jung*. 2nd ed. Edited by Sir Herbert Read, Michael Fordham, Gerhard Adler, and William McGuire. Translated by R.F.C. Hull. Princeton: Princeton University Press, 1970.

Jung, C.G. *Psychology and Alchemy*. Vol. 12 of *The Collected Works of C.G. Jung*. 2nd ed. Edited by Sir Herbert Read, Michael Fordham, Gerhard Adler, and William McGuire. Translated by R.F.C. Hull. Princeton: Princeton University Press, 1968.

Jung, C.G. *The Spirit in Man, Art, and Literature*. Vol. 15 of *The Collected Works of C.G. Jung*. 2nd ed. Edited by Sir Herbert Read, Michael Fordham, Gerhard Adler, and William McGuire. Translated by R.F.C. Hull. Princeton: Princeton University Press, 1966.

Kirkpatrick, Patricia and August, Emily. "An Interview with Brenda Hillman." Hamline University. March 17, 2006. http://maryrockcastle.tripod.com /pdf/2006_excerpts/brendahillmaninterview.pdf

Larimer, Kevin, "An Interview With Poet Brenda Hillman," *Poets and Writers*. August 30, 2001. http://www.pw.org/content/interview_poet_brenda _hillman.

Lennon, J. Robert, "Episode 025: Brenda Hillman." Writers at Cornell interview, Cornell University Podcast Audio. November 7, 2008. http:// jrobertlennon.com/writersatcornell/2008/11/7/interview-brenda -hillman.html

McCabe, Susan. "Platonic Oxygen: On Brenda Hillman's *Pieces of Air in the Epic*." *Denver Quarterly* 41, no. 2 (2006): 65–71. http://www.du.edu/ denverquarterly/media/documents/McCabe.pdf.

Mullins, Brighde. "Brenda Hillman, Introduction." *Readings in Contemporary Poetry* series. November 10, 1995. http://awp.diaart.org/poetry/95_96 /intrhill.html.

Raff, Jeffrey. *Jung and the Alchemical Imagination*. York Beach, ME: Nicolas-Hayes Inc., 2000.

Rosenthal, Sarah. "Our Very Greatest Human Thing is Wild: An Interview with Brenda Hillman." *Rain Taxi Online Edition* (Fall 2003). http://www .raintaxi.com/our-very-greatest-human-thing-is-wild/.

Spiegelman, J. Marvin. *The Divine WABA: A Jungian Exploration of Spiritual Paths*. Berwick, ME: Nicolas-Hays, Inc., 2003.

Wojahn, David. "Survivalist Selves." *Kenyon Review* 20, no. 3 (1998): 180–189.

Joining Spirits

An Interview with Hoa Nguyen (September 2011)
Dale Smith

Dale Smith: Your work expands the range of concerns of feminist discourse to include the environments men and women inhabit, desire, and encounter together. You seek a kind of integration of various life capacities. How does poetry let you accomplish these ethical challenges?

Hoa Nguyen: I admire the open possibilities of poetry, how words, phrases or lines can be laid down with a sonic mathematics of sense that can reach a reader in a fractal or patterning way. A reader can assemble the constellations of meaning for herself then, so that the logic units array themselves in her understanding, an understanding that she can be a co-participant in building.

DS: Would you mind giving an example of a poem of yours that accomplishes this "patterning," and then saying some more about how such poetic constellations extend relationships you desire? I'd like to see an example of how you invite participation, because I think this is essential to your work, though I see it more as a ritualistic space between not only the poem and reader, but between your creative engagement and a larger cultural space.

HN: For example, I wrote this sonnet in July 2011:

RAGE SONNET

Rage on the grinding spot
Independence Day   Rag laundry day
My boy wears shark pajamas
Mother ran large food trays   sore

shoulders   Lobster surf & turf
It's Independence Day 2011
We may have been poisoned
by "Operation Ranch Hand"

I am not dead yet
Ezra Pound in my DC
Charles Olson dream "It is
so much harder to be a poet now"

they say to me   Lack of rain and the #30
Bus may run now all the way to downtown[1]

I'm interested in the resonances of words at the level of the letter—(re-) reading Emily Dickinson earlier this year, I saw that she often dwelt, in her poems, at the level of the letter. Syllable, yes, but also the letter—as in the tiniest units of word-making.

The first stanza opens in an associative way. There is something about "rage" being focused on a single point, being ground in, but also grounded in a specific day (the US's Independence Day). Which leads to the introduction of a domestic moment in the phrase "Rag laundry day."

What you may notice (or sense at an intuitive or somatic level) is how the lines are populated by words that circle the word "rage"—containing the opening letters of the word "rage." reversing them, digressing from the letters as in:

Rage / Rag / Wears / Shark / Ran / Large / Trays / Operation / Ranch / Ezra / Charles / Harder / Rain

The unit is the letter combination/syllable "ar" but then it is also reversed as "ra." The patterns are both visual and sonic.

The sonnet contains, at its opening, a domestic moment—"My boy wears shark pajamas"—which travels to the memory of my mother as a waitress. "Mother ran large food trays" connects to the descriptive/literal and ocean-associative "sore / shoulders   Lobster surf & turf"—the poem continues to relate historical, personal, and situational history: a moment, memory, the massive spraying of defoliants/herbicides in the war in Vietnam, a literary dream of struggle, environmental and civic disorder/order. The poem also includes these, among other, sonic arrays:

(ending in D words) Food / Poisoned / Hand / Dead / Pound

("ow" sounds) / Pound / Now (twice) / Downtown

My sense is that these sound arrays and associative sense frames allow a reader to receive them for personal noetic, physical, and emotional responses.

DS: Well, knowing intimately the "rags" you describe, as well as the complexities of the daily domestic routines, it's extraordinary how you turn the mundane into something completely other. For instance, the purely sonic /ra/ in "rags" and "rage" associates semantically with the Egyptian sun god Ra, and with Ezra Pound's nickname, which is also Ra (I think he received it while still in Wyncote, Pennsylvania, during his Cheltenham Military Academy days). And since the latter figures prominently here, and since the sequence of writing this poem belongs to associates so strongly with light, the correlation of these figures hovers over or within the syllabic voicings in your poem.

Along these lines, you mention Emily Dickinson and I just read a poem of yours that is written after her. I was wondering if you could share it and talk about what you've learned from her as a poet. I find it interesting that this withdrawn though attentive poet of the 19th century inspires your more socially engaged and determined sense of poetics. (Actually this is what distinguishes your writing greatly—you have a strong social commitment, but it all hinges on an equal commitment to words and the art of poetry.) And then shortly, I want to step back a bit and look at the kinds of social engagements your work presents. For while you have an abiding commitment to words and their sonic resonances, you also speak with a fierce determination at times about the cultural conditions we live in.

HN: A fellow poet and participant in the Dickinson workshop I led this year related that a colleague, in studying Emily Dickinson with

Susan Howe, said that Dickinson's words are "like knives."[2] That insight crystallizes some of what I found in her poems: how to pick the right word—words without rhythmic drag—ones that have an excellent precision for sound and meaning. I learned a strategy of compression, observation, and syllabic/letter echoing: how to squeeze words and point them directly and indirectly at matters. In her poems I see that she makes her interior point directly and indirectly—but pointedly—to a social/historical exterior.

Interestingly, the poem you ask after is also one in which I am considering a substance made by Monsanto and Dow chemical companies that was deployed by the US military during the war in Vietnam. The height of Agent Orange spraying coincided with the year I was born—I was born in the Mekong Delta in a town called Vinh Long near Saigon—and I left for the US at the end of the spraying, when I was about two years old.

I encountered Dickinson's line "the zeroes—taught us—phosphorus"[3] and it recalled for me the fires of "white phosphorus," an igniting agent that would allow napalm bombs (a jellied gasoline) to burn for up to ten minutes when aerially dropped. Dow Chemical also made napalm.

AGENT ORANGE POEM

After Emily Dickinson

What justice foreigns for a sovereign
We doom in nation rooms

Recommend & lend   resembling fragrant
Chinaberry spring

Here we have high flowers   a lilac in the nose
"The zeroes—taught us—phosphorus"

and so stripped   the leaves   to none[4]

My poems steps in her steps in terms of cadence, a kind of solemn hymnal, a hymnal of the damned, the horrible. Chinaberry trees (an Asian native and invasive species) appear throughout my gathering of poems, *As Long as Trees Last*. I lived near Chinaberry trees in my adopted city of Austin, Texas. And I feel an affinity with Emily Dickinson in her absolute attention to her locale, the beings that dwell there—plant life. It's a web of attention that captures a constellation of experience.

In this poem, one of the things I'm doing is using the letter "O"—playing against it—its fullness in the mouth, the zero or emptiness that its form recalls, and its exclamatory nature—as well as the contradictions—as in the "or/ore" pairing.

I'm interested in yoking opposites in poems.

DS: Speaking of opposites, your work seems compelled by a broad investigation of myth, ancient religions, practices of devotion, and forms of spiritual attention. Your writing contains symbolic events that create a texture of spirituality. How does poetry feed your spiritual practice, or vice versa?

HN: When I was five years old, I remember standing next to my elementary school underneath a pine during a brief, light rain shower. Water was running down the side of the brick schoolhouse wall, splashing into a pebble-lined puddle, and I arrived at the sense that this was like the resting place for my Vietnamese grandfather, a person I never knew. I think I said some oaths of remembrance to him then.

There was something in that moment, how the elements came together, and the sound of rain falling and this persistent unknown presence just beyond me but also within me came to be felt.

I think of poetry like that: joining spirits and forces beyond one's immediate perception, linked by the phenomenal world through one's faculties, metamorphosed. And as with that moment, I feel that I have always been drawn to the music of poetry as I have always been drawn to the numinous in all its forms. It informs my investigations and my poetics.

DS: Yes, I see that in your work, and I particularly like how spiritual practice is conjoined with other forms of attention that usually are divided in our culture. We're so conditioned to think of our social lives, political investments, or our personal values as all somehow distinct or compartmentalized, though I think in your poetry these are all worked out within the spiritual body of feeling you describe.

There are of course poems like "Great Mother of the Gods" that address the many features of a goddess. You consider mythic terms by which the everyday can be known:

Cybele   among many
other names
Her sacred symbol: a small
meteoric stone (black)

All-begetter
All-nourisher
The Mother of the Blest

Great Nature Goddess:
Mountain Mother
Greater Mother of the Gods
Mother of all Gods and all Men [sic]

also as Ma or Ammas

Caves = Cybele

(hair fragrant with ointment)

Niobe of Mt. Sipylus
is really the Mother

She is generally pictured with 2 lions
under her arms[5]

I like the power of the poem for revealing the chthonic figure of Cybele in her many embodiments, and so the mythic in your writing always helps me see the mundane as something interwoven with the continuous concerns you have for the many aspects of the feminine.

HN: Thanks for looking at this poem so closely. Yes, I think I find these mythic fragments and connect them to a modern present as a way to get at a spiritual articulation. My spirituality is an organic one and I find that it resists a narrative explanation or descriptive discourse. Instead it gets imbedded inside the constellation of words that make up my poems.

Once I performed an English-to-English translation on Shakespeare's sonnet #86 and I "translated" his phrase "by spirits taught to write" as "Spirits taught me to write / countless spirits writing this."[6] Then much later, I consulted with a woman who sensed spirit presences around me. She explained that everyone has these other-dimensional presences near them but often one is not aware they are there. She said that that was not the case with me. The spirits around me loved me, said that I "took good dictation."

DS: Perhaps we should just end with one of my favorite poems—a favorite because of the intimacy it performs. I'm also drawn to it because I've had the privilege of sharing these mundane facts with you:

TOWELS

Towels   What of towels
There are never enough
of them with vomit sickness
in the house

Could I clean them in the creek?

Mama?
What-a?

I need you   I need something
I can't do it alone Papa Mama

What you
I love you Pooh
flying on the balloon
and spitting out bees

Triphala
how long can I store Triphala
to manage upper respiratory complaints
before it becomes pneumonia[7]

Here the power of the Earth Mother is submerged in the tender calling of the child. I find your search to identify both the power and the fragility of life in our most basic relationships to be one of your great accomplishments as a poet. The spiritual power you invoke through myth is also patient and generous, and this is revealed with great strength in your poems.

HN: Through your attention to the poems. I'm noticing how often I recall fabric and how this can appear literally in the poems as towels or rags. I think this is as a route to articulate something toward what I believe to be true of the universe's design—maybe it points back to the unity of opposites as a basis of that design. You know: zeros and ones making up a binary code, that helix form—a way of warp or weave. I'm interested in how poems can make it possible to connect one's prism of time/space to eternal time/space.

Notes

1. Nguyen, "Rage Sonnet," in *As Long as Trees Last*, 2.
2. Nguyen has taught a weekly workshop from her homes in Austin, Texas, and Toronto, Ontario, for nearly two decades. A description of her pedagogy can be found in "Continuing Poetry," *Poets on Teaching*, ed. Joshua Marie Wilkinson (Iowa City: University of Iowa Press, 2010), 229.
3. Dickinson, "The zeroes—taught us—phosphorus."
4. Nguyen, "Agent Orange Poem" in *As Long as Trees Last*, 4.
5. Nguyen, "Great Mother of the Gods," in *Red Juice*, 47.
6. Nguyen, "Blackberries" in *Red Juice*, 122. Poem first published in *Hecate Lochia*, 37.
7. Nguyen, "Towels" in *Red Juice*, 235. Poem first published in *Hecate Lochia*, 101.

Bibliography

Dickinson, Emily. "The Zeroes - taught us - Phosphorus -," #689. 1863 in *The Complete Poems of Emily Dickinson*. Edited by Thomas Johnson. Boston: Back Bay Books, 1976.

Nguyen, Hoa. *As Long as Trees Last*. Seattle/New York: Wave Books, 2012.

Nguyen, Hoa. "Continuing Poetry." *Poets on Teaching: A Sourcebook*, edited by Joshua Marie Wilkinson, 229–230. Iowa City: University of Iowa Press, 2010.

Nguyen, Hoa. *Hecate Lochia*. Prague, Czech Republic: Hot Whiskey Press, 2009.

Nguyen, Hoa. *Red Juice: Poems 1998–2008*. Seattle/New York: Wave Books, 2014.

Ghosting the Line

Susan Howe and the Ethics of Haunting

Dan Beachy-Quick

> *it must acknowledge the spiritual forces which have made it*
> —Marianne Moore

> *Too much and not enough.*
> —Heraclitus

Prefatory

I first read Susan Howe's poems in the spring time. A professor had given me a copy of *The Nonconformist's Memorial,* and one day when the sun shone bright and winter finally felt put away, I walked out from the ratty apartment I shared with my wife, walked across the street, sat under a tree, my back against the rough bark, and began to read. I read the entire book. When I was done I turned back to those mirrored pages in "A Bibliography of the King's Book, or Eikon Basilike," the lines not behaving on the page as lines of poems were supposed to behave, lines crossing each other, clipping across each other's utterances, lines that confuse, lines that confound, that make of themselves a web in the eye, a nest in the eye, lines growing tangible as they grew tangent, not one voice but voices; I could hear them as if in a room in which words gained body, words putting themselves in this difficult and impossible grace called *delay*. Something meant to disappear had not disappeared here: the words of which voice is constructed, these "vibrations of air." These mirrored pages seemed to look at each other; when the book is closed, these pages lie with one face pressed to the face of the other, not a kiss, but a kind of circular breathing, a kind of circulation. I looked and looked at those pages. I read in the middle—

$$\underset{\forall}{\overset{\mathrm{b}_{\wedge}{}^{o^{f}}}{}}$$

and on the facing page—

$$\overset{A}{\underset{p^{i\,v}o_{t^{i}}}{}}$$

the word broken apart letter by letter, but legible through its damage. Here is one form of fearful symmetry: a pivot that pivots itself. See how the word isn't linear, but in orbit around itself, a centerless center. But these two pages mirror each other, reflect each other. The word is not the only thing in circulation. It is as if one page looks at itself in the mirror, but neither page knows which is but image and which is actual, nor does the reader know. There is a question here; it is not a question that asks itself, nor is it a question that can be asked. We feel the medieval philosopher's endless concern with the nature of the reality of the mirrored image. Save here it is not a face reflected, behind which could be seen the room in which the philosopher asks his questions of himself to himself, some self who will not answer, but only mimes back the face in its effort. Here voice reflects voice, an echo chamber in a mirror on a page as still—one might hazard to say—as Narcissus's pond. Origin asks a haunted question. Am I the first?

Am I the first?—that is how I felt reading Susan Howe's poetry. It is the feeling of one who enters into the world and becomes bewildered. It is a wilderness condition. And when I looked up from the pages I looked up into the tree out-branching above me. I felt like my breath had blossomed; and when I breathed in, I breathed in the whole tree.

Breath

The library is a forest, a woods, a wilderness. Leaves of trees and leaves of pages fall from branch and from binding fall. That hush in the dim-lit narrow between stacks? Don't mistake solemnity for the dead-leaf strewn path; don't mistake silence for those thinnest threads voices trail behind them in their song. Even what is wild finds a trail and marks it more legible as it passes. Reading is when the eye falls on some compost the foot can't find. "Often a damaged edition's semi-decay is the soil in which I thrive,"[2] says Howe in her "Personal Narrative" in *Souls of the Labadie Tract*. The damaged voice provides the fertile ground.

Invert the symbol and the library becomes ocean. Melville, quoted by Howe in *The Nonconformist's Memorial*: "But I have swam through libraries." Howe, too (like Coleridge), a "library-cormorant," finds in words' watery depths that which nourishes. There is also the book open and flat on the library's table, the pages gathering as two waves about to crash together (or is it a wave about to crash into its own reflection?). And Dickinson: "There is no Frigate like a Book."

To enter these woods recognizes that the "errand in the wilderness" is still our own, these woods through which voices run more swiftly than do the deer, these savage-haunted, prophet-hunted woods. To enter this ocean is to ship with Bulkington on Captain Ahab's Pequod, where "all deep, earnest thinking is but the intrepid effort of the soul to keep the open independence of her sea."[3] When Susan Howe walks into a library she walks into the woods. In the "vocalized wilderness" she grows bewildered. It is a mark of honesty, this becoming lost, this losing one's way. When she dives down she dies a little and also she denies death. A page is just a surface masking underneath it unfathomable depths. What does the poet-reader, library-cormorant do? She learns to hold her breath.

*

I have heard the wind blow through the woods in such a way that I thought the ocean was near. And I have smelled in the air blown off the ocean a fertile, fecund, rotting smell, as of leaves overturned in a forest. Wind plays tricks, and breath plays tricks, too.

> Sometimes by the seaside
> all echoes link as air
> Not I cannot tell what
> so wanton and so all about[4]

The voice, Howe reminds us not only in *The Nonconformist's Memorial*, but throughout the entire body of her work, is composite in the strangest of ways. A construction of opposites, a voice is word carried on breath, sound borne by silence. The voice lives "a sort of border life,"[5] and the border divides what it divides not flawlessly, but with deep flaw. The voice keeps letting time escape into memory, moment into echo. The body of the word keeps breaking down into no body at all, a kind of silence that is also a kind of soul. The voice marks that border where oppositions fail to be opposite, word and world, syllable and silence, body and spirit. The voice found on the page—that ocean-like blank formed of the forest's wood—navigates a wilderness it contains within itself. It bears in it the marks of "The literature of savagism / under a spell of savagism,"[6] where here, *savage* shakes free of connotation, and returns to Thoreau's etymology, traced from the Latin *sylva*, dividing in Old French and Middle English into *sauvage* and *salvage*, the latter meaning simply *a person of the woods*. Pages are savage. Words make the trails they mark. To read is to enter the woods, and to enter the woods is to become bewildered. Howe: "Who is not a wild Enthusiast."[7]

But the enthusiast wilds herself at more than the music inside the voices she hears. She hears also that in the voice which the voice cannot speak, the silence the voice contains, marked by no words but by the breath words hold within themselves, some blank instant some call now, and some call forever. Thoreau, January 4, 1851: "The longest silence is the most pertinent question most pertinently put." Howe is a poet uniquely suited not to answering this most pertinent question, but through the border life of the poetic voice, letting silence ask its ongoing question within her own words. It is a question by which she brings herself into question. Thoreau, again:

> My life at this moment is like a summer morning when birds are singing. Yet that is false, for nature's is an idle pleasure in comparison: my hour has a more solid serenity. I have been breaking silence these twenty-three years and have hardly made a rent in it. Silence has no end; speech is but the beginning of it. My friend thinks I *keep* silence, who am only choked with letting it out so fast. Does he forget that new mines of secrecy are constantly opening in me?[8]

Thoreau sees that to speak is to speak silence, speech being but silence's beginning. A word strangely reflects the crisis of body and soul. A syllable marks not only the initial sound as it builds into sense, it marks exactly there where time seems to begin—and because of time, suddenly there is history, suddenly there is history in all its suddenness. But the voice is carried in breath's silence; but the voice carries within it that silence on which it is borne. Words contain within themselves that breath that is silence without end, silence larger than the word that contains it—a silence that does not deny expression, but affirms it. That breath affirms that chaos still dwelling within cosmos.

> Words are an illusion
> are vibrations of air
> Fabricating senselessness
> He has shattered gates
> thrown open to himself[9]

When the word is spoken, when the illusion ends, one is left with the senseless air alone. One has put breath then into one's breathing—shattered gate of one's own mouth, one's own mind. That breath is not simply one's own. That breath is not simply the air in the lungs.

Such silence marks the curious terrain of poetic perception. Giorgio Agamben offers to bring such silence into consideration:

> ... not only memory ... but also forgetfulness, are contemporaneous with perception and the present. While we perceive something, we simultaneously remember and forget it. Every present thus contains a part of non-lived experience. Indeed, it is, at the limit, what remains non-lived in every life, that which, for its traumatic character or its excessive proximity remains unexperienced in every experience ... [10]

Howe, who knows to ask through the work of the poem about that toward which the poem itself works, writes in the "unutterable gathering darkness"[11] where "I stray to stray,"[12] toward that *who* "Who is this distance / Waiting for a restoration."[13] It is too simple to say that this poetry's relation to history is one of reclamation and recognition—of bodying the ghosts—for Howe's poetry contains in it the full complexity of memory occurring in the moment. It arrives in its experience containing that which cannot be experienced. Howe speaks her invitation, her voice in which voices might reside, the poem a place of dwelling not unlike the library's wilds where, the poet says, "I am at home in the library / I will lie down and sleep."[14] Howe does this work—a work not wholly unlike how sleep bides in the midst of wakefulness—of bringing herself, and so bringing her readers, into that "excessive proximity" that remains silent, experienced only through the fact of its resistance to experience. She offers what remains "not-lived in every life" and whose spiritual nature belongs, as Howe writes of it, to the "Occult ferocity of origin."[15]

Breath, I mean to say, is an origin. Breath occult in every word. We forget we are speaking silence when we speak. We forget that when we breathe we breathe in some original silence that preserves our relation to a life we forgot we're still living. That breath gains its greatest philosophical weight in the idea of the medieval *pneuma*; it is a breath we still breathe. The *pneuma* is, as Agamben writes of it, "the breath that animates the universe, [it] circulates in the arteries, and fertilizes the sperm [and] is the same one that, in the brain and in the heart, receives forms and phantasms of the things we see, imagine, dream, and love."[16] This breath connects the outermost limits of world to the innermost excess of proximity, threads together the macrocosm and the microcosm, universe and self. That spirit-substance that makes the star shine is the very same spirit-substance that makes the sperm potent, that enlivens the heart with the images that there dwell. Medical knowledge of the time thought that the veins carried blood, but the arteries carried *pneuma*. Circulating through the body entire is this breath of the stars, this world-breath. The *pneuma* connects and keeps livid the uncertain realm where the corporeal and the incorporeal join, maintain through their opposition an unforeseeable unity. The poem is a star-chamber and a self-chamber through which the same breath blows.

> I listen spheres of stars
> I draw you close ever so
> Communion come down and down
> Quiet place to stop here
> Who knows ever no one knows
> to know unlove no forgive
>
> Half thought thought otherwise
> loveless and sleepless the sea

Where you are and where I would be
half thought thought otherwise
Loveless and sleepless the sea[17]

What does the poem do? It learns to listen to the stars, not to know, not to know. How does it learn not to know? How does it learn to listen? The poem learns to breathe.

Body

Reductive, but maybe helpful, perhaps even honest, to say that Howe's poetry over the course of the books entire contain within them a continuous pivot that turning to one side opens onto poems whose nature explores the *pneumatic* line's spiritual implications, and turning to the other side, opens to a language whose nature explores the physical, the body of the voice, or the voice as body. In part, this complexity in her work—work of spirit and work of body—arises as both a natural and an ethical consequence of the poetic ground she finds herself standing on: "I thought I stood on the shores of a history of the world where forms of wildness brought up by memory become desire and multiply."[18] Here the wilderness wilds itself, emerging from history's strict fact and wilding that fact back into complexity, into desire, back into those bodies whose only evidence lurks within the "damaged edition's semi-decay" in which Howe finds her fertile soil. Like Oppen's deer in "Psalm," as she finds voices that are themselves bodies, the startle is that "they are there," roots dangling from their mouths, "scattering earth in the strange woods." It is here, in this location all the more real for needing the imagination to find it, that Howe discovers the necessity for her radical vacillation between body and breath:

domain of transcendental subjectivity
Etymology the this

present in the past now
So many thread[19]

A "transcendental subjectivity" finds itself no longer limited to the self and the self's experience; rather, this self when it says "I" finds this pronoun of greatest intimacy, this word of the self-same, open on every

side rather than closed. The "transcendental subject" finds herself appre-
hensive as a basic condition: fearful, yes, but also grasping, also seeking,
also understanding. Words contain a history that includes us and exceeds
us. A word points back through itself past the definite article to the accu-
sative this (etymology here ambivalent in such a way that it acts almost as
a verb—almost as a verb in the imperative). *This* says we are in the presence
of what has arrived from out the past's wilds, shuttles the opened self into
the past whose nature isn't history's index, but now's experience. A word
is a thread. The poem is a test of the words that fill it, a test that seeks to
discover if the thread is strong enough to pull into itself that wilderness
to which the poem is attached, or strong enough for the poet herself to be
pulled through the poem into that wilderness. Haunted, haunting work.

Howe seeks a way "To write against the ghost."[20] Such writing doesn't
seek to negate, but by pressing against, to bring by the work of language
in the crucible of poetic fervor, the ghost into relief—as if the statue could
step bodily out of the blank stone, or as a child rubs a crayon against the
page until in every detail, down to the very veins, the leaf beneath appears.

The last, short section of *Souls of the Labadie Tract*, "Fragment of the
Wedding Dress of Sarah Pierpont Edwards," re-materializes the body
of the poem in a book remarkable in part for the pneumatic quality of
the long series that precede it. The first poem is the fragment of wedding
dress itself, reproduced in black and white, a square cloth whose selvage
on each side slightly frays, a partial blossom darker than the background
cloth, one thread on the top arching above the whole like a solar flare.
The fragment is as much a poem as the poem to follow—not simply an
artifact for proof, not merely an evidence. Looking at it one feels that
the fragment could be pulled apart thread by thread from any side of
the fabric; likewise, one feels that from every margin threads could
gather and weave themselves into the dress entire.

The fragment is a haunted intimacy—fragment of wedding dress
and fragment of poem. The fabric points back to the body that wore
it. Though the dress fragment appears flat, it has an inside that pressed
against the body of Sarah Pierpont Edwards, and it has an outside that
faces the world. To look at the square swatch of cloth long enough is to
realize that one doesn't know which side of the fabric is seen—am I

outside the body or am I within it? The poem fragment shares the same dilemma. The poems in the section feel comprised of a language pulled from multiple sources: definitions, descriptions archival and speculative, personal notes, notational marginalia, historical facts, categorical ephemera. It is a language found and language assembled and a language created; it is a language frayed, a selvage-language, a language marking the weave of its own construction, marking the schisms of its own damage. Certain lines are revelatory without being revealing:

the space of time into paper. Generation to[21]

And later:

fragile security . when alphabetic characters still
light of twighlight share the approaching sun
carrying traces[22]

The collage work emphasizes not only a pulling from multiple sources, or from differing registers of voice, but the helpless recognition that no voice is singular in its unity. Like some unconscious, inevitable Philomela, we speak by weaving a cloth that depicts our history—save, our history is never merely our own. We seldom see how a line of poetry is simultaneously a vocalized reality and a tangible thread. Less often do we see that the threads with which we weave our voices are not a self-made material. The "alphabetic characters" carry traces. Those traces in part are the indefinite permutations of every use the alphabetic characters have been put to, as if words built of these letters contain in them those experiences which before our own lives they have named. We speak other lives when we speak our own—it is not enough to say we speak *of* them. We speak them. In Howe's poem, there are these traces exerting themselves bodily in word as a material, in the word as fragment, in the fragment of the dress, in the dress's material. These fragments contain within themselves not only traces of history ongoing and so not history at all—Faulkner's "The past isn't dead. It's not even past"—but contain within themselves the "twighlight" of the "approaching sun," that light that turns the material semi-transparent, that reveals behind the fragment, be it cloth or be it poem, the presence of the body or the absence of the body.

More to the difficult point, we find in the fragment itself the intimate definition of the poet's nature. Wordsworth's sense that the poet possesses "a disposition to be affected more than other men by absent things as if they were present"[23] finds both confirmation and complication in Howe's work. Howe's poems *present* absence, and *absent* presence. They make of themselves a fragment of the wedding dress turning itself always inside-out and then outside-in, confusing intimacy with surface, confounding surface with intimacy. Her work is a deeply erotic work, and so the fragment of wedding dress is a fitting emblem to the nature not of the poet necessarily, but of the poetry itself. The poem is both the external evidence of an internal work, as the thought moves into voice and voice exits the body into the vibrating air. But there is air inside the poem's body—breath, *pnuema*—also vibrating. The miraculous pivot in Howe's poetry is an exchange of breath because an exchange of body. We find ourselves within and without at once—wearing the dress we are admiring on the bride, inside the poem we are holding as we read it.

Affirming of Wordsworth's sense of the poet and poetry's work at one level, Howe also refutes him at another. Far from Wordsworth's "egotistical sublime" (cf. Keats's letter to Richard Woodhouse, October 27, 1818), Howe presents the apprehensive self, the open self, the adhesive self, and the permeable self. In *Singularities*, she quotes from Deleuze and Guattari:

> The proper name (*nom propre*) does not designate an individual: it is on the contrary when the individual opens up to the multiplicities pervading him or her, at the outcome of the most severe operation of depersonalization, that he or she acquires his or her true proper name. The proper name is the instantaneous apprehension of a multiplicity. The proper name is the subject of a pure infinitive comprehended as such in a field of intensity.[24]

The voices gather in the name of the poet and give her her name. She is a body for their breath, and then also her breath fills their body. Who isn't a many and a one? Who isn't a ghosted chorus? Who isn't a body filled with breath?—or is it, a breath filled with body?

> Here the poem is the poet.
> Here the poet haunts the haunted ground.
> "Speak to me," Sappho says.
> "Let me in" is a question and an answer.

Ghosts

Howe's poems alternate between materiality and intangibility; they never mark the line that divides their own opposition. We find instead poems built of languages found, gathered, and gleaned which Howe assembles into collages of intimate damage. These poems hover in some uncertain realm between clarity and dispersal, unable to signal within themselves a tendency toward manifestation or decay. Reading such poems, we feel witness to the holy moment when being decides to step into itself and begin to speak. But there are traces that remind one, that in the midst of this bodying forth from *saying* to *said,* that the construction is a wary one, finding in itself, on itself, those marks that map the intent of the construction, and so map the fault lines by which it may also fall apart. The majority of the poems in *That This*—Howe's most recent book whose cover is the slate blue fragment of Sarah Pierpont Edward's wedding dress glimpsed in ghostly black and white in *Souls of the Labadie Tract*—show the spectral lines of the "invisible" tape holding these voices together. Those traces point back at the poet whose adhesive effort leaves a ghostly demarcation. It cannot be helped. The poet ghosts the ghosts.

Conversely, we find poems (as in the majority of poems in *Souls of the Labadie Tract*) whose standard lineation offers only the most basic clue that in them an alternate (read altering; read alterity) work is occurring. The differences are more profound, more mysterious. Here, too, voices arrive manifold, but bear no mark of that multiplicity. Among those voices is Howe's own. It does not designate itself simply by saying *I.* Nor do the other voices name themselves, nor offer their voices up for naming. To do so would be to commit a violence from which the poem itself might not recover—false claim of identity, of naming names, of pinning voice to history as a butterfly is pinned to a mat. Howe's effort opposes such reductions, resists such categorizations. Rather, the ethical effort infusing the poems must be reflected in the reader's ethical effort in experiencing the work. We must learn to hear how many voices dwell in another voice; we must learn to read so other voices may dwell in us. We must learn to hear the haunting chorus, that when we say *I* we say *I* for all.

A haunted voice denies that its primary value is historical. It speaks through itself not merely of the fact of its own occurrence, but of that ongoing source that speaks through the fecund decay of the nearly forgotten words that populate and wild Howe's poems. That ongoing source could be called origin. It could be thought of as before history, as before language. It is precisely here—though "here" is in Howe no precise point—where the historical arrives not as any end in itself, not as any reclamation or revision or recovery, but arrives so as to open within itself another threshold, ontological in nature. History enters into the poem's realm not as a door closing or a wall fitting into place, but enters with a casement window faultily latched in the midst of its certainty, half-open in the midst of its facts. But one must not forget that such openings, ontological in nature, are also violent. They have in them the violence of that which, once open, refuses to close.

We should also see, as Giorgio Agamben encourages,[25] that such violence marks the work of the poem concerned with tradition. Howe's poems radically redefine the nature of the traditional lyric. Ghosts demonize tradition's old dilemmas. They wander through the woods, these sourceless sources. They make the leaves shake. Howe invites them in, not merely into the content of her own poems, but into her voice that opens on the page that metaphysical space the poem must first open within itself. The blank page is the place on which the poem is printed, but within the poem is another space, the haunted realm that occurs only after the words have been written:

Unconscious demarcations range

I pick my compass to pieces

Dark here in the drifting
in the spaces of drifting

Complicity battling redemption[26]

The traditional voice—that is, the voice that invites into it that which haunts it—disorients itself through its own method. It creates the dark space of its own drifting. It realizes it is complicit in the creation of the very condition from which it wants to redeem those it discovers. Those voices:

Oh I see—I have to see
you fresh as those rough
streams are as power is

Caught—and wide awake

Oh—we are past saving
Aren't odd books full of us
What do you wake us for[27]

The voices themselves, "saved" into the poet's poems, ask why it is they're being awakened. (When such ghosts awake they open their mouths and not their eyes.) To see "you fresh as those rough / streams" is to understand that the poem on the page cannot remove itself from a consideration of the history that precedes it. Such a poem doesn't venerate history, but damages it, or is willing to damage it—damage, perhaps, to destruction complete. The traditional poem asks a question of which tradition is not the answer sought, but that origin before tradition, underneath tradition. There is in the poem the furious effort to become its own source. The genuinely traditional poem, of which in my mind Howe's is the necessary example, cannot take for granted the means by which it has come to its knowing, but must pull up its own roots, must tear up and tear apart, the very history that makes its own utterance possible. It must disturb its own roots. It is no simple act of reclamation. Nor is the effort to restore, to repair. It also disturbs the root that is the poet herself:

"Here we are"—You can't
hear us without having to be
us knowing everything we

know—you know you can't

Verbal echoes so many ghosts
poets I think of you as wild
and fugitive—"Stop awhile"[28]

The poet invites the ghosts into the poem and in doing so makes of the ghosts poets. The poem becomes some dwelling the poet writes so as to enter, and in entering becomes less real, less than real, the countermotion of which is the arrival of the ghosts into the same space, an arrival that makes more real, more than real. Then their wildness finds confine; then they are not fugitive. But this poetry does not seek to tame. The nature of the confine is the poetic line which in uttering itself opens itself. In opening itself, it opens to the utterances of the ghosts that fill it; the poet's line loses the narrow subjectivity of identity, and grows multiple: "The tone of an oldest voice / Still one of great multitude." [29]

Howe's work concerns the epistemological repercussions and the ethical consequences of the poem as a realm of gathering proximity. The voice gathers these ghosts; these ghosts gather in a voice. Milton's "darkness visible" seems too legible a construction to speak honestly about how the reader encounters the multiplicity of voices speaking within one another, and against one another, in Howe's poems. But Levinas's sense of the work of art existing in a "dark light" brings us closer to that light in which we might approach Howe's work—approach, as the poems themselves demand, so as to enter ourselves into that shade among the shades.

> I keep you here to keep
> your promise all that you
> think I've wrought what
>
> I see or do in the twilight
> of time but keep forgetting
> you keep coming back[30]

These ghosts, this multiple-you, this other that is always others, this one that is always plural, keep entering into the twilit space of forgetting. These ghosts exist in the very space in which they cease to exist, they find remembrance in these very woods—"Language a wood for thought"[31]—where the non-experiential existing always within experience exerts ceaselessly its paradoxical condition.

This "dark light" illuminates its own obstructions. It alters radically the assumption a reader has towards a poem's own impetus toward formal completion. In these poems, where "Memory was and will be,"[32] incompletion replaces completion as the poem's end. All that exists within the unfinished, unfinishable limits of the poem's utterance— subject and object, speaker and spoken—finds itself fated to incompletion, an uncertain condition, half-lit or dark-lit, in which the poem's ethical complexity finds its difficult, stuttering expression. This ethical stuttering does not belong to the poet, for who now is the poet? Nor does it belong to the ghosts, for who are they? In the dark light of the poem such distinctions can only be falsifications. It occurs in rhythm more than image, as Levinas writes, where rhythm

> represents a unique situation where we cannot speak of consent, assumption, initiative or freedom, because the subject is caught up and carried away by it . . . It is so not even despite itself, for in the rhythm there is no longer a oneself, but rather a sort of passage from oneself to anonymity . . .[33]

Howe's willingness to write so as to create on the page that uncertain realm in which the ongoing work of proximity may continue marks not only the greatness of her project, but its most profound, and most complicated, ethical work. She writes so as to sentence herself to an anonymity that cannot be maintained, slipping back always into the narrow realm of singular self, but doing so in such a way that the traces of that "oldest voice of greatest multitude" require (more than merely make possible) the next poem into whose wilderness she casts her voice so as to open her voice, and opens her voice so as to enter it just as others enter it. Just as we enter it who read her poems. The ethical work isn't one of clarification, but one of mystification. Beyond even the Levinasian framework in which the ethical obligation begins in the discovery of the supervening precedence of the other's face, we find in these bewildered poems a condition in which the face of the other cannot wholly be seen.

The face can't be seen, but the voice can be heard.

That voice is no single voice—though within it, as of the hiss at universe's edge, one can hear, or imagine one hears, that pre-original, pre-language drone that marks the inexperiential edge where chaos hedges into cosmos. One can almost sense the limit, the binding source. But it is only heard by suffering this poetry's ethical difficulty, suffering it just as the poem suffers it:

> Is one mind put into another
> in us unknown to ourselves
> by going about among trees

and fields in moonlight or in
a garden to ease distance to
fetch home spiritual things[34]

Perhaps there is no other home than the home poetry offers, the home the poem is. Open the door to that home and find the wilderness growing in it. The poem contains the forest it wanders through, continual mystical inversion of form and content. The poem contains what contains it. Is it that one writes so as to enter? A word being a door and a wood and a wild leaf and an initiation? To enter is to find in one's own mind another mind, many minds, each with a mind in its own. Confounded among the trees, in the moonlit fields. The effort, as the poem so plainly says, is to "ease distance to / fetch home spiritual things." Such things are ghosts, are phantasms, these images-not-quite-images that invoke in the singular subject that ethereal obligation to dismantle the edifice of one's merest self, ego's iota, and to let the ghosts climb into the poem, dwell in the voice, multiply and sing, accuse and comfort, and make of the poet's mouth only a crooked path in a dark forest, whose trees branch up through the brain, whose leaves open not to the sun but to this dark light, the word's own shining, call it responsibility, and whose echo from the edges calls back, *response*.

Notes

1. Susan Howe, *The Nonconformist's Memorial*, 56-57.
2. Susan Howe, *Souls of the Labadie Tract*, 15.
3. Herman Melville, *Moby-Dick*, 94.
4. Howe, *The Nonconformist's Memorial*, 36.
5. Susan Howe, *Singularities*, 50.
6. Howe, *Singularities*, 49.
7. Howe, *The Nonconformist's Memorial*, 74.
8. Henry David Thoreau, *Journals, Volume 1*, 71.
9. Howe, *The Nonconformist's Memorial*, 38.
10. Agamben, "Philosophical Archaeology," in *The Signature of All Things*, 95.
11. Howe, *The Nonconformist's Memorial*, 69.
12. Howe, *The Nonconformist's Memorial*, 16.
13. Howe, *The Nonconformist's Memorial*, 26.
14. Howe, *The Nonconformist's Memorial*, 75.
15. Howe, *Singularities*, 30.
16. Agamben, "Chapter 13: *Spiriticus phantasticus*," 94.
17. Howe, *The Nonconformist's Memorial*, 42.

18. Howe, *Singularities*, 40.
19. Howe, *Singularities*, 43.
20. Howe, *The Nonconformist's Memorial*, 61.
21. Howe, *Souls of the Labadie Tract*, 120.
22. Howe, *Souls of the Labadie Tract*, 122.
23. Wordsworth and Coleridge, "Preface to the *Lyrical Ballads*," 104.
24. Howe, *Singularities*, 41.
25. Agamben, *The Signature of All Things: On Method*.
26. Howe, *Singularities*, 55.
27. Howe, *Souls of the Labadie Tract*, 50.
28. Howe, *Souls of the Labadie Tract*, 58.
29. Howe, *Souls of the Labadie Tract*, 94.
30. Howe, *Souls of the Labadie Tract*, 55.
31. Howe, *The Nonconformist's Memorial*, 39.
32. Howe, *The Nonconformist's Memorial*, 34.
33. Bruns, "The Concepts of Art and Poetry,"48.
34. Susan Howe, *That This*, 104.

Bibliography

Agamben, Giorgio. "Philosophical Archaeology." In *The Signature of All Things: On Method*, translated by Luca D'lsanto and Kevin Attell, 81–112. New York: Zone Books, 2009.

Agamben, Giorgio. "Chapter 13: *Spiriticus phantasticus*." In *Stanzas: Word and Phantasm in Western Culture*, translated by Ronald L. Martinez, 90–101. Minneapolis: University of Minneapolis Press, 1993.

Bruns, Gerald L. "The Concepts of Art and Poetry in Emmanuel Levinas's Writings." In *The Cambridge Companion to Levinas*, edited by Simon Critchley and Robert Bernasconi, 206–234. Cambridge: Cambridge University Press, 2002.

Howe, Susan. *The Nonconformist's Memorial*. New York: New Directions, 1993.

Howe, Susan. *Singularities*. Middletown: Wesleyan University Press, 1990.

Howe, Susan. *Souls of the Labadie Tract*. New York: New Directions, 2007.

Howe, Susan. *That This*. New York: New Directions, 2010.

Melville, Herman. *Moby-Dick*. Oxford: Oxford University Press, 2008.

Thoreau, Henry David. *Journals, Volume 1. Feb 9, 1841*. New York: Dover Books, 1962.

Wordsworth, William and Samuel Taylor Coleridge. "Preface to the *Lyrical Ballads*." In *Lyrical Ballads 1798 and 1802*, edited by Fiona Stafford. Oxford: Oxford University Press, 2013.

Ecstatic Émigré

Prologue

poetic statement by Claudia Keelan

The work of epistemology, of knowing, in spiritual terms, is countered by the work of Being. Interacting, the two work a dynamic of abandonment. Knowing begat Empire, eventuating in a mouse attached to electrodes, while the scientists pretended they were not dreaming of Elysian Fields. Being is inexorably connected to dispossession, a serial dispossession, an act of becoming ceaselessly, a condition Simone Weil called "decreation."[1] It—that is, Being—is not contained by knowledge, but runs through it. Christian mystics called it by various names, god, soul, love, Buddhists Tao.[2][3] It becomes imperative, embarrassed and anguished by the discredited state of faith in the hands of religion, to rush to the dictionary: It is a noun. Synonyms for It: He, Him, She, Her, this one, that one, the aforementioned, the situation. The subject. Thus "It," aided momentarily by epistemology, involves a living range of possibility, and so the seeker in time is bound to destabilization as she pursues that living.

When I speak of Being, I often call it Her. She must forget what she knows to find what It is. She is at all times aware of the deictic, aware that the referent is dependent on the context in which it is said or written. She says: "I want him to come here now," knowing the words I, here, him, and now are deictic because the determination of their referents depends on who says that sentence, and where, when, and of whom it is said.

I am interested in It, in relation to myself, and to others, which is, among other things, a Christian ethic. It is also a political stance, evident in, among other things, American rhetoric. As Gertrude Stein sees, in *The Making of Americans:*

> Many have a very certain feeling about something inside them. Many need company for it, this is very common, many need a measure for it, this will need explaining, some need drama to support it, some need lying to help it, some are not letting their right hand know what their left hand is doing with it, some love it, some hate it, some never are very certain they really have it, some only think they love it, some like the feeling of loving it, some like the feeling of loving it they would had have if they could have it.[4]

The "It" inside, deictic, determined and indeterminate, progressive-digressive, based in singularity and multiplicity, based in the certainty of contradiction, in the capacity for being in uncertainties—in Gertrude Stein's grammar, the American is one among others in the making, the writer among them seeing in the one the many, seeing a *process* by which something whole is seen.[5] I have worked something like this in my writing, pluralizing the "I," singularizing the "we," allowing Her to script a flow chart of what is a particular—and through its particularity shared—liberation theology. I believe that the central work of poetry, the work that remains in a state of revolution,[6] is attached *via negativa*, to clarifying the *real locale* of our ultimate dispossession, while creating a space for futurity and paradise here:

Pressed beyond zero   I pressed my ear to her

I found a channel   & radioing   Came a colony

Rousseau's rabbits   A dream of population

    A dream of unpreparing   To prepare

A population of rabbits   I would never see   But dream of

    Forever in my absence from them

  In the generation the newest population I and my dream

Of them   Became her   Then it was I was under

I was below stars   I gave up my dream there

Under as in beneath

A light so profound a light very possibly streaming

From a star   Dead already thousands of years

And yet I saw it   So you can see me   As you see her

As I give up me   For generations   To prepare by[7]

Notes

1. Stevens, *The Necessary Angel*, 174–175. This is Wallace Stevens's reading of Weil's notion of decreation: "Weil says that decreation is making pass from the created to the uncreated, but that destruction is making pass from the created to nothingness. Modern reality is a reality of decreation, in which our revelations are not the revelations of belief, but the precious portents of our own powers. The greatest truth we could hope to discover, in whatever field we discovered it, is that man's truth is the final resolution of everything."

2. Porete, "The Mirror of Simple Annihilated Souls," 174–175. "So one must crush oneself, hacking and hewing away at oneself to widen the place in which Love will want to be, burdening oneself down with several states of being, so as to unburden oneself and to attain to one's being." Whoa. Marguerite Porete was a Beguine who was executed as a heretic in Paris in 1310, because she wouldn't stop distributing her book which proposed such a spiritual path. Her Christianity is still heretical. In psychological parlance, she'd be called a hysteric, self-mutilating, perhaps sado-masochistic, given a series of drugs, etc.

3. Lao Tzu, *Tao Te Ching*, 1.
"Tao called Tao is not Tao.
Names can name no lasting name."
This could easily be categorized as New Age, which is an industry. It could sell a series of tee shirts, or be the logo for a yoga studio.

4. Stein, *The Making of Americans*, 305.

5. Stein, *How to Write*. In Gertrude Stein's lexicon of value in "Poetry and Grammar" it is the activity available in the verb, the "mistakenness" of the adverb, the indefinite nature of pronouns, the "work" of the conjunction, the "inevitability" of the period, that garner respect. By contrast, nouns, adjectives, commas, question marks ("it is alright…when it is used as a brand on cattle…"), quotation and exclamation marks are "servile, while semi colons and colons "have no life of their own…they are dependent on use and convenience." Prepositions are king and queen, because they can "live one whole life being nothing but mistaken…" The mistakes of nouns and adjectives, semi-colons, question marks, etc., are their *dependence* upon verbal conventions which to Stein are "unnecessary names" of things that in and of themselves don't "work," don't "have a life of their own." Normative grammar is besieged. By way of mistakenness, activity and work, Stein develops a language that destabilizes the nominative case.

6. NOUN

revolution: (from the Latin *revolutio*, "a turnaround")

1. overthrow of government: the overthrow of a ruler or political system

2. major change: a dramatic change in ideas or practice

Radical poetics might hope that definition two could result in definition one.

7. Claudia Keelan, "Rabbits."

Bibliography

Keelan, Claudia. *Missing Her.* Farmington, ME: Alice James Books, 2009.

Lao-Tzu. *Tao Te Ching.* Translated by Stephen Addiss and Stanley Lombardo. Indianapolis: Hackett Publishing, 1993.

Porete, Marguerite. "The Mirror of Simple Annihilated Souls." In *The Essential Writings of Christian Mysticism,* edited by Bernard McGinn, 172–179. New York: Random House, 2006.

Stein, Gertrude. *How to Write.* Edited by Patricia Meyerowitz. New York: Dover, 1975.

Stein, Gertrude. *The Making of Americans.* Normal, IL: Dalkey Archive Press, 1995.

Stevens, Wallace. *The Necessary Angel: Essays on Reality and the Imagination.* New York: Vintage Books, 1951.

It Didn't Need Believing

Cole Swensen's Gravesend

Elizabeth Robinson

In his essay, "Poetry and Positivisms," Robin Blaser objects that "the institutionalization of imaginary forms has become an immobility of foregone conclusions."[1] Blaser enjoins poets to create a poetry that sets aside positivistic assumptions in order to replace them with poetic practices that "compose the representable alongside the nonrepresentable."[2] Cole Swensen's newly published book, *Gravesend*, engages with exactly such a project as she investigates the phenomenon of ghosts. Our contemporary remove from assumptions and beliefs that grounded previous eras is something that Swensen has clearly considered in this book for she alludes extensively to cultural and historical discussions about ghosts. Yet to engage with this kind of historical and philosophical reflection is not a practice of debunking. Rather, it is, as Blaser says, a shift that

> involves us in a changed view of ourselves and of the range in recognitions of the other. The imagination of wholeness is being undone and displaced by a poetics which [has] to do with movement and change.[3]

Swensen does not endorse "magic" or the "sublime" in the way that Blaser could more comfortably do. At one point in the manuscript, the author even concedes of ghosts, "I really don't think I believe in ghosts, but."[4] This statement, to my mind a central turn in the book, mediates both belief and unbelief through the syntactically incomplete conjunction of "but" as well as the hedging diction of "I really don't think" (which could more assertively and simply have been written as "I don't believe"). Here and elsewhere in the book, Swensen models a mode of movement, attention, and responsiveness that resists ossifying convictions in favor of what I will call the spirituality of a disrupted knowing. Thus, Swensen's poetics open to an inquiry that suspends belief and disbelief alike; the author responds to "information" and experience that are malleable, evasive, and unconfirmable within a poetry that deliberately erodes our confidence in the line between "being and place" so that we enter the process of "place being time." Such a place is uneasy and uncanny and yet it frames itself for the reader as an open question; the aperture of the inquiry, destabilizing though it may be, is also an opening to hospitality through which we "let the stranger in."[5]

Swensen's characteristic mode of writing—that is, book projects that emphasize what I would call lyric research (covering topics from religious paintings, to hands, to opera, etc.)—would seem to be an unexpected site for consideration of the spiritual. Yet it's exactly the straitened metaphysics of Swensen's approach that seems relevant in providing for alternatives within a contemporary spirituality and a poetry that attains the imaginative suppleness that Blaser urges us to foster. The material of *Gravesend* demonstrates the profound ambiguities of not believing, which is to say that this material marks an irresolute space between the positive poles of belief and unbelief. In affirming that she does not believe, she is not exactly saying that she utterly *disbelieves*; notably, the first phrase of the book is, "I sat on the edge."[6] *Gravesend* functions as a mode of alertness and, above all, responsiveness within a disrupted epistemology. It provides a threshold space.

As Bachelard notes in *The Poetics of Space*, the liminal space of the threshold (modeled imagistically in so many instances throughout *Gravesend*), "the door is an entire cosmos of the Half-open."[7] The author's willingness to open this portal onto a site of speculative uncertainty (through a door, so to speak, left ajar) marks a decided engagement with spirituality that functions in a post-belief manner. I would cite here Robin Blaser's claim that "our poetic context involves relation to an unknown, not a knowledge or method of it."[8] Correspondingly, *Gravesend* reflects philosophically and ethically on the limits of what can be known and in so doing affirms that individuals and communities both desire and need to persevere in inquiries that will never yield definitive answers.

The way that Swensen constructs her inquiry in *Gravesend* is significant. Readers of her previous work will recognize the way she has, here as elsewhere, done extensive research into (for example) the literature of the ghost story, historical shifts in conception of what a ghost is, and even the etymology of the word "ghost." Tonally, this gives the material a feeling of detachment that (again characteristically) Swensen disrupts through formal interventions and subtle eruptions of affect and commentary. Fragmentation, shifts of attention, and contradiction (even between historical or literary sources) usefully dislocate the sense of objectivity and authority that the quasi-scholarly resources at first seem to establish.

At the same time, this book also marks a shift in Swensen's process, for, interspersed among the poems, the reader finds three sections in which the author has interviewed others, asking:

~Have you ever seen a ghost? Were you afraid?
~How did Gravesend (in the United Kingdom) get its name (this asked of residents of the town)?
~What is a ghost? Do you think you'll ever be one?

This material based on interviews suggests that there are different forms of authority and, correspondingly, different means of upsetting that authority. Importantly, the interviewees are not identified within the text while the interview text itself is sometimes fragmented with interpolations from the author, as when in the first interview section the author asks individuals if they have ever seen a ghost. This vagueness about who the speaker/respondent is contributes greatly to a sense of uncanniness in the text. Bachelard observes that the "phenomenology of the poetic imagination allows us to explore the being of man [sic] considered as the being of a *surface*, of the surface that separates the region of the same from the region of the other."[9] Here, the boundaried surfaces are effaced and the reader is haunted by a "not knowing" that compels not so much a suspension of disbelief as something akin to the bewilderment that Fanny Howe describes as the disorientation necessary to meet a poetic text on its own defamiliarized terms. One gets a sense of this in "Going Home," when Swensen asserts that "this story is told in many versions . . . as if a man // slipped on his own name and became a repetition in tongues."[10] The usual points of orientation, the borders that mark as self and an other, have eroded.

Pressing on the interview as a formal trope that permits one to "find out" about a topic, to partake of the authority of the interviewee, Swensen not only evokes the uncanny, but she is more overtly humorous than I have observed her to be in other books. For of course she is asking about a matter for which there can be no empirical, verifiable evidence and she is attuned to the potentially absurd aspect of such conjecture. Further, multiple voices—sometimes roundly, even absurdly—contradicting each other's utterances, set up knowing/knowledge as dialogic, lofted lopsidedly *between* voices or speakers. The reader's suspension between these voices is, arguably, an experience of the supernatural; through them, perception comes at the reader devoid of attributable origin. Swensen's informal research (conducted in an historic tavern in Gravesend) into the origin of the name "Gravesend" deliberately muddies the water further. This query deviates from the ostensible subject at hand—ghosts— and shows the wildly unreliable nature of any purportedly factual or historical report. Implicit here are the questions: What is history? What about a place makes it susceptible to being named *or* haunted? Credulity (or incredulity) is revealed as communal and consensual in the hands of Gravesend's populace, even though (the reader quickly discovers) there is no communal consensus to be had in Gravesend.

When Swensen returns to the matter of ghosts in the last third of the book, asking, finally, "What *is* a ghost?" seemingly objective discourse or epistemology ruptures into material that is freely and compellingly speculative. It is here that the material has earned and achieved a freedom that takes it beyond the question of the verifiable. To employ a cliché, doubt has here become an adjunct of faith. Indeed, no statement of credulity/suspended disbelief is necessary here because "proof" is no longer the point. The acknowledged disruption of knowledge has opened epistemology into a dynamic and buoyant disequilibrium that has its own eros and charge. The very act of inquiry is a beguilement which pulls the participant into its continuous, albeit inconclusive, orbit, where "a gathering mist / is a migration."[11]

Looking closely at the three interview sections is a necessary way of gaining a deeper intimacy with the book.[12] Because they are formally distinct from the poems, they impress themselves strongly on the reader's attention, thereby creating compass points around which the poems constellate. These sections serve as an almost architectural element in the book (and this is complemented by Swensen's repeated reliance on such structural images as doors, windows, and houses) because they force the reader to ask: What is inside and what is outside? Who is speaking? Are the poems distinct and therefore outside the interview? What is the relation of one form to the other and how do the liminal spaces between formal shapes help the reader enter a state of productive wonder?

The initial interview section comes after the manuscript has already established its concerns with twenty pages of poetry. At this juncture, Swensen introduces the following questions: "Have you ever seen a ghost?" and "Were you frightened?" Immediately, her respondents shift the nature of the inquiry. The first reply is "It depends on what you mean / by seen."[13] A few lines on, the respondent adds, "No, it's not that I *didn't* see him; what / I'm calling into question here is the notion of seeing," (25) and still further down the page we get, "Well, yes . . . just glimpses— something out of the corner of my eye, something crossing a room; I didn't exactly see it," (25) and ". . . hmmm . . . *seen*—it's a complex word. What I mean is that I've perceived presences" (25). Swensen amplifies this tension in a dense little paragraph in which she repeats the word "look" almost to the point of making it nonsensical:

> And yet, would you have thought it, just *looking* around the room? Would you have thought that over 70% of these people who *look* so untroubled have ever seen anything that they couldn't in any way explain? They don't *look* like it to me. And do they speak of it? And will they if I ask them? And if they do speak of it, will they start to '*look* like it'?" (25, italics mine.)

What Swensen does here is not only show the reader that she is asking the wrong question, but underlines this "wrongness" with the parodic repetition of the word "look." On the following page, a voice admits with a sigh that he or she has never seen a ghost but then with a figurative shrug adds, "Who knows? Sometimes I think they're all around us; I mean, so all around us they're simply the background. We don't see air either, or wind. We live in them" (27). The difficulty of response leapfrogs from the poet's ostensibly innocent query, to the realization that the question itself is wrong. The further recognition is that what one hopes to perceive and confirm is so pervasive that it transcends perception. This realization clarifies that, amid the omnipresence of ghosts, "a ghost is a form of privacy" (26) and at the same time, due to the inexplicable nature of its presence, a violation of privacy. Thus, the comment "it didn't need believing" (26) is not a form of skepticism but a new form of knowing that relegates conventional definitions of belief to irrelevance. Suddenly, the intimacy of the subject with the ghost becomes threatening. The ghost breaks down the surface and structure that order knowledge and certainty.

Correspondingly, we often say "haunted houses" in the same breath that we say "ghosts." It's as though the ghost's amorphousness begs for a structure in which it can be held. The elusiveness of the ghost suggests that a supernatural entity is itself lost and, in the process of haunting, needs to return to a familiar site in order to express itself or reclaim form. As I mentioned earlier, Swensen calls upon liminal architectural elements—doors, windows, stairs, and bridges—to show how location itself is an unstable category. On what side of any border does the ghost reside? To what has it "returned," (if, after all, the ghost can ever be said to have returned) when it exists on these "verges"? There *is* no place to come back to in much the same way that there is no final resting point for any conviction that extends beyond what can be empirically authenticated. Swensen frames the problem of location as something between physical and epistemological worlds when she asks, in the second interview section, how the town came to be named Gravesend. The name, read literally, implies a siteless place: the place where a discrete marker, the grave, has ended. The name can then be read theologically as the location at which death itself has ended. Yet where does death end? Mortality may be the one inevitability that all humans face, but even here there is disagreement: is death a passage or a stopping point? The utter lack of agreement on the origin of the name is an appropriate part of the larger investigation.

Two prelude poems precede the second interview (both called "Gravesend"). In the first of these, Swensen presents several seemingly objective accounts of how the town got its name, in each instance following the explicatory stanza with a negation ("No, London does not go to the sea," "No, he is dead," "They are wrong," "No, a grave is a grievance" (45). This mirrors elements of the first interview in which Swensen shows the wrongheadedness of her query by emphasizing the misdirected word "look." The poem's interruptive contradictions are almost outlandish; they thwart any progress toward the origin of the town's name. The claim that "a grave is a grievance" is to the point here, for the impossibility of any final resting place will halt all inquiry, whether about ghosts or towns.

Throughout the manuscript, Swensen repeatedly employs terms for return and recurrence; this poem models the import of these terms as, six lines from the end of the page, the poem suddenly breaks into first person, saying, "I never returned" before moving into its final stanza:

Gravesend swings back and forth
like a window in the wind. It is named
for the fact that you never returned. It bears
the name of a man who disappeared in plain sight
in the town square on a sunny day. (46)

Note here the curious shifts of pronoun, the first person speaker ("I") who has never returned becomes the "you" who never returned and, finally, the oxymoronic "man who disappeared in plain sight." In this instance, Swensen neatly overturns the concept of a ghost as a haunting, recurring presence, turning it instead into a mortal man who disappears on a sunny day. The formal device of shifting pronouns unsteadies any ready image. The reader cannot settle the boundaries of the poem's protagonist(s) as they come and go, and that's how Swensen enacts a form of haunting. Bachelard has observed, when we try to enter such an image, "we learn to know, in one of its tiny fibres, a becoming of being that is an awareness of the *being's inner disturbance*."[14] This disturbance is additionally evidenced in the way Swensen uses the architectural elements that have come to so define her image bank—in this section, for example, the window that swings back and forth in the wind. The significance of such images is further foregrounded in the next poem, also called "Gravesend." Here, Swensen juxtaposes forms of absence against identifiable structures such as a nave, the "sill of a window or a door," a deadbolt, a door, a hinge, and a bridge. For instance, the nave "is you walking out" where the trees surround "the things left behind" an eerie deadbolt made from thumbs purports to latch "the something that won't // quite shut." The arresting conclusion of this poem states that a grave "is a door laid flat in the earth, worked into a hinge, which articulates a gulf // without being a bridge" (47). In the interview that follows, the diction changes abruptly. Swensen conducted her interviews in a pub, and her interchanges with the people there are chatty and informal. Once again, the speakers are anonymous and the poet expresses herself both via conventional first person discussion ("I was told I couldn't buy a ticket," or telling someone that she is from San Francisco) and through lyric interruptions. This interview is the longest of the three and digresses in surprising directions, as with a description of press gangs, the town's underground tunnels, and the rumor that Pocahontas died in Gravesend. It commences, however, with a response that marks the tenuousness of all responses to follow:

> Why is it called Gravesend? Now that you mention it, that's an interesting question. I've lived here all my life, and I've heard a lot of stories, but I don't know if any of them are true [. . .] it makes me think of engravings and grayscales and all sorts of things to do with printing, but I doubt that has anything to do with the real history—but then history isn't real anyway, is it? (48)

This casually meditative response highlights a key question in the book, namely the unreliable character of history. Beginning the section this way certainly threatens the legitimacy of the interviewing enterprise. In addition, Swensen reprises ideas from her first interview when a pub employee says, "No, I've never seen a ghost, but I've heard one [. . .] Everyone who works here has a different story; we all feel them" (49). Swensen is thus undermining her own procedure by quietly reminding the reader of her inapt question about how a ghost might be perceived (apparently not visually) and then by pointing out that historical accounts have no more viability than perceptual experience. In a section that contains some groan-worthy puns (Tillbury—"till bury" as a repository for bodies until they could be interred in Gravesend, or the town as named for its proximity to an apple orchard full of Gravensteins), Swensen essays her own telling pun, "shifted out of light in a way most / unbecoming, it unbecame" (49). The centrality of *unbecoming* is marked as analogous to belief; stories proliferate and, in the process, undo each other. As they dissolve, though, they resurge as "some slight slippage that streamed beneath" (50). That slippage is part of a "rapt commerce in which none of the merchants is seen" (50). The section ends by showing the futility of burying a body in Gravesend, for "as soon as they stick them in the ground, they start to rise" (52). Questions that refuse to be put to bed once and for all, in a sense, resurrect themselves from what the poet elsewhere calls a "spiral grave" (64). A spiral is a fitting metaphor for this intermediary state of being. Like Swensen's emphasis on returns and arrivals, it clarifies that "in being, everything is circuitous, roundabout, recurrent . . . a refrain with endless verses."[15] Unraveling the viability of her questions even while insisting on the process of *asking* means that Swensen's emphasis is really on the un-becoming of knowledge and being, therefore she can ally with the interviewee who says, "and why not believe it?" (48). The final interview is the shortest at only one and a half pages, but it is rich with speculation and insight. Swensen asks, "What do you think ghosts are?" and "Do you think you'll ever be one?" The first response is, "I don't know . . . I think they're communication, simply that; a ghost is simply a connection" (69). The ghost as discrete, stable entity is effaced throughout the responses. Instead, ghosts become phenomena. The fascinating catalogue of responses includes the following:

they are "a way to get on with it," a passage through time or a crossroads, "what will not fit within," "an accident," or "a broken window, though the window does not end the room; it only breaks the seal," "that fractional moment of suspension that all laws pass through as they're changing," or "tangled electricity" (69–70). One provocative comment suggests that a ghost is "a gap between two clarities, a void and as such, it cannot possibly make sense, at which point, we must admit that we are lacking crucial information on our own state." This last description causes the speaker to reflect further that he or she might very well be a ghost right now, "if viewed from another state." Interestingly, this interview section is without the lyric interpolations that are a feature of the other sections. Perhaps this is because Swensen feels no need to comment on or amend the possibilities that her interviewees have posed: they clearly elaborate the ghost as a site of epistemological irresolution. Moreover, this isn't a site of stasis but an active process, "an electrical storm in a jewelry box" (70). Tension abounds, and the definitions clearly include efforts to contain this mysterious phenomenon, this excess that "will not fit within." Here we indeed see an enactment of the mobile, dynamic poetics that Blaser described, one which does implicate us "in a changed view of ourselves and of the range in recognitions of the other."[16] *Gravesend's* remodeling of our understanding of time, presence, and knowing makes clear that our very partiality and lack of mastery are strange assets—apertures to perception that can be sustained through gulfs of apprehension. This is one way of proceeding with poetry as both a spiritual and an ethical project.

Jean-Luc Nancy proposes that those who want a world that is perceptible through the senses and which makes any sort of rational sense "demand of the world that it signify itself as dwelling, haven, habitation, safeguard, intimacy, community . . . as the signifier of a proper and present signified, the signifier of the proper and present as such."[17] In *Gravesend*, Cole Swensen finds ways to acknowledge that desire while guiding the reader to a construal of "world" that haunts us gracefully with the impossibility of clear signification. She tells us that a "ghost is a hearing is a calling and every gesture that builds the pressure that then through unknowing becomes in pieced the inner ether so larger grows the mansions and larger grows the wind, undid" (30). The ghost, we realize through her tutelage, is neither present nor absent, neither local nor transcendent, neither interior nor exterior. The ghost refuses to yield absolute knowledge of itself or its conditions. It is instead a fertile rumor that helps us respond, as Nancy says, "in the very opening of the abandonment of sense, as the opening of the world."[18] Ghosts and their hauntings force us from the comfortable havens of meaning and knowing that we have clung to. In entertaining the possibility of these indeterminate and intermediary presences, we find the opportunity to interact with the "world" in a more ethically and, yes, spiritually rich manner. Belief, thereby, becomes a suspension that refuses the lure of dialectical resolution. Nancy encourages us to think of this responsiveness as a vibrant openness to experience that circumvents "the appropriation of signification" and can "hold the step of thought suspended over this sense that has already touched us."[19] Belief becomes something other than gullibility or a revised form of mastery. Rather, we might refer to Bachelard who describes something similar:

> In that region where being *wants* to be both visible and hidden, the movements of opening and closing are so numerous, so frequently inverted and so charged with hesitation, that we could conclude on the following formula: man [sic] is half-open being.[20]

Swensen offers us the opportunity to use the ghost as a slippery, evocative metaphor, where the ghost "erodes the line between being and place   becomes the place of being time." The awareness that emerges through living this "half-open being" shows us that poetry's real value isn't solace which "as if a little / trap door slowly spread through every room."[21] As one of the respondents says, "It's meaningless to ask if ghosts are real—*they have an effect in the world. They work.* Can you say that the fright was real and yet that what caused it was not?" (27, italics mine) By emphasizing the text as a site, centrally, of inquiry (as opposed to acquisition of knowledge), Swensen emphasizes the import of nurturing curiosity amid the limits of what can be known. This is a form of faithfulness. Living "ajar" this way, we may more freely make our own departures and returns, guests in the blurred domicile where "we wash [. . .] our hands // in its liminal spaces" (58).

Notes

1. Blaser, *The Holy Forest*, 40.
2. Blaser, *The Holy Forest*, 43.
3. Blaser, 47.
4. Swensen, *Gravesend*, 26. Note that the statement is further mediated as appearing in a section which is ostensibly an interview. Attribution to a single speaker (for instance,

the author) is problematic, since the sentence might be variably read as the author's own assertion or something that an interviewee said.

5. Swensen, *Gravesend*, 9.

6. Swensen, 5.

7. Bachelard, *The Poetics of Space*, 222.

8. Blaser, 54.

9. Bachelard, *The Poetics of Space*, 222.

10. Swensen, 17.

11. Swensen, 81.

12. The poems are not at all secondary to the interviews but part of a complexly constructed whole; however, because of limitations of space, I will devote extended attention to the interviews which are a distinctive element of the text.

13. Swensen, 25. The poetic lines in the rest of the essay are cited from *Gravesend* and page numbers are hereafter cited in the body of the essay.

14. Bachelard, 220.

15. Bachelard, 214.

16. Blaser, 47.

17. Nancy, *The Sense of the World*, 3.

18. Nancy, *The Sense of the World*, 3.

19. Nancy, 11.

20. Bachelard, 222.

21. Swensen, 44.

Bibliography

Bachelard, Gaston. *The Poetics of Space*. Translated by Maria Jolas. Boston: Beacon Press, 1969.

Blaser, Robin. *The Holy Forest*. Edited by Miriam Nichols. Berkeley: University of California Press, 2006.

Nancy, Jean-Luc. *The Sense of the World*. Translated by Jeffrey S. Librett. Minneapolis: University of Minnesota Press, 1997.

Swensen, Cole. *Gravesend*. Berkeley: University of California Press, 2012.

Biographies

Editors

Jennifer Phelps is a poet, writer, and editor in the Denver area where she currently works with authors of academic essays, full-length books, personal essays, and memoirs. (See www.jenniferphelps.com.) She graduated in 2009 with a MFA in Writing and Poetics from Naropa University. Her publications include *Grandmother God* (Eyries Press, 1998), *Memory: a space between breaths* (Shadow Mountain Press, 2013), "Stepping In" in the anthology *Fearless Nest* (Lulu Press, 2010), and other literary reviews and essays in *Bombay Gin* and *Jacket2*.

Elizabeth Robinson is the author of sixteen books, most recently *Rumor* (Parlor Press), *Counterpart* (Ahsahta), *Blue Heron* (Center for Literary Publishing). *On Ghosts* (Solid Objects) was a finalist for the *Los Angeles Times* Book Award. Robinson has been a winner of the Fence Modern Poets Prize and the National Poetry Series and has been awarded grants from the Fund for Poetry and the Foundation for Contemporary Arts. Robinson has also been awarded fellowships from the MacDowell Colony, the Djerassi Resident Artists Program, and the Marin Headlands Center for the Arts. Her poems, essays, and reviews are widely published.

Contributors

Kazim Ali is a poet, essayist, fiction writer and translator. His books include several volumes of poetry, including *Sky Ward* (Wesleyan University Press, 2013), *The Fortieth Day* (BOA Editions, 2008), and the cross-genre text *Bright*

Felon: Autobiography and Cities (Wesleyan University Press, 2009). Translations include *Water's Footfall* by Sohrab Sepehri (Omnidawn Press, 2011), *Oasis of Now: Selected Poems* by Sohrab Sepehri (BOA Editions, 2013) and (with Libby Murphy) *L'amour* by Marguerite Duras (Open Letter Books, 2013). His novels include *Quinn's Passage* (blazeVox books) and *The Disappearance of Seth* (Etruscan Press, 2009), and his books of essays include *Orange Alert: Essays on Poetry, Art and the Architecture of Silence* (University of Michigan Press, 2010) and *Fasting for Ramadan* (Tupelo Press, 2011). In addition to co-editing *Jean Valentine: This-World Company* (University of Michigan Press, 2012), he is founding editor of the small press Nightboat Books. In addition, he is the series co-editor for both *Poets on Poetry* and *Under Discussion*, from the University of Michigan Press. He is an associate professor of Creative Writing and Comparative Literature at Oberlin College.

Michelle Auerbach's most recent novel, *Alice Modern,* was published by XOXOX Press in 2016. She is also the author of *The Third Kind of Horse* (2013 Beatdom Books). Her writing has appeared in (among other places) *The New York Times*, *The Guardian*, *The Denver Quarterly*, *Chelsea Magazine*, *Bombay Gin*, and the literary anthologies *The Veil* (UC Berkley Press), *Uncontained* Baksun Books, and *You. An Anthology of Essays in the Second Person* (Welcome Table Press). She is the winner of the 2011 Northern Colorado Fiction Prize and can be found at www.michelleauerbach.com.

Faith Barrett is Associate Professor of English at Duquesne University where she teaches courses in American literature and culture and creative writing/poetry. With Cristanne Miller, she co-edited *Words for the Hour: A New Anthology of American Civil War Poetry* (U Mass, 2005); she is the author of *To Fight Aloud Is Very Brave: American Poetry and the Civil War* (U Mass, 2012). She has published articles on the poetry of Abraham Lincoln, George Moses Horton, Phoebe Cary and Emily Dickinson among others. Her chapbook *Invisible Axis* was published by Etherdome Press in 2001.

Dan Beachy-Quick teaches poetry workshops and literature courses at Colorado State University. He is the author of five books of poetry, *North True South Bright* (2003), *Spell* (2004), *Mulberry* (2006), *This Nest, Swift Passerine* (2009), and *Circle's Apprentice* (2011, Winner of the Colorado Book Award in Poetry). He is also the author of a book of interlinked meditations on Herman Melville s *Moby-Dick*, titled *A Whaler s Dictionary* (2008) and a collection of essays, meditations, and fairy tales, *Wonderful Investigations* (2012). Two book-length collaborative projects are also available: *Conversities* (2012, with Srikanth Reddy) and *Work from Memory* (21012, with Matthew Goulish). His poems have appeared widely in such journals as *The Boston Review, The New Republic, Fence, Poetry, Chicago Review, VOLT, Colorado Review,* and *New American Writing.* His essays and reviews have appeared in *The Southern Review, The Poker, The Kenyon Review, The New York Times, The Denver Quarterly, Interim,* and elsewhere. He is the recipient of a Lannan Foundation Residency and has been a finalist for the Colorado Book Award, The William Carlos Williams Award, and the PEN/USA Literary Award in Poetry.

Laynie Browne is a poet, prose writer, teacher and editor. She is author of thirteen collections of poems and three novels. Her most recent collections include a book of poems *You Envelop Me* (Omnidawn 2017), a novel *Periodic Companions* (Tinderbox 2018) and short fiction in two editions, one French, and one English in *The Book of Moments* (Presses universitaires de rouen et du havre, 2018). Her honors include a 2014 Pew Fellowship, the National Poetry Series Award (2007) for her collection *The Scented Fox,* and the Contemporary Poetry Series Award (2005) for her collection *Drawing of a Swan Before Memory.* Her poetry has been translated into French, Spanish, Chinese and Catalan. Her writing has appeared in many anthologies including *The Norton Anthology of Post Modern Poetry* (second edition 2013), *Ecopoetry: A Contemporary American Anthology* (Trinity University Press, 2013), *Bay Poetics* (Faux Press, 2006) and *The Reality Street Book of Sonnets* (Reality Street, 2008). She teaches at University of Pennsylvania and at Swarthmore College.

Beverly Dahlen's first book *Out of the Third,* was published by Momo's Press in 1974. Two chapbooks, *A Letter at Easter* (1976) and *The Egyptian Poems* (1983) were followed by the publication of the first volume of *A Reading (1–7)* (1985), a serial poem that continues to be in process. Since then, four more volumes of *A Reading* have appeared, *A Reading 11–17* (1989), *A Reading 8–10* (1992), *A-Reading Spicer & Eighteen Sonnets* (2004), and *A Reading 18–20* (2008). Dahlen was a co-founder, with Kathleen Fraser and Frances Jaffer, of the feminist poetics newsletter *(HOW)ever.* In 2011, Dahlen received a Small Press Traffic Lifetime Achievement Award and in 2013 was recognized with a Foundation for Contemporary Arts Grants to Artists Fellowship. Dahlen earned her B.A. from Humbolt State University and continued her studies at San Francisco State.

Kythe Heller is a poet, essayist, artist, and scholar completing a doctorate at Harvard University in Comparative Religion, with a secondary field in Critical Media Practice. She is author of the poetry collections *Immolation* (Monk Honey, 2008) and *The Thunder Perfect Mind* (Wick: Harvard Divinity School, 2011), and of the monograph "An Ethnography of Spirituality" in *White Light* (Cambridge University Press, 2017). Her poetry and essays have been published in *The American Poetry Review*, *Tricycle*, *The Southern Review*, and elsewhere, and she has been the recipient of grants and fellowships from the Mellon Foundation, Harvard University, The MacDowell Colony, Vermont Studio Center, Virginia Center for the Creative Arts, Squaw Valley Community of Writers, and the Laurels Foundation/PSU. Recent film and interdisciplinary work has been presented at the Harvard Film Studies Center, Open Engagement, SEEDS Festival/Earthdance, Sonoma State University, WAXworks (NYC), BAX (NYC), Virginia Center for the Creative Arts, and in various collaborations and street performances in NYC and elsewhere. She is a teaching fellow at Harvard University and a poet on the faculty of the Language and Thinking Program at Bard College.

Claudia Keelan was born in Southern California when it was still covered with orange groves and NATO started the embargo, still in place, against lovely Cuba. Her writing and teaching career has spanned all corners of the US, as she has taught in many writing programs, including the University of Iowa Writers' Workshop, the University of Alabama, where she held the Coal Royalty Chair in Poetry, Boston College, Rhodes College, and the University of Nevada, Las Vegas, where she is a Barrick Distinguished Scholar. In spring of 2018, Barrow Street published her selected poems *We Step into the Sea* and *Ecstatic Émigré : An Ethics of Practice* was published in the Poets on Poetry series from the University of Michigan Press. A poet, literary scholar, and translator, she lives in the Mojave Desert with the poet Donald Revell, son Ben, daughter Lucie, standard poodle Miss Margaret Jarvis, and a worried schnauzer named Dugan.

Joanne Kyger was born in 1934 and died in 2017. She attended Santa Barbara College. One credit short of a degree, she drove up to San Francisco "one day in January 1957 with [her] Siamese Cat." She arrived at the height of the *Howl* obscenity trial, and a friend introduced her to The Place, the bar that served as headquarters for Jack Spicer and other poets of the

San Francisco Renaissance. At the invitation of Joe Dunn and John Wieners she attended the Sunday Meetings lead by Spicer and Robert Duncan and gave her first reading at the Bread and Wine Mission in 1959 before moving to Japan with Gary Snyder. Out of respect for local custom, they married in Japan, living there and also travelling to India (with Allen Ginsberg and Peter Orlofsky), events that are chronicled in Kyger's *Japan and India Journals 1960–64*. Kyger moved back to San Francisco, was divorced from Snyder, published her first book *The Tapestry and The Web*, travelled in Europe with Jack Boyce, and lived in New York briefly before returning to California. She moved to Bolinas in 1968, where she lived until her death in 2017, writing poetry, editing the local newspaper, travelling to Mexico, and teaching occasionally at Naropa University. The volume, *About Now: Collected Poems*, was published in 2007.

Myung Mi Kim is a Professor of English at the State University of New York at Buffalo. She has been awarded the Multicultural Publisher's Exchange Award of Merit for *Under Flag* (Kelsey St. Press, 1991). She has also received a fellowship from the Djerassi Resident Artists Program, and awards from the Fund for Poetry, a Daesan Foundation Translation Grant, and the State University of New York Chancellor's Award for Excellence in Scholarship and Creative Activity. Her collections of poetry include *Under Flag* (Kelsey St.), *The Bounty* (Chax Press), *DURA* (Sun & Moon), and *Commons* (University of California).

Hank Lazer has published twenty-seven books of poetry, including *Evidence of Being Here: Beginning in Havana (N27)* (2018), *Thinking in Jewish* (2017), *Poems Hidden in Plain View* (2016, in English and in French), *Brush Mind: At Hand* (2016), *The New Spirit* (2005), and *Days* (2002). His *Selected Poems and Essays* was published by Central China Normal University Press in 2015. Lazer's *Selected Poems* have also been published in Italy and will appear shortly in Cuba. In 2015, Lazer received Alabama's most prestigious literary prize, the Harper Lee Award, for lifetime achievement in literature. His books of criticism include *Opposing Poetries* (two volumes, 1996) and *Lyric & Spirit: Selected Essays 1996–2008* (2008). With Charles Bernstein, he edits the Modern and Contemporary Poetics Series for the University of Alabama Press. Lazer retired from the University of Alabama in January 2014 from his positions as Associate Provost for Academic Affairs and Professor of English.

Kimberly Lyons is the author of books of poetry including most recently *Capella* (Oread, 2018), *Approximately Near* (Metambesenddotorg, 2016) and *Calcinatio* (Faux Press, 2014). Her essays on the poetry of Bernadette Mayer and Joseph Ceravolo appeared in *Aufgabe* and *Jacket2*. She has given talks on the poetry of Alice Notley, Pierre Joris, Barbara Guest, and the Poetry Project in the 1980s. She is the publisher of Lunar Chandelier Press and has recently organized events at Anthology Film Archives in NYC. She lives in Chicago.

Laura Moriarty's *Personal Volcano* is forthcoming this spring from Nightboat Books. Her recent publications include *Verne & Lemurian Objects*, *The Fugitive Notebook*, *Who That Divines*, the long essay poem *A Tonalist*, and the novel *Ultravioleta*. Her awards include The Poetry Center Book Award, a Wallace Alexander Gerbode Foundation Award in Poetry, a New Langton Arts Award in Literature, and a Fund for Poetry grant. She lives in Richmond, California.

Tracie Morris is Professor and Coordinator of Performance and Performance Studies at Pratt Institute and has worked extensively as a page-based writer, sound poet, and multimedia performer. Her sound installations have been presented at MoMA and The Jamaica Center for Arts and Learning among others. Tracie is the recipient of the NYFA, Creative Capital, Yaddo, and MacDowell along with other grants, fellowships and awards. Publications include *Intermission* (Soft Skull Press, 1998), *Rhyme Scheme* (Zasterle Press, 2012) and *Collaborations: 4 Kinds* (Kore Press, 2015).

Rusty Morrison's poems and/or essays have appeared in *Boston Review*, *Colorado Review*, *Fence*, *Gulf Coast*, *Iowa Review*, *Kenyon Review Lana Turner*, *Pen Poetry Series*, *Poem-a-Day from the Academy*, *Prelude*, *VOLT*, and elsewhere. Her five books include *After Urgency* (Tupelo), which won The Dorset Prize and *the true keeps calm biding its story* (Ahsahta), which won the Sawtooth Prize, the Academy of American Poet's James Laughlin Award, the Northern California Book Award, and the DiCastagnola Award from Poetry Society of America. Her poems have been anthologized in the *Norton Postmodern American Poetry 2nd Edition*, *The Arcadia Project: Postmodern Pastoral*, *Beauty is a Verb*, and elsewhere. She has been co-publisher of Omnidawn (www.omnidawn.com) since 2001. Her website: www.rustymorrison.com.

Born in the Mekong Delta and raised in the Washington DC area, **Hoa Nguyen** currently makes her home in Toronto. Her poetry collections include *As Long As Trees Last, Red Juice, Poems 1998–2008*, and *Violet Energy Ingots* from Wave Books. Nguyen teaches at Ryerson University, for Miami University's low residency MFA program, for the Milton Avery School for Fine Arts at Bard College, and in a long-running, private poetics workshop.

Sara Nolan teaches personal essay writing—for college admissions and beyond—to teens and tweens through Essay Intensive (www.essayintensive .com). She works with stellar young people at NYC partner nonprofits—The TEAK Fellowship, JPMC The Fellowship Initiative, and Brooklyn Youth Sports Club. She edits broadly. Her work has appeared in *TeenLife Mag, The Manifest Station, Kestrel, Laundry Line Divine*, and *The St. Ann's Review*. Sara has a quirky blended family of four, two children under three who plunder her writing time, and too many noisy parrots.

Alice Notley lives in Paris and is the author of numerous books of poetry, including *Mysteries of Small Houses* (1998) that won the *Los Angeles Times* Book Prize, and her collection *Disobedience* (2001) that was awarded the Griffin International Poetry Prize. Notley's recent work includes *Alma, or the Dead Women* (2006), *Grave of Light: New and Selected Poems 1970–2005*, which received the Lenore Marshall Poetry Prize, *In the Pines* (2007), *Culture of One* (2011), and *Songs and Stories of the Ghouls* (2011). Among her two newest volumes are *Benediction* (Letter Machine Editions, 2015) and *Certain Magical Acts* (Penguin Books, 2016). In addition to collections of poetry, Notley has published the autobiography *Tell Me Again* (1982), the play *Anne's White Glove* (1985), and a book of essays on poets and poetry, *Coming After* (2005). She edited and wrote the introduction for the reissue of Ted Berrigan's *The Sonnets* (2000), as well as editing, with her sons, *The Collected Poems of Ted Berrigan* (2005). Her honors and awards include an Arts and Letters Award from the American Academy of Arts and Letters and the Shelley Memorial Award from the Poetry Society of America. She has also been a finalist for the Pulitzer Prize. She was married to the British poet Douglas Oliver until his death in 2000. In 2015, she was awarded the Ruth Lilly Poetry Prize.

Peter O'Leary was born in 1968 in Detroit, where he was educated by the LaSallian Christian Brothers. He studied literature and religion at the University of Chicago. He is the author of five books of poetry, most recently *The Sampo*, as well as two books of literary criticism, including *Thick and Dazzling Darkness: Religious Poetry in a Secular Age*. He lives in Oak Park, Illinois, and teaches at the School of the Art Institute of Chicago and at the University of Chicago. With John Tipton, he edits Verge Books.

Colleen Lookingbill is the author of *a forgetting of*, from lyric & press. Her previous book of poetry, *Incognita*, was published by Sink Press, and her writing was also published in *New American Writing*, *26*, *Ploughshares*, and *Ambush Review*, among other literary periodicals. She was co-publisher with Elizabeth Robinson of EtherDome Press and was a longtime curator of San Francisco's Canessa Park reading series with her husband Jordon Zorker. She passed away in 2014.

Jaime Robles has two poetry collections from Shearsman Books: *Anime Animus Anima* and *Hoard*. An e-book of essays on poetic theory, *Dark Lyrics: Studying the Subterranean Impulse of Contemporary Poetry*, was published by the Argotist Online in 2016. A visual artist and writer, she has produced many of her texts as artist books, including *Loup d'Oulipo* and *Letters from Overseas*, and her bookworks are in collections at the Bancroft Library, University of California, Berkeley; the Beinecke Library, Yale University; and the Oulipo Archive in Paris, among others. *Three Propositions*, her short film mixing imagery with poems written in response to Wittgenstein's Tractatus, can be found on YouTube. She holds a doctorate in Creative Writing from the University of Exeter, UK.

Elizabeth Savage is a professor of English at Fairmont State University and poetry editor for *Kestrel: A Journal of Literature & Art*. Her recent essays on twentieth and twenty-first-century poetry and poetics appear in the *Cambridge History of Twentieth-Century American Women's Poetry*, *Contemporary Women's Writing*, *Journal of Modern Literature*, and *J2*. She is author of two books of poetry, *Grammar* (2012) and *Idylliad* (2015), and a new chapbook, *Woman Looking at a Vase of Flowers* (2017). In 2016, her poetry won the Denise Levertov Prize and, with Ethel Rackin, the Thomas Merton Prize in Poetry of the Sacred.

Andrew Schelling teaches poetry, Sanskrit, and wilderness writing at Naropa University in Boulder, Colorado. Author of twenty books, he is a translator as well as poet and essay writer. Two recent books of poetry work largely with lore of the American West, ecology of the Rocky Mountains, and the Arapaho language. Translations are from the old languages of India. His latest collection of essays is *The Real People of Wind & Rain*. He edited *Love and the Turning Seasons: India's Poetry of Spiritual and Erotic Longing*. In 2017,

Counterpoint Press published *Tracks Along the Left Coast: Jaime de Angulo & Pacific Coast Culture*—an ideogrammic study of West Coast poetry, California Indian lore, linguistics, and salvage ethnography.

giovanni singleton is the author of *Ascension* and the poetry/art collection *AMERICAN LETTERS: works on paper*. She has received the California Book Award Gold Medal and the African American Literature and Culture Society's Stephen E. Henderson Award for literary achievement. Her writing has also been exhibited in the Smithsonian Institute's American Jazz Museum, San Francisco's first Visual Poetry and Performance Festival, and on the building of Yerba Buena Center for the Arts. singleton is the founding editor of *nocturnes (re)view of the literary arts*, a journal committed to experimental work of the African Diaspora. She teaches poetry in the San Francisco Bay Area where she also coordinates UC Berkeley's Lunch Poems series.

On the faculty of the Department of English at Ryerson University, Toronto, **Dale Smith** has published five books of poetry and a critical monograph, including, most recently, *Slow Poetry in America* (Cuneiform, 2014), a book of narrative writing, and *Poets Beyond the Barricade: Rhetoric, Citizenship, and Dissent after 1960* (University of Alabama, 2012), a critical study of poetry as public art. He is the co-editor with Robert J. Bertholf of *An Open Map: The Robert Duncan/Charles Olson Correspondence* and *Imagining Persons: Robert Duncan's Lectures on Charles Olson*, both published by University of New Mexico Press in 2017. From 1999-2004 he co-edited with Hoa Nguyen the journal and book imprint *Skanky Possum*.

Sasha Steensen is the author of four books of poetry: *House of Deer* (Fence Books), *A Magic Book* (Fence Books), *The Method* (Fence Books), and *Gatherest* (Ahsahta Press). She has published several essays including *Openings: Into Our Vertical Cosmos*, which can be read at Essay Press (http://www.essaypress.org). She lives in Fort Collins, Colorado, where she tends chickens, goats, and children. She serves as a poetry editor for *Colorado Review* and teaches Creative Writing and Literature at Colorado State University.

Brian Teare is the author of five critically acclaimed books, most recently *Companion Grasses*, which was a finalist for the Kingsley Tufts Award, and *The Empty Form Goes All the Way to Heaven*. His sixth book, *Doomstead Days*, will be out from Nightboat Books in 2019. His honors include a Lambda Literary Award and fellowships from the NEA, the Pew Foundation, the American

Antiquarian Society, and the MacDowell Colony. An Associate Professor at Temple University, he lives in South Philadelphia, where he makes books by hand for his micropress, Albion Books.

Acknowledgments

We would especially like to acknowledge Brenda Hillman, who encouraged us to pursue "a book of essays about women poets and weird matters of the spirit and experimental writing" back in 2009, the spark that grew into *Quo Anima*. Many thanks to all our authors and contributors—we are forever grateful for your work and the care and attention you have given to innovation and spirituality as a poetic practice. We are thankful to AWP who, in 2012, accepted our panel proposal "Quo Anima: Women, Spirit, and Poetic Innovation," and our panelists—Laynie Browne, Andrew Schelling, Dan Beachy-Quick, and Rusty Morrison—who presented to a full, engaged room and kept the flame alight. We are grateful for the help and support of Jennifer Heath and Faith Barrett for their professional expertise and support. Special thanks to the wonderful staff at the University of Akron Press for your hard work and dedication to this anthology: Jon Miller, Amy Freels, Thea Ledendecker, and especially Mary Biddinger, who took a chance on this project. Thank you to the UA Press Editorial Board for your support. And with heartfelt gratitude to Ray Smalley and Randy Prunty for your love and bearing witness to this project for the many years it has taken to come to fruition.

Grateful acknowledgment is made for permission to reprint the following work:

Kazim Ali's essay "Third Eye Who Sees: On the Source of Spiritual Search in *Sappho's Gymnasium* by T Begley and Olga Broumas" was originally queried by Elizabeth Robinson and Jennifer Phelps for *Quo Anima*, and then first published in *Resident Alien: On Border-crossing and the Undocumented Divine* (University of Michigan Press 2015). Reprinted by permission.

Michelle Auerbach's essay "Can I Do this Spiritual Drag: on kari edwards" was first published in *Bombay Gin* Vol. 39, no. 1 (2013). Reprinted by permission.

Dan Beachy-Quick's essay "Ghosting the Line: Susan Howe and the Ethics of Haunting" was first published by the *Denver Quarterly* Vol. 47, no. 4 (2013). Reprinted by permission.

Laynie Browne's "Devotional Practice: Writing and Meditation" originally appeared in *Talisman: A Journal of Contemporary Poetry and Poetics*, Vol. 32, no. 33 (Summer/Fall 2006). Reprinted by permission.

Kythe Heller's essay "Living Backwards: Cecilia Vicuña's Fleshly Language of Unsaying" was first published online in "Imaging the Ineffable: Representation and Reality in Religion and Film," Zoe Kelly-Nacht and Lina Verchery, eds. Reprinted by permission.

Claudia Keelan's interview "I Find Out Everything I Believe Through Writing: An Interview with Alice Notley" was first published in: *American Poetry Review* Vol. 33, no. 3 (May/June 2004) and then in Elisabeth A. Frost and Cynthia Hogue, eds. *Innovative Women Poets: an anthology of contemporary poetry and interviews* (University of Iowa Press 2006). Reprinted by permission.

Myung Mi Kim's poem "from *Penury*" was originally published by Omnidawn Publishing (2009). Reprinted by permission.

Pieces of Hank Lazer's essay "Thinking of Spirit and Spiritual: Lissa Wolsak's *Squeezed Light*" have appeared in *Golden Handcuffs Review* Vol. 1, no. 14 (Winter-Spring 2011) and *The Poetic Front*, Vol. 4, no. 1 (2011). Reprinted by permission.

Colleen Lookingbill's poem "leap with nature)" was first published in *Incognita* (Sink Press 1992). Reprinted by permission.

Kimberly Lyons's poem "Empty Sleeve" was first published in *Rouge* (Instance Press 2012). Reprinted by permission.

Rusty Morrison's essay "The Exact Temperature of a Hand: Melissa Kwasny and the Mystical Imagination" was published in *Gulf Coast* Vol. 25, no. 1 (Winter/Spring 2013). Reprinted by permission.

Hoa Nguyen's poems "Rage Sonnet" and "Agent Orange Poem," which appear in Dale Smith's interview "Joining Spirits: An Interview with Hoa Nguyen (September 2011)," were first published in *As Long As Trees Last* (Wave Books 2012). Her poems "Great Mother of the Gods," "Blackberries," and "Towels" were first published in *Red Juice* (Wave Books 2014). All poems were reprinted with permission of the author and Wave Books.

Jennifer Phelps's essay "Mysticpoetics: Writing the Alchemical Self in Brenda Hillman's Poetry" was first published in *Jacket2* (2013).

Elizabeth Robinson's essay "It Didn't Need Believing: Cole Swensen's *Gravesend*" was first published by the *Denver Quarterly* Vol. 47, no. 4 (2013). Reprinted by permission.

Andrew Schelling's interview "A Rangy Sense of Self: An Interview with Joanne Kyger" was published online by *The Conversant: Interview projects, talk poetries, embodied inquiry* (April 2014). Reprinted by permission.

giovanni singleton's poem "eye of the be/holder" was first published in *Ascension* (Counterpath Press 2012). Reprinted by permission.